Praise for... *Trauma Treatment - Healing the Whole Person*
Meaning-Centered Therapy & Trauma Treatment Foundational Phase-Work Manual

"Drs. Marie Dezelic and Gabriel Ghanoum have created a comprehensive and innovative manual for the meaning-centered treatment approach to heal past trauma. Their work and approach are commendable; their ability to convey it to other clinicians is superb."

~ Amir Levine, M.D.
Assistant Professor of Clinical Psychiatry
Division of Child and Adolescent Psychiatry
Department of Psychiatry, Columbia University
Co-Author, *ATTACHED: The New Science of*
Adult Attachment and How it can Help You Find and Keep Love

"To categorize *Trauma Treatment - Healing the Whole Person* as a conventional "manual" would only marginalize its inherent value as a supportive resource for all people experiencing life transitions, whatever they may be. Informed by Viktor Frankl's System of Logotherapy and Existential Analysis, and guided by their own innovative model of meaning-centered trauma treatment, Drs. Dezelic and Ghanoum aptly demonstrate how finding meaning in life—under ALL circumstances—is both within, and within reach. Importantly, it is along this pathway to meaning where the healing process ultimately takes place and where wholeness in spirit, mind, and body can be found."

~ Alex Pattakos, PhD
Co-Founder, The Global Meaning Institute, Canada, Greece, USA
Co-Author, *Prisoners of Our Thoughts: Viktor Frankl's Principles for*
Discovering Meaning in Life and Work; and
The OPA! Way: Finding Joy & Meaning in Everyday Life & Work

"The paradigm shift in the traditional treatment model is currently upon us; the idea behind living a fulfilling and authentic life is paramount in the therapeutic community and addiction industry. The missing links are self-actualization, self-transcendence, and meaning in the everyday experience when talking about recovery and sobriety. Dr. Dezelic and Dr. Ghanoum provide a clear and concise trauma training platform for professionals across disciplines where meaning is woven throughout all interventions."

~ Cali Estes, PhD
CEO, The Addictions Coach and The Addictions Academy, USA
Author, *The Recovery Coach Workbook*
www.theaddictionsacademy.com
www.theaddictionscoach.com
www.caliestes.com

"Once again Drs. Marie Dezelic and Gabriel Ghanoum have developed an easy-to-use manual not only for clinicians but also for clients. Their Trauma Treatment Foundational Phase-Work model is the combination of the latest evidence-based interventions for the treatment of trauma with the humanistic and existential ingredients of Meaning-Centered Therapy. As a trauma specialist and a trainer, this book is an excellent visual resource to use with clients dealing with trauma-related symptoms, and a valuable resource to use when conducting trainings for trauma clinicians. This manual provides a practical guide for helping our clients to go beyond their trauma narratives to discover and enhance their personal meaning and healing of the traumatic event(s) during the process."

~ **Irene M. Rodriguez, MS, LMHC, CAP, CCTP**
Certified Traumatic Incident Reduction Trainer and Dancing Mindfulness Trainer
Affiliate Trainer of the Institute for Creative Mindfulness
CEO, The Mindful Journey Center, USA
www.mindfuljourneycenter.com

"How do we heal from the pain of traumatic events? How do we survive in the face of unavoidable suffering and loss? Welcome to Dr. Marie Dezelic and Dr. Gabriel Ghanoum's newest book entitled *Trauma Treatment - Healing the Whole Person*, a clinical manual that combines Viktor Frankl's *Meaning-Centered Therapy* and their innovative *Trauma Treatment Foundational Phase-Work (TTFP)* model. This multi-disciplinary approach is based on their extensive clinical expertise and experience helping patients heal from traumatic events. Once again, Dezelic and Ghanoum have developed innovative, colorful and informative Conceptual Pictographs to illustrate their model of recovery. *TTFP* is flexible enough to be appropriate for individual and group counseling, as well as for self-exploration. This manual is an invaluable addition to the treatment plan for clinicians dedicated to helping trauma survivors heal from and discover meaning in the face of tragedy and sorrow."

~ **Ann-Marie Neale, PhD**
Diplomate in Logotherapy
Distance Learning Education Consultant & Faculty Member
Viktor Frankl Institute of Logotherapy, Abilene, TX, USA
Karen Horney Professor of Counseling and Psychology
Graduate Theological Foundation, Mishawaka, IN, USA
Editor, *Meaning-Centered Therapy Workbook:*
Based on Viktor Frankl's Logotherapy and Existential Analysis
Editor, *Meaning-Centered Therapy Manual:*
Logotherapy and Existential Analysis Brief Therapy Protocol
For Group and Individual Sessions

"Trauma and traumatic impacts are found across the spectrum in psychological services, regardless of socio-economic status, culture and gender groups. Specifically, in the forensic population, we can see the lasting and devastating longitudinal, psycho-social effects of a developmental trauma history on their personhood and subsequent behaviors. *Trauma Treatment - Healing the Whole Person* is not only a clinician's manual for trauma treatment and recovery, but is also a psychoeducational book full of imperative information when dealing with any trauma population; a must-have for trauma clinicians or specialists, as well as all those they serve."

~ **Michele Quiroga, PhD**
Clinical Neuropsychologist
Forensic Psychology and Expert Witness
www.forensicneuro.com

Trauma Treatment - Healing The Whole Person

Meaning-Centered Therapy & Trauma Treatment Foundational Phase-Work

Manual

*~ Stabilize, Revive, and Thrive through
Meaning-Centered Therapy and Trauma-Informed Interventions ~*

Marie S. Dezelic, PhD
Diplomate in Logotherapy

Gabriel Ghanoum, PsyD
Diplomate in Logotherapy

Trauma Treatment - Healing the Whole Person:
Meaning-Centered Therapy & Trauma Treatment Foundational Phase-Work Manual
Copyright © 2016 Marie S. Dezelic and Gabriel Ghanoum – Dezelic & Associates, Inc.
All artwork—Conceptual Pictographs © 2013-2016 by Marie S. Dezelic, and Marie S. Dezelic & Gabriel Ghanoum.
All rights reserved.

Edited by Ann-Marie Neale, PhD

Cover artwork—"Shades of Life" © 2013 by Artist Chady Elias. All rights reserved.
Cover Design © 2016 by Artist Chady Elias. All rights reserved.
For more information, contact Chady Elias at www.CHADYELIAS.com

All rights reserved. Tous droits réservés.
No part of this publication may be reproduced through any mechanical, photographic, electronic or phonographic process, stored in a retrieval system or transmitted in any form, without prior written permission from the copyright owner, except in the case of brief quotations embodied in articles or reviews. "Conceptual Pictographs" may not be reproduced in any form unless permission is granted by the copyright owner. Unauthorized usage is prohibited. For permission or additional information contact Dezelic & Associates, Inc. at *info@DrMarieDezelic.com.*

> *Reproduction of the Conceptual Pictographs—Clinician and Client Handouts is permitted under the following conditions:*
>
> It is reproduced solely by the original purchaser/owner of this book for professional and private use designed to aid in professional psychotherapy, clinical pastoral support, and personal growth. The purchaser agrees not to charge or make a profit for any copyrighted material; all handouts must include the copyright notice and may not be modified from their original format.

Trauma Treatment - Healing the Whole Person: Meaning-Centered Therapy & Trauma Treatment Foundational Phase-Work Manual is designed and intended for the professional clinician as a manual and guide for existential psychotherapy and spiritual-pastoral support in trauma-informed treatment, as well as for those seeking personal theoretical understanding and growth. No part of this book or any information contained within it constitutes professional treatment for any condition or clinical disorder, and is not considered an adequate substitute for professional or medical help. When distress in any form is experienced, one should seek professional guidance immediately.

Library of Congress Cataloging-in Publication Data
Includes bibliographical references and handouts
ISBN 978-0-9846408-8-1 (Paperback)
ISBN 978-0-9846408-9-8 (Electronic edition)

Presence Press International
Miami, FL
Printed 2016

This Book is dedicated to:

To our Clients

For allowing us to enter your world of pain and suffering, walk by your side, and
and shine the light of Meaning Discovery in your path.

To our fellow Clinicians

For your ongoing, tireless dedication and courageous choice to enter
the battlegrounds of trauma and tragedy day in and day out;
and for shining an unwavering light and sharing your wisdom with
clients as they learn to cope with and heal from the painful aspects of human existence.

Table of Contents

The Taste of Your Teardrop, Poem	xi
Shades of Life Artwork, Chady Elias	xii
Foreword by Pavel Somov, PhD	xiii
Editor's Foreword by Ann-Marie Neale, PhD	xv
How to Use this Manual	1
Introduction	5

I.
MEANING-CENTERED THERAPY & TRAUMA TREATMENT FOUNDATIONAL PHASE-WORK (TTFP) IN PRACTICE

Part I- Overview of Meaning-Centered Logotherapy & Existential Analysis

Logotherapy & Existential Analysis Definition	9
The Main Tenets of Logotherapy	10
The Meaning of Suffering	11
Mind-Body-Spirit Approach	12
The Meaning Triangle	12
Ultimate Meaning & Meaning in the Moment	13
Existential Vacuum	13
The Tragic Triad	13
The Neurotic Triad	14
Tragic Optimism of Logotherapy	14
The Existential Triangle	15
Defiant Power of the Spirit	16
Primary Methods of Logotherapy	17
Complementary Methods of Logotherapy	18

Part II- Meaning-Centered Therapy in Action

Meaning-Centered Therapy: Integrative Meaning-Centered, Existential and Humanistic Treatment Concepts	21
DARE Existential Therapy: Live Life in Each Moment & REACH Beyond Limitations	22
Existential Therapeutic Process: Logotherapy & Existential Analysis	24
Meaning Construct Model: Through a Bio-Psycho-Social-Spiritual Context	26

Hope from a Meaning Perspective: The Hope Equation … 29
The Gift of Meaning in Trauma and Tragedy: Responses to Trauma … 31

Part III- Trauma Treatment Foundational Phase-Work (TTFP)

Trauma: Acronym … 35
Trauma Definitions … 36
Trauma Elements: Trauma Affects Each Person Differently … 37
Window of Tolerance- Trauma/Anxiety Related Responses:
 Widening the Comfort Zone for Increased Flexibility … 43
The Body Hold the Memory, The Mind Acts it Out, Applying Logotherapy:
 How Each Process Impacts our Internal Feeling and Outward Doing … 45
Trauma Treatment Foundational Phase-Work (TTFP) Model
 Integrative Trauma-Informed Treatment: Core Elements for
 Stabilization, Recovery, & Reconnection … 48
Trauma Experience Through Meaning-Centered Therapy Exploration:
 Bringing Awareness, Becoming Curious and Discovering the
 Mind-Body-Spirit … 54
Core Relational Wounds: Initial Impact on Self-Concept and Identity,
 Secondary Impact on Relational Development … 56
When Getting Triggered Takes Over: Taking a Time Out from the Situation to
 Take a Time In for Self-Discovery … 59
The Meaning-Action Triangle: Becoming Existentially Aware … 63
Noögenic Activation Method: LTEA Applied to the Stages of Change in
 Clinical Practice … 64
The Trauma-Addiction Cycle: How Life Behaviors are Used to
 Avoid/Receive Physiological and Psychological Responses … 68
Meaning-Centered Grief Model: An Existential Approach for
 Addressing the Lifelong Phase in Grief … 70
Addressing Anger: A Multi-Dimensional Construct … 81
Forgiveness- ACCESS Model: How to Release Blocked or
 Stuck Energy and Move Toward Existential Healing … 86

Part IV- Meaning Discovery & Exploration Interventions

Sources of Discovering Meaning in Life & Adversity:
 Through Meaning-Centered Therapy … 91
Meaning Exploration Topics: "Meaning-Legacy Project" … 93
Mind-Body-Spirit Rejuvenation Method: Simple Techniques for
 Stress Reduction & Healthy Living … 98

Appealing Technique: "Accessing the Defiant Power of the Spirit"
  Guided Meditation 103
Peaceful and Comforting Place Meditation: Relaxation for
  Stressful-Anxious Moments 106
Seek & Find Meaning Every Day: A Daily Method of Observation,
  Mindfulness Practice 108
REACH Beyond the Limitations: Sources of Meaning in Life 111
Connect—Create—Convey: Living Life with Meaning and Purpose 113

Part V- Conclusion

Meaning-Centered Therapy in Trauma Treatment: Healing and Lasting Recovery ... 115
Epilogue by Brent Potter, PhD 117
Into the Light, Poem 121

II.
MEANING-CENTERED THERAPY & TRAUMA TREATMENT FOUNDATIONAL PHASE-WORK (TTFP) APPLICATIONS "CLINICIAN AND CLIENT HANDOUTS"

Meaning-Centered Therapy Handouts 125
Trauma Related Handouts 151
Trauma Treatment Foundation Phase-Work (TTFP) Handouts 178
Meaning Discovery & Exploration Handouts 205

III.
"CLINICIAN AND CLIENT HANDOUTS" BLACK-AND-WHITE VERSION FOR PHOTOCOPYING

Clinician and Client Handouts (Black-and-White versions) 217
References 263

The Taste of Your Teardrop

Tell me your tale as if it were not you
Describe the torture, the anguish, the fear, the unknowing
Let me understand how you separated yourself from the body
From the feeling, from the confusion
Where did you go
Where was that peaceful place in your mind and in your soul
How did you pass through those years of torment
Did you go unnoticed
Where did your rage for the injustice go

Did I ever tell you the tale of you as if it were not you
Did I describe to you the beauty that is inside of you
Did I help you to understand that you and your body are not the same
Only partners on this journey who have to help each other to grow
Did I tell you that it is a gift to be able to go
And that this experience was meant to show you how
Did I tell you that your trial was to surpass the greatest test of torment
To see if you would notice
To capture the suffering and surround it with freedom

As I sit before you now
Holding your heart in the cradle of unconditional love
I see only grace
Exquisite creation, sentiment and source
Radiating light
Nothing less than all of this is you
And silently you let go

The taste of your teardrop
I know
Deep inside of it, I meet with you now
And here we shall heal all the pain held from long ago

-M. Dezelic, 2008

Cover Artwork: **"SHADES OF LIFE"**
by Artist, **Chady Elias**
www.ChadyElias.com

"Shades of Life" is an art piece created and carved out of repurposed paper. This piece represents the beauty, grace, and dignity of our spirit, always there and always present, regardless of our experiences inherent in our human condition. These life experiences, including the traumatic and tragic ones, have the possibility of shaping us into the masterpieces that we are, and were created to be. Let our different shades become the aspects of our stories and our exquisite uniqueness.

Foreword ..... *by Dr. Pavel Somov*

Gautama, an Indian Logotherapist from twenty five hundred years ago, observed (in his "first noble truth") that suffering is inevitable. It is exactly this kind of philosophizing that is a hallmark of applied Logotherapy: Life forces lessons upon us; we either reject them or integrate them into our ever-evolving predictive models of reality.

The "smooth sailing" upon the ocean of life is good as long as it lasts. But eventually, along comes a wave of circumstance and crushes our understandably naïve conceptions about how life should be. Shipwrecked, our psyches hide out – sometimes only for days, but not infrequently, for months, and even years, and sometimes for good - in the labyrinthine fiords of grief, buffeted further on by the never-ceasing waves of compounding complications of the core wound.

Eventually, tired of looking for solutions outside, we turn inward, and, if fortunate, we stumble upon something that lifts us up, upon a force that counters the gravity of what happened. We stumble upon the levity of Meaning.

"Meaning" – to many an utterly meaningless word! What does "meaning" mean? Before we center upon meaning, let us try to define this curious manifestation of mind. I have a simple, perhaps, offensively simple, way of seeing this. Meaning - to me – is an information-processing event. You see, we are, for all intents and purposes, information-processing beings. It is information-processing (and not our puny canines!) that helped us survive the jungle of evolution. Information-processing and meaning-making are not two. Information-processing is meaning-making, as well as meaning-discovery. The reason why we process information is to make meaning (make sense) and discover meaning (ascertain significance). The reason why we make and discover meaning is to understand the order – the cosmos, if we choose to speak Greek – of "What Is."

Seen as such, meaning is an information-processing event that helps us integrate the seemingly disparate data-points into a conceptual whole, into an orderly cosmos of reassuring predictability. Understanding meaning this way helps us make sense of trauma. Trauma is a loss of understanding of "What Is." There is a reason why we feel that our worlds, as we know them, come to an end in trauma. Trauma deconstructs the carefully constructed understanding of life. Trauma disorganizes the prior harmony of our assumptions. Trauma is a loss of pattern. Just like meaning, trauma too is an information-processing event. Meaning is when we see the pattern of "What Is." Trauma is when we can no longer make sense of "What Is."

Understanding trauma this way helps us make better sense of meaning. (And if you feel like we are going in a circle, it's exactly because we are. "Meaning" – just like the word "being" – is a gerund. There is an "-ing" in it to point out the process of unfolding. Meaning-making has the circularity of paragliding – as in a thermal column that gives wings life, meaning-making is a perpetual soaring to an ever bigger "bird's eye" view.) So, if trauma is a loss of pattern, a fragmentation of an understanding of life into a chaos of data-points, then meaning-making and meaning-discovery is a Gestalt-like moment of re-gathering and re-collecting and re-integrating the disorganized data-points into a larger philosophical whole.

The moment-of-meaning is when the picture of Reality comes back into focus – when mind turns the chaos (disorder) into cosmos (order) again. That is the alchemy of meaning-making and meaning-discovery.

Meaning-centered trauma work does not only center around meaning. Meaning-centered trauma work centers us through meaning. The point is not to just philosophize for the sake of philosophizing, but to transcend the gravity of circumstance through the levity of meaning.

In this day and age of reductionistic "protocol-ing" of psychotherapy, we tend to fear the hand-holding connotation of a manual. Dezelic and Ghanoum offer no hand-holding. This manual, metaphorically speaking, is a fleet of Socratic dirigibles that are designed to uplift a weighed-down mind with endless meaning-discovery questions. (That is, by the way, I think, the subtle reason why the questions come with that *up*-talk intonation.) Dezelic and Ghanoum offer a profound understanding of the structure of trauma. Reading this manual is akin to taking a walk around a grounded airship, weaving around the steel vines of assumptions and expectations that keep a given psyche aground. Dezelic and Ghanoum – a dynamic duo of clinical provocateurs (and I mean this as an utmost compliment!) – help you see how to sever the ballast of "What Was" so as continue with the life-journey.

Logotherapy is perhaps best understood as a journey to a launch site. The art of a Logotherapist is to guide a client towards a bluff with a spectacular view – towards a platform for a new life-flight. This walk, this therapeutic collaborative journey involves no cognitively combative dragging, no cheerleading tug-of-war, no patronizing prodding – but merely a series of questions and encountering. When questioning, we look up and away. When we find an answer, we look down. A Logotherapist keeps the questions coming and this wind of inquiry keeps the wounded mind aloft until a final question crystallizes, until a wounded mind and body arrive at a launch site: "Am I ready to fly again – despite all that happened, despite all that changed, despite it all?!"

Pavel Somov, PhD, Licensed Psychologist
Author of *Present Perfect; Lotus Effect;*
Choice Awareness Training: Logotherapy and Mindfulness for Treatment of Addictions;
www.DrSomov.com

Editor's Foreword ..... *by Dr. Ann-Marie Neale*

It is both an honor and a privilege to be the Editor of Dr. Marie Dezelic and Dr. Gabriel Ghanoum's newest publication entitled *Trauma Treatment - Healing the Whole Person,* a clinical manual that combines Viktor Frankl's *Meaning-Centered Therapy* and the authors' innovative *Trauma Treatment Foundational Phase-Work* (TTFP). Dezelic and Ghanoum's treatment protocol stays true to Viktor Frankl's teachings and philosophy; while at the same time, they share their own clinical knowledge and expertise based on extensive experience working with patients who are attempting to heal from past or present traumatic events. Once again, they have developed innovative, colorful and informative Figures and Conceptual Pictographs, as well as individual and group exercises. By presenting the information and exercises in both written and visual format, the authors give readers several ways to both comprehend and utilize the treatment options. As before, Dezelic and Ghanoum have designed a manual that is flexible enough to be appropriate for individual or group counseling, as well as self-exploration. This manual can be used in many diverse settings such as inpatient hospitals, outpatient facilities, and spiritual centers.

In Part 1 of the Manual, the basic tenets of Viktor Frankl's Meaning-Centered Logotherapy and Existential Analysis (LTEA) are detailed and explored. Rather than taking considerable time defining and explaining the philosophy, theory of personality and psychotherapy principles of LTEA, I will simply mention what I consider the most important aspects of Frankl's teachings. First and foremost, Viktor Frankl maintained that there is Ultimate Meaning in the Universe and that there is meaning to be discovered in each moment of life. Secondly, he believed that we have a will (or desire) to discover meaning in our lives, and lastly, he stated that we all possess the free will (freedom) to discover our own unique meaning and purpose. In addition, Frankl suggested that there are three general ways we can discover meaning: First, through the use of our creative gifts, such as work, career, or raising children; second, through our love for and from others, and/or through our love for and appreciation of art, nature and beauty; and third, through our attitude in the face of unavoidable suffering, guilt and death. Frankl also states that, in addition to our soma (body) and psyche (thoughts, emotions), we have a nöetic or spiritual dimension. This spiritual dimension is incapable of getting sick and is, therefore, the healthy aspect of ourselves. Frankl is using the term "spiritual" in a secular way, and is not talking about a religious concept; rather, our Nöetic Dimension is that which makes us distinctly human. In our Healthy Human Spirit we find our Personal Conscience, our creativity, our sense of humor, our compassion, our ability to forgive a hurt, and our intuition. Finally, Frankl did not believe that our primary goal should be self-actualization; rather, he felt that it should be Self-Transcendence. Therefore, the question that Life is asking each of us to consider is this: What am I going to give to others and the world through my creative gifts, my experiences, and my attitude in the face of unavoidable pain, guilt or death? Happiness, suggested Frankl, is a byproduct of doing the next right thing. It is never achievable directly. Meaning is always present—Life has meaning until the last breath!

With Frankl's theory in mind, how do we begin to understand and heal from trauma? This is the question that is at the heart of Dezelic and Ghanoum's new Manual and why they developed their *Trauma Treatment Foundational Phase-Work (TTFP)* model. In their own words:

> *Trauma Treatment Foundational Phase-Work (TTFP)* is an integrative trauma-informed treatment modality. The framework of trauma-informed treatment and therapeutic care combines the

most recent, researched information available in the field of trauma treatment and development. It builds upon existing theories and strategies; however, this model utilizes a holistic and existential methodology, attending to the "Whole Person in Trauma Treatment," which necessitates a multi-dimensional therapeutic approach.

Dezelic and Ghanoum's *Trauma Treatment Foundational Phase-Work* (TTFP) model covers such topics as anger, forgiveness, core wounds, current social support networks, grief, losses, triggers, memories, hope and resilience. While I would love to discuss all of these concepts, instead I will comment on the act of forgiveness. As Dezelic and Ghanoum remind us, forgiveness is primarily for the forgiver—the one who was hurt. It is not about condoning or excusing the behavior that caused the hurt; nor is it about reconciliation—resuming or beginning a relationship with the one who has hurt us. Rather, as a spiritual retreat leader, Sister Cathy Cahill, wisely reminds me every time I attend one of her retreats: Forgiveness is the willingness to let go of a hurt. In *Trauma Treatment - Healing the Whole Person*, I was pleased to see that Dezelic and Ghanoum also espouse the theory that forgiveness can help us heal from and let go of a hurt. Through their *Trauma Treatment Foundational Phase-Work (TTFP)* model, they gently guide all of us who have been hurt by others or by any trauma, to open our hearts to the healing power of forgiveness. By doing so, we are better able to move forward with our lives, to once again experience hope, to begin a new phase of healing filled with limitless opportunities for self-transcendence, and ultimately to discover new meanings in each and every moment of our life.

I have no doubt that the professional experience and expertise Dr. Marie Dezelic and Dr. Gabriel Ghanoum generously share in this Manual will help those who work daily to care for the many trauma survivors who seek their guidance. Finally, may their wisdom, combined with limitless compassion and understanding, bring solace, peace and hope to the many patients and other trauma survivors who seek healing and relief from their pain and suffering.

Ann-Marie Neale, PhD
Diplomate in Logotherapy
Distance Learning Education Consultant & Faculty Member
Viktor Frankl Institute of Logotherapy, Abilene, TX, USA
Karen Horney Professor of Counseling and Psychology
Graduate Theological Foundation, Mishawaka, IN, USA
Accredited Member
International Association of Logotherapy and Existential Analysis,
Viktor Frankl Institute Vienna
Editor, *Meaning-Centered Therapy Workbook:*
Based on Viktor Frankl's Logotherapy and Existential Analysis
Editor, *Meaning-Centered Therapy Manual:*
Logotherapy and Existential Analysis Brief Therapy Protocol
For Group and Individual Sessions

How To Use This Manual

> This manual is based on Viktor Frankl's *Meaning-Centered* and *Spiritual-Ontological, Existential* theory of personality, philosophy of life and psychotherapy known as Logotherapy & Existential Analysis (LTEA). The term "Meaning-Centered" has been added before "Logotherapy" to highlight the fact that Logotherapy is a meaning-oriented theory and therapy. Since the Greek word "Logos" can be translated as "Meaning," Frankl named his existential theory and therapy "Logotherapy." Logotherapy focuses on the concept of "Meaning" in its many forms and constructs, and is therefore, a Meaning-Centered existential approach. The term "Meaning-Centered" emphasizes that Frankl's theory is about discovering meaning in our lives. In addition, we have also expanded on Frankl's original theory of personality and psychotherapy while remaining true to its basic concepts.

Clinician/ Facilitator Manual:

This manual covers the foundations of Logotherapy & Existential Analysis (LTEA), additional adaptations of Meaning-Centered Therapy, as well as specific topics related to trauma and our Trauma Treatment Foundational Phase-Work (TTFP) model. Clinician and client handouts—Conceptual Pictographs are included to enhance and facilitate treatment. Trauma-informed clinicians, who mainly function as mental-health therapists or are involved with spiritual care and chaplaincy, can use this book to help guide clients in addressing trauma and seeking meaning in life, as well as explore existential concerns. Other clinicians, or those who are rooted in a particular theoretical model other than existential theories, can use this book to further familiarize themselves with deeper existential questioning, concerns, and distress that our clients will go through as a result of trauma, traumatic and overwhelming experiences, as well as methods of existential treatment, in order to provide more holistic, well-rounded care grounded in theoretical practice.

Any topic can be adapted and tailored specifically to the type of population—type of symptoms being treated, and can be modified for individual, family and group therapy as well as psycho-educational lectures, and teaching. Topics and exercises can be offered as "take home" assignments for further exploration. Everyone is encouraged to adjust or enhance exercises according to their own unique and personal experiences as well as for the specific needs of your clients. **Make this work your own, allow your essence to shine through your personal creativity, and let your talents and experience be your guiding force,** while staying true to the spirit and main concepts of Meaning-Centered Therapy and Trauma Treatment Foundational Phase-Work (TTFP).

Self-Help and Self-Exploration:

When using this book in a *self-help* and *self-exploration* manner to understand concepts, individuals can follow use this book as a source of discovery about themselves and in finding meaning to their suffering. However, we do recommend that you work with a trained therapist, counselor, or spiritual mentor/ advisor/ director for guidance and assistance when addressing trauma and traumatic events.

Information about "Clinician" and "Client":

Throughout this manual, the words "clinician(s)" and "client(s)" are used. Feel free to substitute therapist, counselor, chaplain, facilitator, or leader, for "clinician"; and client, individual, group member, or self, for "client," or whatever terms work best for your particular situation or setting.

> The **Conceptual Pictographs—Clinician and Client Handouts** included in this book provide a visual way for understanding and applying **Meaning-Centered Logotherapy & Existential Analysis and Trauma-Informed Treatment**. They each address existential issues, including suffering and growth, as well as the notion of existence itself. The Conceptual Pictographs will not only improve interaction with clients, but also offer techniques to help motivate clinicians as well as clients to discover **Meaning** through **Creativity, Experiences, Attitudes,** and **Self-Transcendence, *even in spite of pain and suffering due to trauma and tragedy.***

Conceptual Pictographs—Handouts

The *"Conceptual Pictographs"* (visual graphic, representations of concepts and terms), can be used as client handouts or instructive guidelines for clinicians learning about Meaning-Centered Therapy and Trauma Treatment Foundational Phase-Work.

More information for how to use these handouts as therapeutic tools specifically for Meaning-Centered Logotherapy & Existential Analysis can be found in:

Meaning-Centered Therapy Workbook: Based on Viktor Frankl's Logotherapy (Dezelic, 2014);

Meaning-Centered Therapy Manual: Logotherapy & Existential Analysis Brief Therapy Protocol for Group & Individual Sessions, 8 Session Format (Dezelic & Ghanoum, 2015).

Break-Down... Break-Through... Break-Free!

Meaning-Centered Therapy, combined within the Trauma Treatment Foundational Phase-Work (TTFP) model, assists clients to **break-down** old assumptions, **break-through** maladaptive patterns, and **break-free** from the bonds that trauma holds over the mind, and body, while allowing their unique spirits to shine through.

Introduction

Meaning in relation to self and the world, meaning in life, meaning in suffering, and meaningful engagement have long been addressed in trauma treatment as both general concepts and aspects of clinical treatment. Through this workbook we bring together elements of Viktor Frankl's Meaning-Centered Logotherapy & Existential Analysis and our Trauma Treatment Foundational Phase-Work (TTFP) model. The clinical concepts are presented with a clear and concise understanding of existential topics relative to developmental trauma, psychological trauma, Post Traumatic Stress Disorder (PTSD), trauma-and-stressor related disorders, and core elements that trauma-informed therapists need to include in order to promote recovery and healing.

Physical, psychological and emotional trauma can disrupt our lives, causing us to possibly become hypervigilant, wary of human connection, and fearful or uncomfortable in our own bodies. The experience of traumatic events is stored in our brain's memory system, in our body's memory cells, and often as fragmented pieces of sensations, emotions, and physical postures. These fragmented memories become current triggers (something in the present that links with the fragment of memory of the past) for staying safe (our body's natural response system in order to stay alive), and may cause exaggerated responses. When this happens, our fearfulness often becomes exacerbated. We can even become disconnected and isolated from the rest of humanity in order to stay safe and survive. Finally, our deep-rooted existential beliefs about self and our existence can become altered and re-shaped by the traumatic experiences.

What is Trauma Treatment Foundational Phase-Work (TTFP)?

Trauma Treatment Foundational Phase-Work (TTFP) is an integrative trauma-informed treatment modality. The framework of trauma-informed treatment and therapeutic care combines the most recent, researched information available in the field of trauma treatment, trauma-informed care, and development. It builds upon existing theories and strategies; however, this model utilizes a holistic and existential methodology, attending to the "Whole Person in Trauma Treatment," which necessitates a multi-dimensional therapeutic approach.

Because trauma manifests itself in a variety of ways, clinicians working in the trauma field understand that they must have a therapeutic toolbox full of treatment interventions, strategies, and skills. Often, in addition to Post Traumatic Stress Disorder (PTSD), the manifestations occur as several diagnosable clinical disorders, including a disorganization in early personality development and possibly ongoing social/relational interactions (referred to as personality disorders). Multiple disorders and symptoms are indications of traumatic experience that may occur as a result of developmental trauma, a one-time traumatic event, or chronic traumatic events in childhood, adolescence and/or adulthood. The chronic effects of trauma are often perpetuated by the ongoing symptoms and reaction cycles. One of the most important considerations clinicians should keep in mind is that the variety of maladaptive behaviors exhibited by trauma clients are actually coping strategies for survival and safety. These self-regulatory behaviors are means of sensory and affect management, are often self-soothing, and are aimed at a desired connection or disconnection with the outside world. If therapists seek to remove these behaviors too quickly or do not help trauma clients replace them with healthier behaviors that they can tolerate, accept, and work with for self-regulation, the original coping behaviors will likely manifest in other unhealthy or dysfunctional ways or even increase in propensity.

One of the main purposes of this manual is to share and highlight our clinician and client handouts—the **conceptual pictographs** that visually depict important psychological concepts that we use in treatment with our trauma clients, and in psycho-educational seminars for clinicians, spiritual or pastoral counselors, and coaches.

Topics Covered

Section I: **MEANING-CENTERED THERAPY & TRAUMA TREATMENT FOUNDATIONAL PHASE-WORK (TTFP) IN PRACTICE – PHILOSOPHY, THEORY & CLINICAL APPLICATIONS** offers an overview of the general concepts of (1) Meaning-Centered Therapy approaches, (2) Meaning-Centered Therapy in action, our (3) **Trauma Treatment Foundational Phase-Work (TTFP)** model, and (4) Meaning discovery and exploration interventions, with mini Conceptual Pictographs—client handouts as visual aids for the topics addressed.

Section II: **MEANING-CENTERED THERAPY & TRAUMA TREATMENT FOUNDATIONAL PHASE-WORK (TTFP) APPLICATIONS – "CLINICIAN AND CLIENT HANDOUTS"** contains handouts for applying Meaning-Centered Therapy in Trauma-Informed practice. These handouts will not only help clinicians comprehend and understand the therapeutic concepts; when shared with their clients, the handouts will also aid and facilitate treatment. It will be up to clinicians to decide whether to show clients the handouts during sessions or ask them to purchase their own book, so that they can take advantage of the "My Notes" section directly behind each handout.

Section III: **"CLINICIAN AND CLIENT HANDOUTS" IN BLACK-AND-WHITE FOR PHOTOCOPYING** contains the black-n-white versions that clinicians (or anyone who owns the book) can photocopy and use in individual and group therapy formats, or coaching sessions.

All of the clinician and client handouts are designed to facilitate deeper understanding. We know that trauma is often saved and re-experienced in pictures, images or scenes. These visual memories are often not accompanied by language or verbal narrative, (or are accompanied with maladaptive narratives and beliefs); therefore, it is often helpful to initially explain concepts using a visual image, as this may enable the language faculties to re-engage. Meaning is always available for us to discover, even in the most difficult, traumatic and tragic situations found in human existence. Discovering meaning even in the face of trauma can provide a pathway toward healing the mind and body, and enable us to access our healthy Human Spirit. According to Viktor Frankl and Meaning-Centered Logotherapy, the Human Spirit is incapable of becoming sick or in need of healing. Although Existential crisis originates in the Spiritual Dimension, the dimension itself is not neurotic or sick. If we believe, as Frankl did, that we are Spiritual Beings with a Soma (body) and Psyche (mind), then the Human Spirit remains whole and healthy. This fact can be very reassuring and comforting to someone who is coping with the after effects of trauma.

I.
MEANING-CENTERED THERAPY & TRAUMA TREATMENT FOUNDATIONAL PHASE-WORK (TTFP) IN PRACTICE

PHILOSOPHY, THEORY, & CLINICAL APPLICATIONS

Ultimate Question:
What is Meaning-Centered Logotherapy & Existential Analysis?

We live in a world where suffering, tragedy and despair may be waiting around every corner and upon every step we take; yet, at the same time, it is a world full of wonder, precious moments, extraordinary experiences, and astonishing triumphs that fill our hearts and souls with ultimate excitement, knowledge, courage, resilience and strength. Meaning-Centered Logotherapy & Existential Analysis is the unique, dynamic, experiential therapy of the spirit and psyche; the metaphorical midwife, birthing the inner wisdom held deep within the tapestry of our fabric and design. It reaches and touches our spiritual wells, which contain the wealth and purity of all the distinctive capacities of our spirits. It is an evolutionary approach that celebrates the possibilities and potentialities of the ongoing transformation and transcendence of human beings through the existence we call "Life."

Those who practice Meaning-Centered Logotherapy & Existential Analysis passionately ignite and empower their clients to develop and explore the creativity central to our essence and being. They recognize our unbroken wholeness as our simple strength that allows us to discover a life worth living—one we will be both grateful and happy to fully experience each and every day, and will be thankful to have lived. Meaning-Centered Logotherapy & Existential Analysis is a multi-perspective philosophy and therapy that utilizes a multi-disciplinary methodology and encourages the celebration of life, existence, possibilities, growth, and new beginnings. Logotherapists join clients on their unique path, are willing to journey with them in their fully experiential existence, and empower them through the interconnectedness of the artful Logotherapeutic-Nöetic encounter. The gift that Meaning-Centered Logotherapy & Existential Analysis brings to the world is its subtle yet distinctly crafted existential approach, which gently guides us to an awareness of our unique essence as well as our unique purpose and meaning in life, even in spite of life's tragic and traumatic events.

-M. Dezelic
(Dezelic, 2014; Dezelic & Ghanoum, 2015)

Part I
Overview of Meaning-Centered Logotherapy & Existential Analysis

(Dezelic, 2014; Dezelic & Ghanoum, 2015)

Logotherapy & Existential Analysis Definition

Logotherapy & Existential Analysis (LTEA) Definition:
(M. Dezelic, PhD and G. Ghanoum, PsyD)

Logotherapy & Existential Analysis (LTEA), widely known as the "Third Viennese School of Psychotherapy," is a **meaning-centered psychotherapy, theory of personality,** and **philosophy of human existence** developed in the 1920s by the psychiatrist and neurologist, **Viktor Emil Frankl**. **LTEA** centers on **"Logos"—denoted as Meaning,** as the primary motivational and striving force in human beings; and focuses on the **meaning of human existence,** one's **search for the unique Meaning of the Moment,** the **Overall Meaning in Life,** as well as **Ultimate Meaning.** Frankl viewed humans as **ontological beings,** comprised of three interconnected and in-extractable dimensions—mind (psyche), body (soma), and spirit (existential, non-religious context).
The three **Primary Tenets of LTEA:**
 * Freedom of Will
 * Will to Meaning
 * Meaning in Life

The **Main Methodologies of LTEA:**
 * Existential Analysis—analysis of one's existence and meaning in life.
 * Socratic Dialogue—open-ended dialogue to promote discovery of meaning.
 * Paradoxical Intention—intending with humorous exaggeration an over-amplification of a behavior in order to eliminate it.
 * Dereflection—shifting focus from symptoms to other meaningful encounters or activities in order to reduce hyper-intention or hyper-reflection, and increase self-distancing.
 * Modification of Attitudes—the ability to change, or alter thoughts or mindsets in the face of unavoidable difficult, limiting, traumatic or tragic situations.
 * Medicine Chest—located in the Nöetic (Spiritual) Dimension, the unique, internal personal resources of the human being, (such as personal conscience, creativity, love, forgiveness, and intuition).

With the Primary Tenets of Logotherapy & Existential Analysis as the starting point, and through the use of its main methodologies and many complementary methods, LTEA therapists assist clients in utilizing their own **Personal Freedom, Choice** and **Responsibility,** and also in developing an awareness of **Inner Strengths and Resources.** Ultimately, Logotherapists practice the principles and techniques of LTEA and guide individuals to recognize and respond to their unique meaning in life, uniqueness as human beings, and responsibility to and for their existence.

> LTEA is the only existential therapy that stresses the importance of **Self-Transcendence** as a way to discover and fulfill our unique meaning and purpose in life.
>
> By a process of discovering and activating our **Meaning Triangle:**
> * Creativity
> * Experiences
> * Attitude
>
> LTEA addresses the **Existential Realities of Life, Existential Frustration** and the **Existential Vacuum**, which are often byproducts of:
>
> **The Tragic Triad:**
> * Unavoidable Suffering
> * Inescapable Guilt
> * Death
>
> **The Neurotic Triad:**
> * Aggression
> * Depression
> * Addiction
>
> Finally, LTEA rejects the view that human beings are pre-determined or fated by drives, instincts, or solely by genetic endowment, and instead, sees humans as ontological, self-determining individuals with **Free Will** and the capacity for change, empowered by their **Unique Existence** and **Search for Meaning.**

(Batthyany & Levinson, 2009; Batthyany, 2010; Dezelic, 2014; Frankl, 1978, 1986, 1988, 2006; Graber, 2004; www.logotherapyinstitute.org, *Official Viktor Frankl Institute of Logotherapy, TX, United States*; www.viktorfrankl.org, *Official Viktor Frankl Institute, Vienna, Austria*).

The Main Tenets of Logotherapy

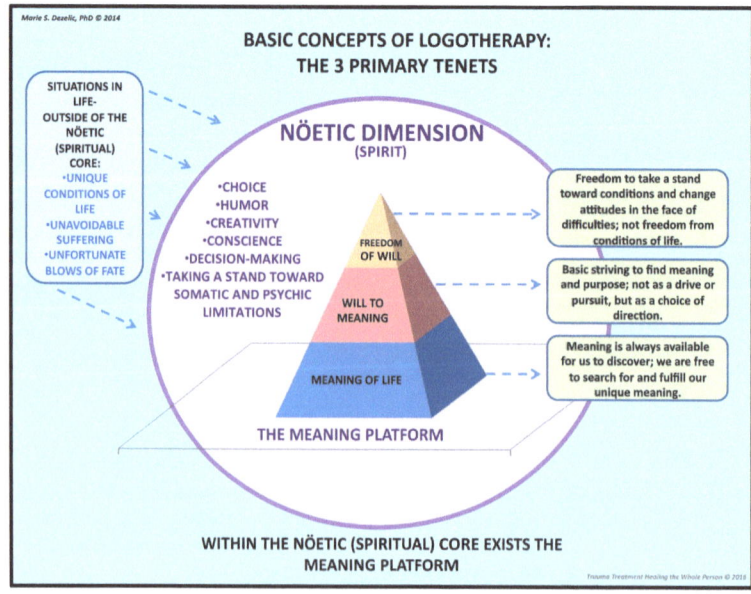

(Handout included in Section II)

In Frankl's formulation of Logotherapy & Existential Analysis, he stated that:
- Life has meaning under all circumstances
- People have a will to meaning
- People have freedom under all circumstances to activate the will to find meaning

The main *Tenets of Logotherapy* consist of:
- **Meaning in Life:** Through our spiritual dimension—our unique essence, the meaning of the moment is continually discovered. Frankl emphasized that the meaning in the moment is present for each individual. He also discussed ultimate meaning, the overall meaning of life that is not knowable until the point of death or beyond. Frankl maintained that life never ceases to have meaning; however, how we discover meaning may change throughout the years of our lives. Finally, meaning differs for each individual, and in each moment of our lifetime. As Frankl was known to say: Life has meaning 'till the last breath.
- **Will to Meaning:** The ultimate striving of human beings is to sense and discover our unique meaning in life. We each possess an innate desire that pulls us toward meaning.
- **Freedom of Will:** Human beings have the freedom and the ability to pursue, to choose, and to experience meaning in life regardless of circumstances.

The Meaning in Suffering

For centuries, seeking an answer to the question of suffering has been the age-old struggle in religion as well as in philosophy. Why should we suffer? What is the benefit from it? Why does God allow suffering? Suffering is any encounter that causes us to confront and attempt to conquer our limitations. Frankl responded to the question of suffering through an existential perspective using experiential evidence. He suggested that when we are confronted with and facing a hopeless, unchangeable situation, such as being diagnosed with an incurable disease, we are challenged to change ourselves through our attitude about the disease; therefore, we have the ability to turn the tragedy into a personal triumph. Here we are able to witness the uniquely human potential of altering our experience of the situation by changing our attitude toward [the situation.

Frankl often wrote that suffering ceases to be suffering once we discover a meaning related to it. That is, when individuals find meaning in their suffering, it changes their perception of the suffering; there is now a purpose to the suffering, a significance that retains meaning. For example, during his years in the concentration camps, Frankl discovered that, when prisoners believed that they still had something significant to accomplish when they were freed, or when they recalled that someone they loved was waiting for or needed them, these same prisoners were better able to endure their suffering and trauma. They felt that their lives continued to have meaning. Thus, their attitude towards their suffering helped many prisoners discover their own unique meaning of the moment. Therefore, suffering can enhance and possibly, even help us discover meaning.

Mind-Body-Spirit Approach

Meaning-Centered Logotherapy & Existential Analysis, differing from most other psychotherapies and psychological schools of thought, for it views individuals as comprised of 3 interconnected dimensions:
- *Body (Soma)*
- *Mind (Psyche)*
- *Spirit (Noetic Core)*

"Human spirit is not a substance, it is pure dynamic (dynamic=movement). Logotherapy would not say 'Man has a spirit.' Instead, **man is spirit.** We have a body (soma) and a mind (psyche), but **we are a spirit**" (Barnes, 2005, p.37).

The Meaning Triangle

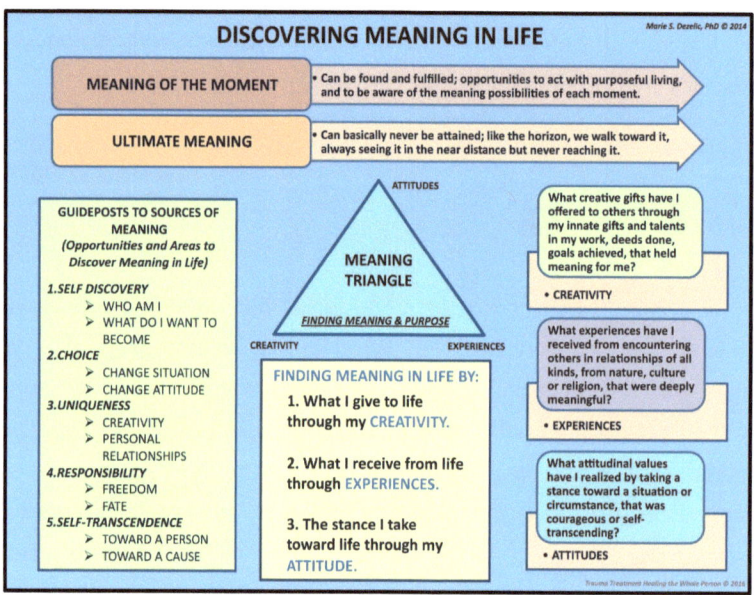

(Handout included in Section II)

In the Meaning Triangle, Frankl identified three categories and areas in which we find meaning, fulfillment and self-transcendence—an experience of going beyond ourselves:
- **Creativity:** By giving something to the world through self-expression; using our innate gifts and talents within our work, deeds, hobbies, parenting, or the services that we offer in life.
- **Experiencing:** By receiving from the world and engaging with others, receiving and giving love to others, or by appreciating the beauty of nature, the arts, and awe-inspiring moments.
- **Attitudes:** A change of attitude is possible in spite of the situation or the circumstances, that is, we can still choose an attitude toward any condition or act of fate. This change in attitude leads to the self-transcending way we find meaning, especially in unavoidable suffering.

Dr. Ann Graber, *(Viktor Frankl's Logotherapy,* 2004), in *Reflections on the Meaning Triangle,* has developed a *"Strengths Awareness Instrument"* (p.94), to help us understand each component of the **Meaning Triangle:**
- A. What I give to life through my *creativity;*
- B. What I receive from life through *experiences;*
- C. The stance I take toward life through my *attitude.*

Ultimate Meaning & Meaning in the Moment

Frankl believed that meanings are always present, are unique, and are ever changing; in other words, life is never lacking a meaning. Logotherapists consistently assist clients in reorienting toward and activating *Meaning* in life. Frankl distinguished between two different kinds of meanings that are possible for human beings to attain:

- *Meaning of the Moment*—which can be found and fulfilled, where individuals have the opportunity to act with purposeful living, and to be aware of the meaning possibilities of each moment through creativity, experiences, and the attitude they take toward life.
- *Ultimate Meaning*—which can be defined in terms of an existing order in the Universe or by our concept of God/Divine. Ultimate Meaning can never be fully attained during our lifetime on earth, for like the horizon, no matter how close we seem to approach it, we are far away from its unreachable and elusive reality until the moment of death or beyond.

Existential Vacuum

Frankl asserted that to *"be human is to be directed to something other than self."* It is through self-transcendence that we can find fulfillment and meaning. The lack of finding meaning leads to what Frankl called the **"Existential Vacuum;"** a state of inertia, inner void, boredom and apathy that we sometimes try to fill with drugs, violence, work, or in which we experience complete despair and no will for life. The existential vacuum should not be viewed as a pathological state; rather, it should be a sign that the Nöetic (Spiritual) Dimension has become blocked.

If this state persists, it progresses into **"Existential Frustration"** and eventually becomes a **"Noögenic Neurosis,"** a neurosis that arises out of the spiritual component when our will to meaning has been halted.

Existential Vacuum and Existential Frustration are often the result of **2 Triads:**
- *Tragic Triad:* resulting from (1) unavoidable Pain, (2) inescapable Guilt and (3) Death;
- *Neurotic Triad:* resulting from (1) Depression, (2) Aggression and (3) Addiction.

The Tragic Triad—people in *despondency* experience:
- *Unavoidable Suffering*: Pain experienced from suffering that is caused by situations that could not be prevented or escaped, or arises from acts of fate or situations over which we have no control.

- **Guilt**: Responsibility, fault, or self blame we experience due to a situation we have caused, been a part of, or even sometimes have been affected by. An example of the latter is the self-blame we feel when reflecting back on missed opportunities with people or situations, or when we wanted to do something that, for whatever reason, was not possible.
- **Death**: The deep sadness and/or questioning we experience upon the realization of the transitoriness of life after the death of someone, or the realization of our own mortality.

The Neurotic Triad—people in *despair* turn toward or experience:
- **Depression**: The feelings we experience in our inner world when we have had a significant tragedy or loss, or have given up our will toward life; feelings of hopelessness or helplessness.
- **Aggression**: An outward expression of violence perhaps caused by the anger and rage experienced internally. Often a means of controlling others; or aggression turned inward—the attempt to harm ourselves through self-mutilation or, at the extreme end, a suicide attempt—to extinguish our existence from this world completely.
- **Addiction**: The attempt to numb or dull pain and despair through substance abuse or a particular behavior. This can also be exhibited as thrill-seeking behavior in order to feel a bodily sensation, experience invincibility and appear larger-than-life, without regard to consequences.

Tragic Optimism of Logotherapy:
Optimism In The Face of Tragedy

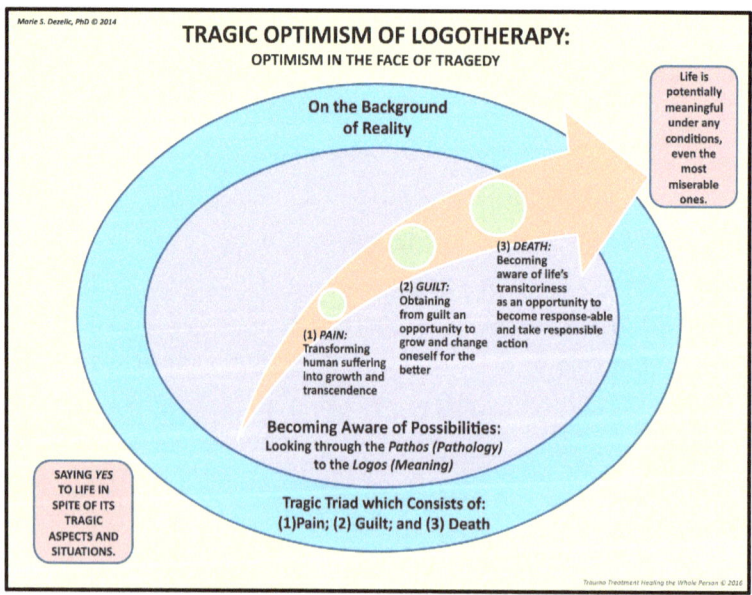

(Handout included in Section II)

Another specific goal of Logotherapy is to contend with what Frankl calls *"the case for Tragic Optimism"* (Frankl, 2006, p.137). Specifically, to remain or become optimistic in the face of tragedy requires a modification of attitude that allows us to become optimistic or positive when it appears we could become discouraged or lose hope.

Tragic Optimism:
- Turning suffering and pain into a human achievement and accomplishment.
- Extracting from existential guilt the opportunity to change ourselves for the better.
- Extracting from the awareness of life's transitoriness an incentive and the possibility to take responsible action.

"The Existential Triangle":
From Meaningless to Meaningful Existence

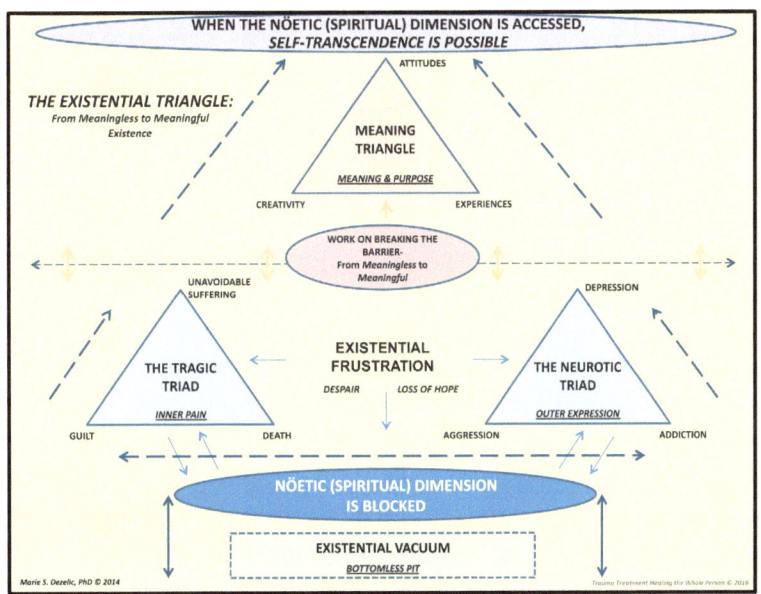

(Handout included Section II)

Marie Dezelic (2014) has coined the term *"The Existential Triangle," From Meaningless to Meaningful Existence,* a larger Triangle that is comprised of Frankl's three basic Logotherapy triangles— **The Tragic Triad, The Neurotic Triad,** and **The Meaning Triangle.** Conceptualizing a client's movement through **The Existential Triangle** offers clinicians a holistic view of inherent possibilities within the difficulties experienced. Therapists can use this concept to help their clients create awareness of and responsibility for the *meaning potentials,* which are always possible regardless of *The Tragic Triad, The Neurotic Triad, Existential Frustration* and the *Existential Vacuum.*

At the base, in the two lower angles of the main triangle *(The Existential Triangle),* are **The Tragic Triad** (Unavoidable Suffering, Guilt, and Death) and **The Neurotic Triad** (Depression, Aggression, and Addiction). *Existential Frustration*—fed by the inner pain and outer despair experienced from the two triads, respectively—exists in this area.

When clients experience inner emptiness and despair, they feel the force of the *Existential Vacuum* pulling them down, maintaining desperation, and ultimately blocking access to the *Nöetic-Spiritual Dimension.*

The main triangle *(The Existential Triangle)* leads toward a peak, where we cross an invisible barrier into the positive areas of growth, possibilities and meaningfulness. In this upper area of the main triangle, we become engaged in **The Meaning Triangle** through *Creativity*, *Experiences*, and *Attitudes*, culminating in **Self-Transcendence** and ***meaningful living.*** Utilizing the methods and tools of Logotherapy, clinicians can assist clients who are experiencing the lower aspects of this *Existential Triangle;* namely, the thoughts, emotions and behaviors of *The Tragic Triad* and *The Neurotic Triad*, to cross the invisible barrier into the realm of *Meaning*, through *The Meaning Triangle* and beyond—toward *Self-Transcendence*. It is important to recognize that, due to the unpredictability of life, human beings will always fluctuate throughout **The Existential Triangle.** It is precisely for this reason that clinicians who practice the principles of Logotherapy & Existential Analysis meet clients exactly where they are at any given point in time, and do their best to assist these clients in their quest to discover their own unique ultimate goals and possibilities.

Defiant Power of the Spirit

Finally, Frankl designated **The Defiant Power of the Spirit** as the area that is activated in Logotherapy through the **Meaning Triangle.** The Defiant Power of the Human Spirit helps us cope with issues arising from the Tragic and Neurotic Triads; issues that can cause human suffering leading toward Existential Frustration and the Existential Vacuum. The Defiant Power of the Human Spirit is exhibited when we push past the Existential Frustration and Existential Vacuum to discover Meaning via the Meaning Triangle and Self-Transcendence. Spirit, (Geist), according to Frankl, refers to the human dimension that is **free, responsible, can make choices,** and is **directed toward finding meaning in life.**

Viktor Frankl's existential and meaning-centered therapy focuses on the basic Tenets of Logotherapy as ways in which we can attend to the difficulties inherent in life and find meaning and purpose within it! We cannot remove human experiences or personal meanings, nor can we dismiss the unique essence of each individual; however, we can apply Logotherapy in all cases. Even in the very last moments of life, all of us are unique individuals who have dignity and value. Thus, in our End-of-life moments, we are still living and breathing, and the Logotherapist can even on some minuscule level, connect with our human spirit (Noös). Clinicians who practice Logotherapy foster a meaningful and meaning-filled encounter and acknowledge the **dignity of human beings** and their existence in this world.

Primary Methods of Logotherapy

(Dezelic & Ghanoum, 2015, p.26-27)

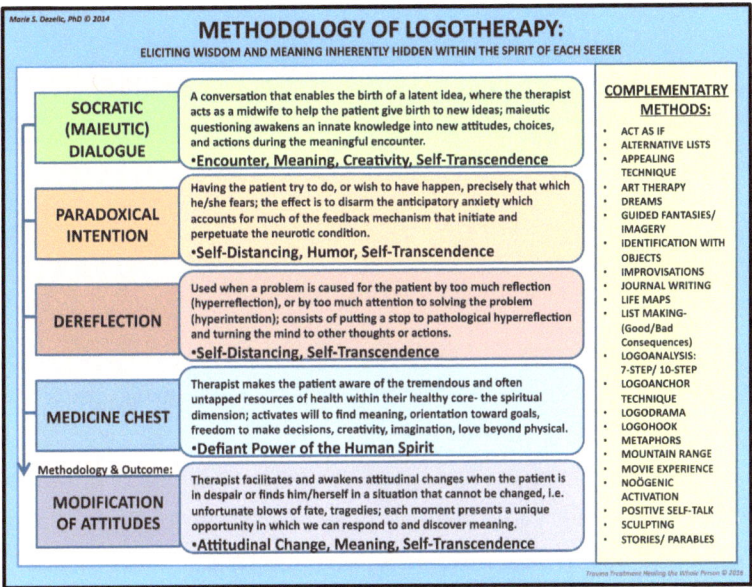

(Handout included in Section II)

- *Socratic (Maieutic) Dialogue*: A conversation that enables the birth of latent ideas—inherent meanings of the moment that are present in our Nöetic (Spiritual) dimension. Therapists act as "midwives" assisting clients to birth new ideas; maieutic questioning awakens innate knowledge so that new attitudes, choices, and actions are revealed during the meaningful encounter.
    Produces: **Positive Therapeutic Encounter, Self-Transcendence, Activation of Meaning, & Creativity**
- *Paradoxical Intention*: Directs or suggests that clients try to do, or wish to have happen, precisely what they fear; the effect is to disarm the anticipatory anxiety, which accounts for much of the feedback mechanism that initiates and perpetuates the neurotic or anxiety producing condition.
    Produces: **Self-Distancing, Self-Transcendence, & Humor**
- *Dereflection*: Used when there is too much reflection *(hyperreflection)* on a problem or when too much attention is focused on solving a problem *(hyperintention)* causes discomfort; consists of putting a stop to pathological *hyperreflection* and turning the mind to other thoughts or actions; reflecting away from self-focus and towards another interest, person or task.
    Produces: **Self-Distancing & Self-Transcendence**
- *Medicine Chest*: The gifts contained within our *Nöetic Dimension* such as creativity, sense of humor, personal conscience and forgiveness. Assist clients to become aware of the tremendous and often untapped resources of health within their healthy core—the *Nöetic Dimension*—the spiritual dimension; activates will to find meaning, orientation toward goals, freedom to make decisions, creativity, imagination, and love beyond the physical.
    Produces: **Engagement with the Defiant Power of the Human Spirit**

Method and Outcome of Treatment:
- **Modification of Attitudes:** Facilitating and awakening attitudinal changes when clients are in despair or find themselves in a situation that cannot be changed (i.e. unfortunate blows of fate, tragedies); each moment presents a unique opportunity that clients can respond to and discover meaning.

    Produces: Attitudinal Change, Meaning, & Self-Transcendence

Complementary Methods of Logotherapy
(Dezelic & Ghanoum, 2015, p.27-28)

- *Act As If*: Ask clients to *act as if* they have already accomplished their goal or achieved their meaningful task, and describe what it feels like to have done this; role play can assist in connecting to these feelings.
- *Alternative Lists*: Ask clients to make a list of desirable activities that would provide meaning, as well as alternative things they can still do despite their current situation/ diagnosis.
- *Appealing Technique*: Use this Autogenic training combined with positive affirmations and guided imagery to strengthen the client's *Nöetic*—spiritual resources.
- *Art Therapy*: Ask clients to use artistic expression as a means to illustrate a meaningful experience; clients can give the art to someone significant as a gift, or keep as a legacy-building piece. This can be accomplished through writing, painting/ drawing/ sculpture/ woodworking/ any artistic medium, photography, videography, or creating something unique such as a scrapbook, cookbook, photo book, short story, poetry, knitting, etc.
- *Dream Analysis*: Identify the dream content which is giving a voice and vision to the client's unconscious— *Nöetic*—spiritual dimension; free association is used to connect to meaningful cues and new meaning possibilities.
- *Guided Fantasies/ Imagery*: Take clients on a journey through guided fantasies and imagery toward achieving meaningful tasks; meditational and mindfulness based.
- *Identification with Objects*: Ask clients to share stories related to significant objects that they have collected over the years. They can bring in the actual object or, if this is not possible, they can take a photograph of it instead; identify ways clients can continue to use the object as a means of activating *will to meaning.*
- *Improvisations*: Create "On the spot," techniques that focus on clients' uniqueness and assist in activating their *Meaning Triangle.*
- *Journal Writing*: Ask clients to write about particular topics in order to look for meaningful cues that will enhance their search for meaning.
- *Life Maps*: Ask clients to map out their significant lifetime experiences, both positive and negative; have them map out where they would like to see themselves in one, five, ten and fifteen years.
- *List Making—(Good/Bad Consequences)*: Ask clients to make lists of good and bad consequences, as well as meaning interpretations of each.

- ***Logoanalysis-7 Steps***: Utilize this modality developed for the treatment of addictions; The 7-step process consists of: (1) Identifying one's belief system; (2) Experiencing loss of value; (3) Developing self-confidence through meditations, relaxation, exercise, and using the *Power of Freedom*; (4) Learning to cope with future problems; (5) Exploring Relationships; (6) Administering the *MILE (Meaning in Life Evaluation Scale)*; (7) Committing to daily work on activating their *will to meaning* to reinforce their uniqueness as human beings.
- ***Logoanchor Technique***: Ask clients to recall and share meaningful or significant experiences, events and images that previously filled them with wonder and a sense of uniqueness. This will enable them to use these past meaningful moments as meaning-anchors for the present.
- ***Logodrama***: Ask clients to imagine a future time when they are close to death, and to reflect back on their major accomplishments and meaningful moments, in order to ignite possible goals and plans.
- ***Logohook***: Make use of a meaningful experience expressed, or object the client has shown, and use it to activate and ignite meaning in the present moment.
- ***Metaphors***: Use metaphors of ideas or goals that interest clients, in order to impart helpful information that will connect them to meaningful concepts in their lives.
- ***Mountain Range***: Ask clients to draw a mountain range, and place significant people/situations who touched their lives on the distant peaks; meaningful individuals/ encounters can be discussed or written about.
- ***Movie Experience:*** Have clients create a movie of their life. The Movie has three parts: (1) Life In Review, (2) Life in Preview, (3) Fast-Forward Experience. Ask them to choose which actors or historical/current figures would play them and other key members in each part, describe the setting, the budget, and the story lines.
- ***Noögenic Activation Method:*** Utilize this seven stage method for Logotherapeutic change which consists of: (1) Pre-contemplation; (2) Contemplation; (3) Preparation/ Determination/ Freedom of Will; (4) Action/ Will to Meaning; (5) Maintenance/ Living Meaningfully; (6) Relapse/ Existential Distress & Frustration; (7) Noö-dynamics and Self-Transcendence. There is also a seven-step protocol to be explored within each stage of change: (1) Access to the Noetic Dimension; (2) Recognize the Uniqueness of the individual; (3) Examine choices; (4) Be aware of responsibility to… not from; (5) Activate the Will to Meaning; (6) Recognize Freedom of Will; (7) Examine Meaning in Life, Meaning in the Moment, Ultimate Meaning.
- ***Positive Self-Talk***: Assist clients in strengthening and building internal resources and strengths, and accessing their *Noetic Dimension.*
- ***Sculpting***: Assist clients as they sculpt, shape and adapt a story or experience into something that provides meaning.
- ***Stories/Parables***: Use stories/parables to illustrate a point that or idea that will help clients discover meaning in their lives.

PART II
Meaning-Centered Therapy In Action

Meaning-Centered Therapy:
Integrative Meaning-Centered, Existential and Humanistic Treatment Concepts

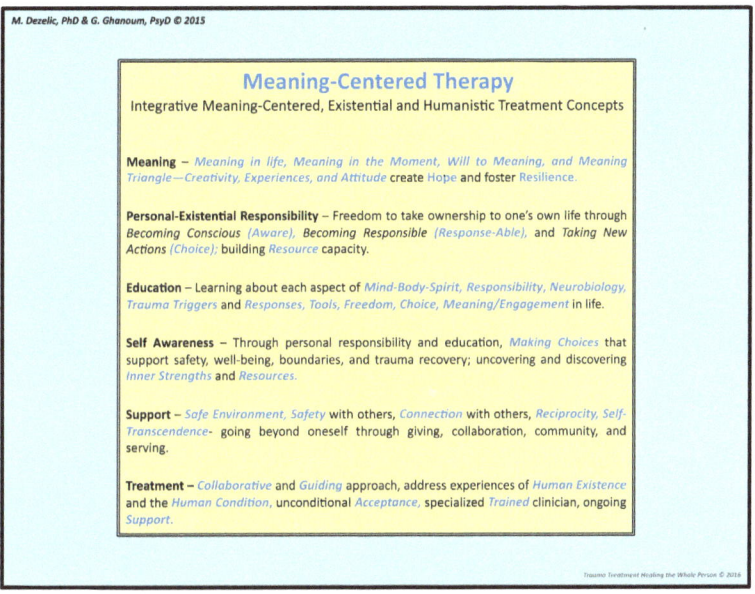

(Handout included in Section II)

The 6 areas of focus in the therapeutic process:

(1) Meaning – *Meaning in life, Meaning in the Moment, Will to Meaning, and Meaning Triangle—Creativity, Experiences, and Attitude change in the face of unavoidable pain, guilt or death* create Hope and foster Resilience.

(2) Personal-Existential Responsibility – Freedom to take ownership for our own life through *Becoming Conscious (Aware), Becoming Responsible (Response-Able),* and *Taking New Actions (Choice);* building *Resource* capacity.

(3) Education – Learning about each aspect of *Mind-Body-Spirit, Responsibility, Neurobiology, Trauma Triggers* and *Responses, Tools, Freedom, Choice, Meaning/Engagement* in life.

(4) Self Awareness – Through personal responsibility and education, *Making Choices* that support safety, well-being, boundaries, and trauma recovery; uncovering and discovering Inner *Strengths* and *Resources.*

(5) Support – *Safe Environment, Safety* with others, *Connection* with others, *Reciprocity, Self-Transcendence-* going beyond ourselves through giving, collaboration, community, and serving.

(6) Treatment – *Collaborative* and *Guiding* approach, address experiences of *Human Existence* and the *Human Condition*, unconditional *Acceptance,* specialized *Trained* clinician, ongoing *Support*.

DARE Existential Therapy:
Live Life in Each Moment & REACH Beyond Limitations

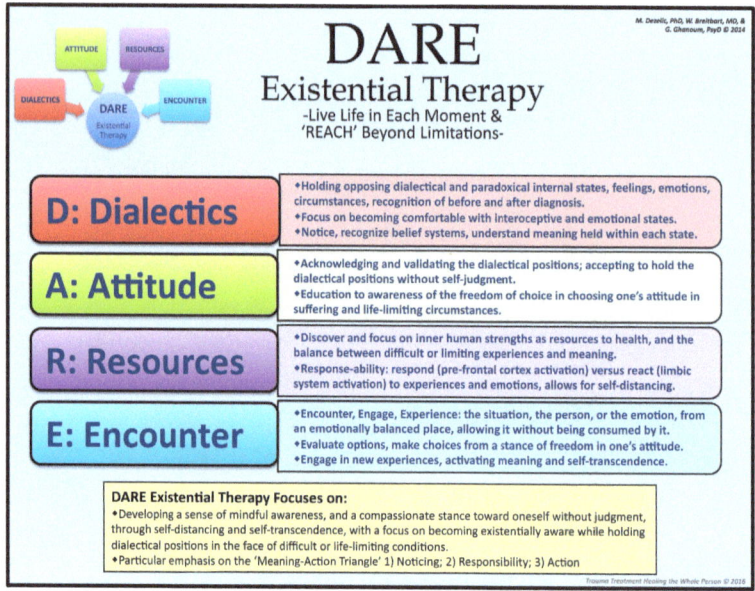

(Handout included in Section II)

DARE (Dialectics, Attitude, Resources, and Encounter) Existential Therapy is a treatment style and approach developed by M. Dezelic, PhD, W. Breitbart, MD, and G. Ghanoum, PsyD. DARE Existential Therapy is rooted in and stands upon an existential, humanistic and meaning-centered foundation, combined with a mindfulness stance, while being able to incorporate neurobiology, positive psychology, and cognitive-behavioral techniques. It is a style that emphasizes "being;" that is, being with clients and their families, being present and open, and being their guide as they face the various difficulties they will encounter, and as they learn to accept the human condition, as well as life's limitations. DARE Existential Therapy incorporates the most vital elements of our belief systems that we have come to understand through our combined decades of research and working on the front lines with clients and families who are in extreme crisis, who have experienced severe trauma and tragic situations, and who are facing life-limiting illnesses, as well as various psychological disorders and difficulties. Our motto for DARE Existential Therapy is "Live Life in Each Moment & REACH Beyond Limitations." With this motto we are proposing a mindfulness presence (openness and awareness) to be in the current moment and an existential responsibility to live life fully.

REACH (Responsibility, Experiences, Attitude, Creativity, and Historical sources of Meaning discovery); handout on p.111, is designed to activate Meaning Possibilities; that is, through an active "agency" of reaching into each area of meaning discovery, to live life with Meaning and on purpose, beyond the limitations presented in the human condition. This approach provides Trauma-informed clinicians with a theoretical model and approach for attending to clients during the entire therapeutic experience. Clinicians can utilize **REACH** in combination with other methods and techniques in their repertoire and training.

DARE Existential Therapy Method:

D- Dialectics:
- Holding opposing dialectical and paradoxical internal states, feelings, emotions, circumstances; recognition of before and after diagnosis/situation.
- Focusing on becoming comfortable with interoceptive states (internal perception of bodily and emotional sensations).
- Noticing and recognizing belief systems, understanding the meaning held within each state.

A- Attitude:
- Acknowledging and validating the dialectical positions; accepting and holding the dialectical positions without self-judgment.
- Educating process that increases awareness of the freedom of choice in choosing our attitude in suffering and life-limiting circumstances.

R- Resources:
- Discovering and focusing on inner human strengths as resources for positive health, and the balance between difficult or limiting experiences and meaning.
- Response-ability: responding (pre-frontal cortex activation) versus reacting (limbic system activation) to experiences and emotions, allows for self-distancing.

E- Encounter:
- Encountering, Engaging, Experiencing the situation, the person, or the emotion from an emotionally balanced place; thus, allowing it without being consumed by it.
- Evaluating options, making choices from a stance of freedom in one's attitude.
- Engaging in new experiences, activating meaning and self-transcendence.

Therapeutic Focus:
- Developing a sense of mindful awareness (open, awake, aware, present), and a compassionate stance toward ourselves without judgment, through self-distancing and self-transcendence, with a focus on becoming existentially aware while holding dialectical positions in the face of difficult or life-limiting conditions.
- Particular emphasis on the **"Meaning-Action Triangle"**
  1) Noticing: Becoming conscious and aware.
  2) Responsibility: Existential response-ability and accountability to our life and to others in our life.
  3) Action: Freedom and personal choice to take initiative, whether in thought or behavior, and discover Meaning, even within limitations.

Existential Therapeutic Process:
Logotherapy & Existential Analysis
(Dezelic & Ghanoum, 2015)

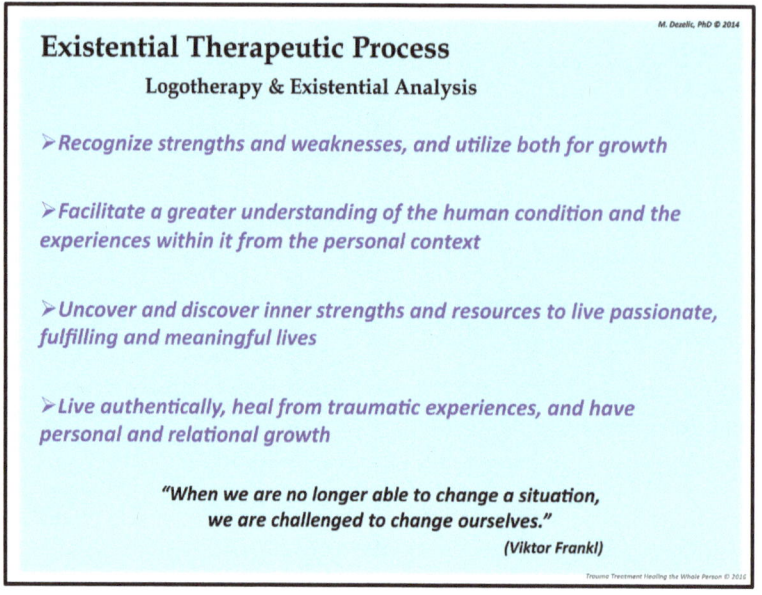

(Handout included in Section II)

The search for meaning, even up until our last moments, is our internal, unconscious (out of awareness) thriving life force. As we become conscious of our search, we are able to capture and discover the essence of Meaning in our life, and fully experience it with a mindful awareness and presence. This awareness of our search for a meaningful life allows us to integrate feelings of satisfaction, fulfillment, peace, contentment, and self-transcendence when we are trying to answer existential questions *(What is the meaning and purpose of my life? Why am I here? Why did I experience these circumstances? Will my life matter after I am gone? etc.)*. During the existential therapeutic process, experienced clinicians provide an atmosphere of acceptance that honors the dignity of clients, thus allowing them to explore the legacy of their lives, find meaningful cues, explore meaningful moments, and continue discovering meaning in life despite traumatic events.

Meaning-Centered Logotherapy & Existential Analysis assists individuals to:
- Recognize their strengths and weaknesses, and utilize both for personal and relational growth.
- Facilitate a greater understanding of the human condition and the experiences within it from the personal context.
- Uncover and discover inner strengths and resources to live passionate, fulfilling and meaningful lives.
- Live authentically, heal from traumatic experiences, and have personal and relational growth.

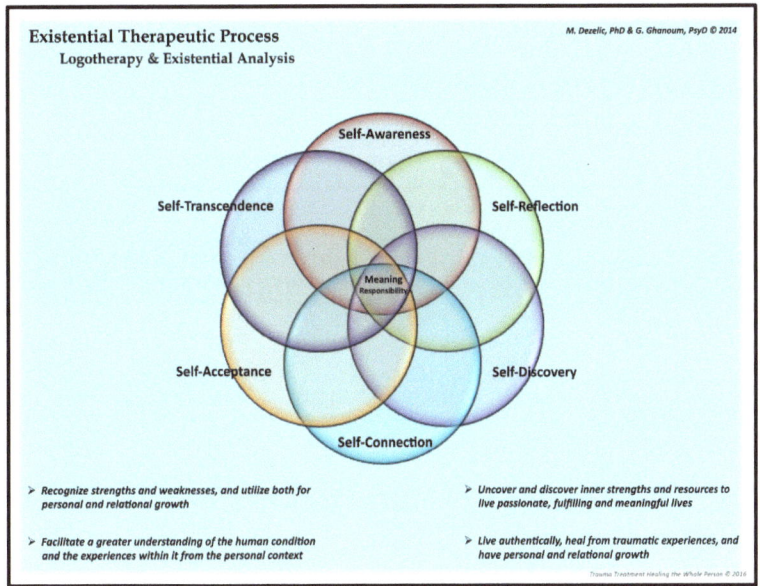

(Handout included in Section II)

This process promotes accessing and **Discovering Meaning,** and fulfilling our **Existential Responsibility** to life through:
- Self-Awareness
- Self-Reflection
- Self-Discovery
- Self-Connection
- Self-Acceptance
- Self-Transcendence

Clinicians who practice Meaning-Centered Logotherapy & Existential Analysis respect the unique essence of their clients. This respect builds an atmosphere of trust and collaboration that allows and encourages clients to increase their inner awareness, deepen their existential connectedness, and demonstrate compassion toward themselves and others, to go beyond themselves by connecting with others, and to utilize their creative talents in pursuit of important endeavors and causes. Thus clients achieve happiness through their acts of self-transcendence.

Meaning Construct Model:
Through a Bio-Psycho-Social-Spiritual Context
(Dezelic & Ghanoum, 2015, p. 12)

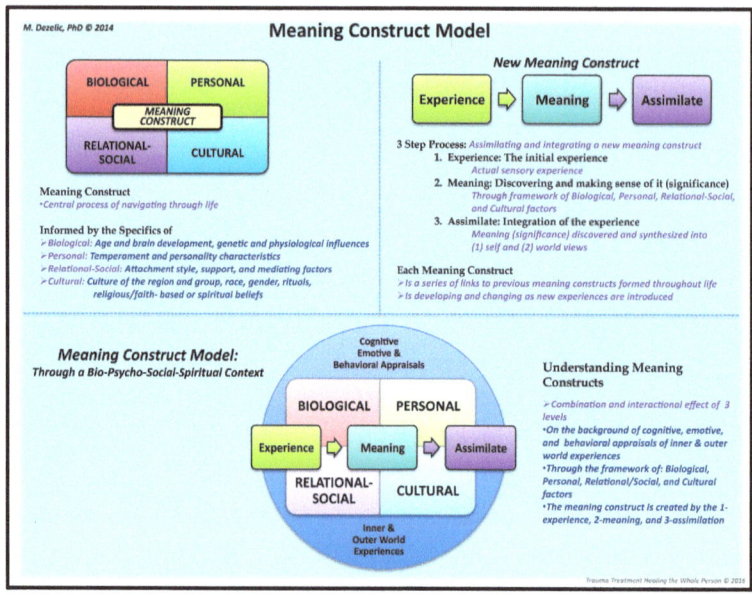

(Handout included in Section II)

The inner motivation to uncover, discover, maintain and embrace meaning is present despite the inevitable challenges, pain, suffering and discomfort that can result from conflict, loss, traumas, tragedies, setbacks and limitations. Since it is an unavoidable fact that all of us will face these difficult situations at one point or another during the course of our lifetime, we may experience despair, hopelessness or meaninglessness—what Viktor Frankl termed the existential vacuum (Dezelic, 2014; Frankl, 1986, 2004, 2006; Graber, 2004; Lukas, 2000; Rice et al., 2004).

One of the difficulties we encounter when faced with the challenge of uncovering, discovering, maintaining, and embracing meaning is the lack of a universal definition of Meaning itself. While most would agree that Meaning is a universal concept, there is no operational definition that has been agreed upon by researchers, personality theorists and other professionals. This is likely due to the many and varied biological, personal, social-relational and cultural differences in individuals, groups and societies as a whole.

In addition, the word Meaning is referenced from two different perspectives. One aspect of *Meaning* refers to the "understanding" or "making sense" of a concept or situation, (i.e. when something happens, it "means"...); *Meaning* can also refer to a "greater purpose" or "significance" (i.e. the "meaning of life," "meaning in the moment" or "discovering meaning within the suffering"). What often happens is that each of us defines meaning according to our own inner and outer worldviews, within our unique cognitive, behavioral and emotive appraisals of experiences. We often base our understanding on current biological, personal, relational-social, and cultural aspects of our lives. Thus "Meaning" can be viewed as an ongoing creative and dynamic process.

Merriam-Webster's Collegiate Dictionary (2005) has several **definitions of the word "Meaning"**:
1) *a: the thing one intends to convey especially by language; (purport)*
   b: the thing that is conveyed especially by language; (import)
2) *something meant or intended; (aim)*
3) *significant quality; (implication of a hidden or special significance)*
4) *a: the logical connotation of a word or phrase*
   b: the logical denotation or extension of a word or phrase

> Throughout this manual, **Meaning refers to a "significance" or "greater purpose,"** such as the "meaning of life," or "discovering meaning within the suffering or situation"; this is the most compatible with Meaning-Centered Logotherapy and Existential Analysis.

"Meaning Construct Model"

A *Construct* is a theoretical description of several factors or complex ideas that are not necessarily directly observable, such as self-esteem, self-confidence, or Ultimate Meaning. The ***"Meaning Construct Model: Through a Bio-Psycho-Social-Spiritual Context,"*** lists the factors that influence or impact the discovery of our own unique and individual Meaning in Life. These factors are based on theoretical concepts that are found in Developmental Psychology, Cognitive-Learning Theory, Constructivist Psychology, Neurobiology, Attachment Theory, Family Systems Theory, Multicultural Psychology, Trauma-Informed Treatment, and Grief Therapies, along with Logotherapy & Existential Analysis, and inform the developmental and navigating process of discovering Meaning throughout the course of our lives.

A **Meaning Construct** for each unique individual is established through:
- ***Biological Influences:*** Age and brain development, genetic and physiological influences.
- ***Personal Influences:*** Temperament and personality styles.
- ***Relational-Social Influences:*** Attachment style (i.e. secure, anxious-ambivalent, avoidant, disorganized), support network, and mediating factors. Mediating factors include situations that create a positive or negative impact, such as a safe and secure environment during developmental years, caregiver support and connection, caregiver neglect and disconnection, peer support or disengagement, mental illness within the family, traumatic and tragic situations, grief, poverty, education.
- ***Cultural Influences:*** Family, geographic region, race, gender, rituals and religious, spiritual/existential or faith-based beliefs.

The **Meaning Construct Model** shows that discovering Meaning is a three-step process of assimilating and integrating new and novel experiences as they unfold throughout our lifetime:
1) *Experience*: the initial event occurs.
2) *Meaning:* the appraisal and "significance" of the experience discovered and informed through Biological, Personal, Relational-Social, and Cultural factors.

3) ***Assimilation:*** the integration of the Experience and Meaning (or significance) into our understanding of ourselves (self-view), and our world views (others-view).

We are continually discovering new Meaning constructs and appraisals, often through the process of refining or adapting previous understandings of Meaning in our lives. We may even choose to disregard or abandon some of our older Meaning constructs as new ones are discovered and assimilated. And likewise, when we look back on our lives, we may discover Meaning in past moments, happenings or events. For, as we know, there are many changes in the Biological, Personal, Relational-Social, or Cultural domains throughout our lives. There are also times when we may actually feel stuck in step 2, the "Meaning" stage. Sometimes it can be difficult to make sense of a situation, especially if we are feeling overwhelmed or influenced in any of the Biological, Personal, Relational-Social, or Cultural domains; thus making it challenging to discover "Meaning" within the experience. Likewise, we may experience difficulty moving from the "Meaning" stage to the "Assimilation" stage, where we can make sense of the new experience. There are times when we may even be confused and have trouble finding adaptive ways of integrating difficult yet potentially meaningful experiences into the context of our lives. Should this pattern become extreme or maladaptive, we might see the emergence of PTSD (Posttraumatic Stress Disorder) symptoms or symptoms of other diagnoses such as Depression or Anxiety disorders.

As therapists and facilitators, we may think we understand the Meaning others experience in a particular circumstance; however, it is always wise and necessary to explore our clients' own unique understanding and appraisal of the situation. This assures that we are not projecting our own life circumstances and Meanings onto others, and that we are instead assisting them in discovering and uncovering their own unique, personal Meanings. The three-step process (1-Experience, 2-Meaning, 3-Assimilation) is incorporated and integrated into our lives through the ongoing and ever changing framework of Biological, Personal, Relational-Social, and Cultural influences. The process is always based on the background of cognitive, behavioral and emotive appraisals of self and world views.

As mentioned above, Meaning, significance and purpose in life, central concepts in Meaning-Centered therapies (Batthyany & Levinson, 2009; Dezelic 2014) can have different interpretations across cultures. One person's "meaning in the moment" or "ultimate meaning in life" will be completely unique to that individual through the framework of the four domains. It is important to remember that the search for "meaning in life" is an innate and inherent pulling force within human beings (Dezelic, 2014; Frankl, 1986, 2004, 2006; Graber, 2004; Lukas, 2000), yet what is discovered and interpreted as meaningful and significant varies across the globe.

Hope from a Meaning Perspective:
The Hope Equation

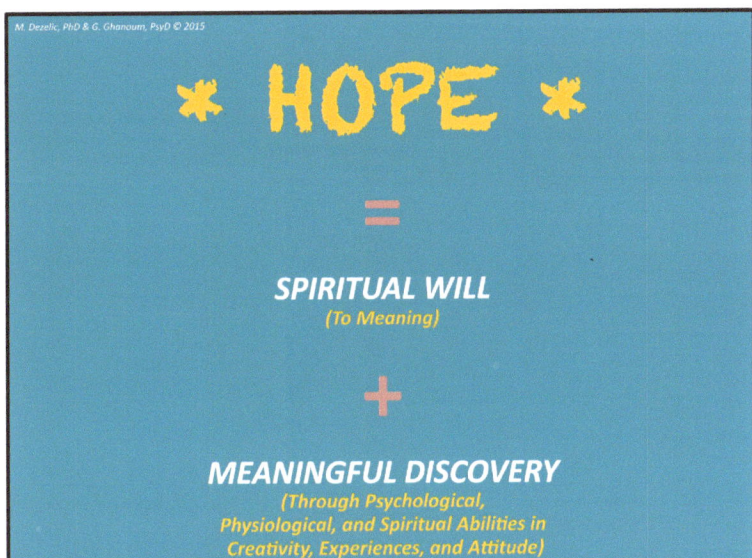

(Handout included in Section II)

When clinicians practice Meaning-Centered Logotherapy & Existential Analysis, they can often help their clients experience hope—hope that they will be able to discover the meaning of each moment in their lives. From our perspective, Hope, like Meaning exists within the spiritual dimensions, and is a byproduct and outcome of meaning-directed focus. **The HOPE Equation:** Spiritual Will plus Meaningful Discovery equals Hope (See box below).

> **HOPE = SPIRITUAL WILL + MEANINGFUL DISCOVERY**

Breaking down this equation, we look at the two aspects that are complementary and collaboratively awakened—spiritual will and meaningful discovery—to generate a sense of hope in situations such as terminal illness or the many adversities we face in life.

HOPE is the sum of:
- **Spiritual Will:** Our Will to Meaning, and Ultimate Meaning in Life, both of which are present under all circumstances.
- **Meaningful Discovery:** The avenues toward uncovering Meaning in every moment of our lives, through our Mind (Psyche), Physical Body (Soma), and Spirit (Spiritual/Existential) within the Meaning Triangle of Creativity, Experiences, and Attitude in the face of unavoidable circumstances or acts of fate.

When we assist clients to access their spiritual will and uncover meaningful moments, we follow a path and focus on how to ignite their multidimensional and multidynamic sense of hope. This moves clients toward an optimal sense of "being" within the limitations of illness, trauma, tragedy, and the transitoriness of life.

The Gift of Meaning in Trauma and Tragedy:
Responses to Trauma

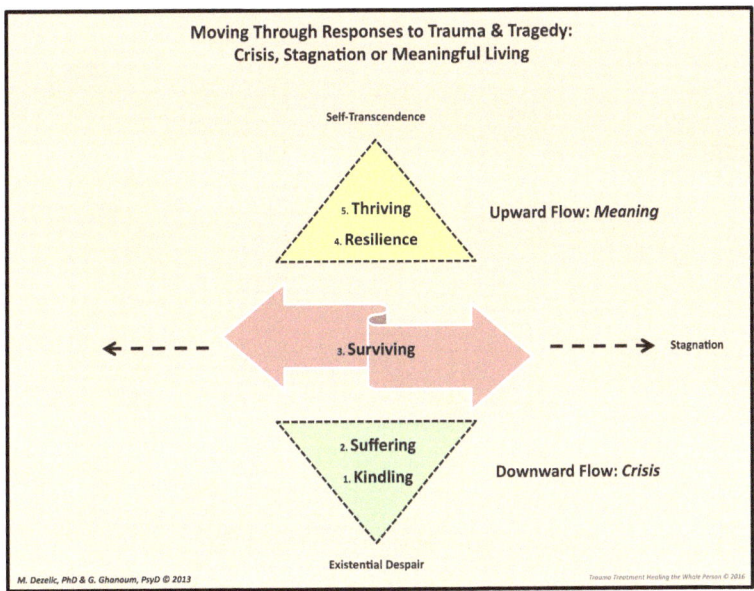

(Handout included in Section II)

The "gift of Meaning" in trauma and tragedy offers clinicians that come face-to-face with clients and families who are affected by chronic illness, death, and tragic life-altering events an avenue to transcend into meaning. As mental health and healthcare providers, it is important to examine the "**Initial Feelings**" experienced by our clients. It is also important to recognize the "**Emotional Impacts**" of any devastating event. For example, the devastating event may be news of a difficult or life-threatening medical diagnosis, overwhelming and chronic grief in reaction to significant loss or tragedy, or the experience of traumatic physical, emotional or psychological abuse.

Initial Feelings and Emotional Impact of traumatic news

- Anger
    - Why me?
    - Why did this have to happen?
    - Why now?
- Sadness/Despair:
    - How can I go on?
    - Why do I feel such extreme pain?
    - What was my life's purpose?
- Fear:
    - What happens now?
    - Where do I go from here?
    - What about my family?

- Overwhelmed:
    - I can't handle this.
    - I can't think straight, and don't know where to begin.
    - How do I take care of myself and my loved ones through this?

There are no absolute right answers to the above questions and statements that clients often express. These questions and statements are usually intermingled with heavy emotions and feelings. Clinicians who are able to build an atmosphere of trust and safety can help clients feel less isolated as they explore each of these common questions. By exploring what each of these questions signify to their clients, clinicians can help them identify and label the accompanying emotion; thus, the process of helping clients to investigate what is happening can reveal many pathways of responding to the situation and shifting understanding and attitudes.

All responses to trauma and tragedy, for example, how we view the situation, what coping strategies were or are being utilized— what has or has not worked, can be further explored. Our actions, thoughts, feelings, and emotions can affect and/or change the perception of our experience. Sometimes clients fail to recognize meaning in the particular moment either because they are too overwhelmed by the traumatic event to look for meaning, or they are unable to accept the gift of meaning due to the nature of the tragic or traumatic experience. Meaning-seeking cannot be forced. Taking care to allow sufficient time to process the event is crucial. The goal we seek when exploring possible responses to the situation is to promote emotional flexibility rather than emotional suppression. Within the framework of emotional expression, flexibility is created and expanded, thus allowing us to eventually recognize meaning, even in the face of tragedy. At that point, we can move from a victim stance to one of freedom and choice, and be able to activate our Will to Meaning, and discover Meaning once more.

Clients often resist finding meaning because they need time to be with the pain. However, long-term resistance can lead to extreme suffering, despair, hopelessness, and even suicidality. Pema Chödron, Buddhist nun and teacher, has often said that: **PAIN x RESISTANCE = SUFFERING.**

We try to show clients that Pain multiplied by "Meaning" equals Resilience, Healing, Hope and Transcendence (see Box below).

> **PAIN x "MEANING" = RESILIENCE, HEALING, HOPE, and TRANSCENDENCE**

Pain can be transformed by the meanings discovered in the tragic situation; it has the potential to change our perceptions, our attitude, and can also allow us to move with a forward momentum in our lives. Pain can even allow us to endure suffering. Meaning has the power to transform us, alter the situation, and even positively affect those around us.

Responses to Tragedy

- **Kindling:** Bringing all negative things together, making things worse
- **Suffering:** Despair, victim stance, "I have no choice in my response"
- **Surviving:** Existing, stagnating, no Meaning, no Will to Meaning
- **Resilience:** Defiant power of the human spirit, courage, freedom
- **Thriving:** Flourishing, Meaning in Life, connections, creativity, authenticity, responsibility, self-transcendence

Kindling (a term used in neurology signifying a brain event that is initiated and whose recurrence is more likely when coupled with similar stimuli) and **Suffering** urges a downward flow motion in our lives, resulting in **Existential Crisis**—Existential Frustration and the Existential Vacuum. Merely **Surviving** refers to maintaining the status quo, simply existing with no meaning in our day-to-day lives. **Resilience** and **Thriving** encourages an upward flow motion in our lives, resulting in **Meaning**—Meaning discovery, having the courage to push forward in life, recognizing our freedom and responsibility to our lives so that we can engage in living authentically, regardless of limitations, and to experience self-transcendence, going above and beyond ourselves.

Through the Meaning Triangle (Creativity, Experiences, Attitude), we can begin to make our way toward finding **Meaning in Tragedy.** As clinicians, we can assist clients who are facing a tragic situation to examine and understand how new meanings can be discovered in each of these areas. And likewise, they can show clients how they can experience **Self-Transcendence,** going beyond themselves and the limiting situation. Once clients begin to experience meaning and engage in finding meaning, even in the midst of the tragedy, **Post Traumatic Growth and Resilience** is often the result. There is a change in their self-perception and self-acceptance; there are newfound connections or deepening of previous relationships, and overall changes in attitude and perceptions of life.

Finally, **Meaning in Life** is regained through a **Sense of Coherence**—(a concept coined by A. Antonovsky), being able to comprehend the situation (comprehensibility), being able to manage it (manageability), and discovering meaning in the process (meaning).

We aim to assist clients, faced with the difficulties of trauma and tragedy, to regain their sense of meaning and purpose in life. Meaning-Centered Logotherapy & Existential Analysis provides the therapeutic pathway, as well as Sacred Encounter of connection, to foster the sense of meaning in clients and their families. The **Gift of Meaning** in the face of tragedy is precisely what allows us to go on living!

Part III
Trauma Treatment Foundational Phase-Work (TTFP)

Trauma:
Acronym

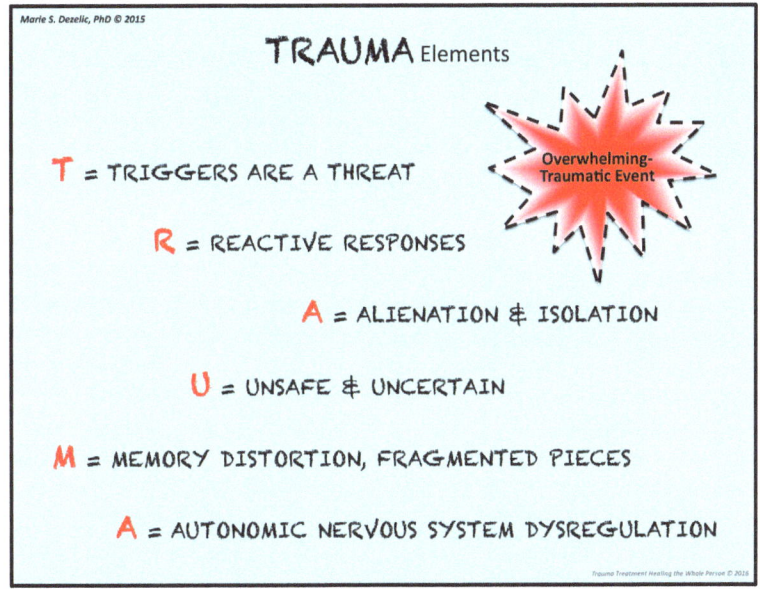

(Handout included in Section II)

Trauma is an overwhelming bio-psycho-social-spiritual event that causes a variety of ongoing disruptive responses and symptoms to occur within the biological and psychological domains. These responses and symptoms can also have an after effect in the social and spiritual domains. Although from a Meaning-Centered Logotherapy & Existential Analysis perspective, our spirit cannot be damaged, when trauma occurs, the resultant overactive symptomatology in the biological and psychological domains produces existential angst, frustration, questioning of meaning, self, life, and God/Universe, which often causes an inability to access the gifts in our spiritual dimension. Viktor Frankl calls this phenomenon "Existential Vacuum," which can lead to "Noögenic Neurosis."

We can also use the word "trauma" as an Acronym; thus "TRAUMA" means:

- **T** = Triggers are threat
- **R** = Reactive responses
- **A** = Alienation & isolation
- **U** = Unsafe and uncertain
- **M** = Memory distortion, fragmented pieces
- **A** = Autonomic nervous system dysregulation

Trauma Definitions

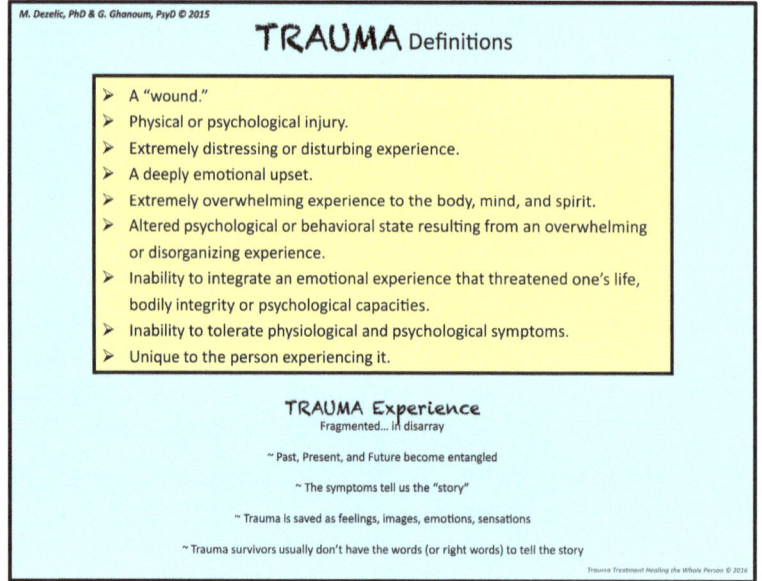

(Handout included in Section II)

Trauma refers to:

- A "wound."
- Physical or psychological injury.
- Extremely distressing or disturbing experience.
- A deeply emotional upset.
- Extremely overwhelming experience to the body, mind, and possibly blocking access to the spirit.
- Altered psychological or behavioral state resulting from an overwhelming or disorganizing experience.
- Inability to integrate an emotional experience that threatened one's life, bodily integrity or psychological capacities.
- Inability to tolerate physiological and psychological symptoms.
- Unique to the person experiencing it.

The **TRAUMA Experience:**

- Fragmented... in disarray.
- Past, Present, and Future become entangled.
- The symptoms tell us the "story."
- Trauma is stored in body and brain memory as feelings, images, emotions, and sensations.
- Trauma survivors usually don't have the words (or right words) to tell the story.

Trauma Elements:
Trauma Affects Each Person Differently

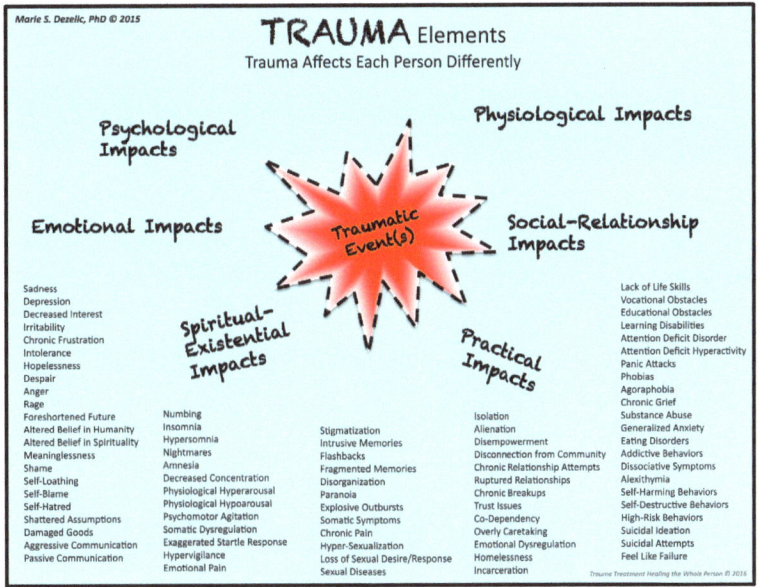

(Handout included in Section II)

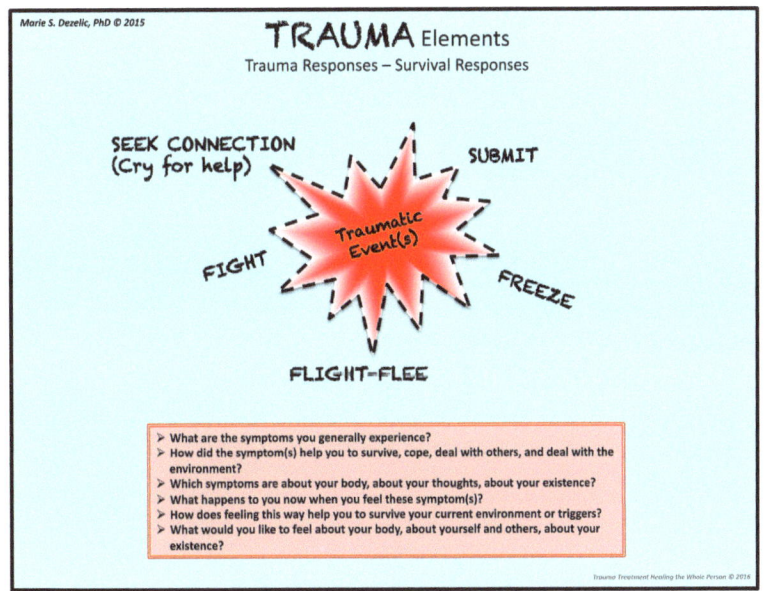

(Handout included in Section II)

Trauma affects each person differently and has **physiological, psychological, emotional, social-relationship, spiritual-existential, and/or practical impacts** on our functioning, while our survival responses (brain-body) follow a pattern of: **seek connection (cry for help), fight, flight-flee, freeze, and/or submit.** These impacts appear as bio-psycho-social-spiritual symptoms, or clusters of symptoms that fit diagnostic criteria for mental health disorders. These symptoms relate to our sense of self, sense of others and the world, sense of self in relationship to others and the world, as well as how we function in life.

Symptoms or Disorders often associated with Trauma:

Depressive Symptoms
- Sadness
- Depression
- Decreased Interest
- Irritability
- Chronic Frustration
- Intolerance
- Hopelessness
- Despair
- Anger
- Rage

Beliefs about Self and World
- Foreshortened Future
- Altered Belief in Humanity
- Altered Belief in Spirituality
- Meaninglessness
- Shame
- Self-Loathing
- Self-Blame
- Self-Hatred
- Shattered Assumptions
- Damaged Goods
- Feel Like Failure
- Aggressive Communication
- Passive Communication

PTSD Symptoms
- Numbing
- Insomnia
- Hypersomnia
- Nightmares
- Amnesia
- Decreased Concentration
- Physiological Hyperarousal
- Physiological Hypoarousal
- Psychomotor Agitation
- Somatic Dysregulation
- Exaggerated Startle Response
- Hypervigilance
- Emotional Pain

- Stigmatization
- Intrusive Memories
- Flashbacks
- Fragmented Memories
- Disorganization
- Paranoia
- Explosive Outbursts

Physiological Symptoms
- Somatic Symptoms
- Chronic Pain
- Hyper-Sexualization
- Loss of Sexual Desire/Response
- Sexual Diseases

Connection with Others
- Isolation
- Alienation
- Disempowerment
- Disconnection from Community
- Chronic Relationship Attempts
- Ruptured Relationships
- Chronic Breakups
- Trust Issues
- Co-Dependency
- Overly Caretaking
- Emotional Dysregulation

Practical Issues
- Homelessness
- Incarceration
- Lack of Life Skills
- Vocational Obstacles
- Educational Obstacles

Disorders and Behaviors
- Learning Disabilities
- Attention Deficit Disorder (ADD)
- Attention Deficit Hyperactivity (ADHD)
- Panic Attacks
- Phobias
- Agoraphobia
- Chronic Grief
- Substance Abuse
- Generalized Anxiety
- Eating Disorders
- Addictive Behaviors

- Dissociative Symptoms
- Alexithymia
- Self-Harming Behaviors
- Self-Destructive Behaviors
- High-Risk Behaviors
- Suicidal Ideation
- Suicidal Attempts

Alphabetical Order of Symptoms or Disorders often associated with Trauma that are listed above:

- Addictive Behaviors
- Aggressive Communication
- Agoraphobia
- Alexithymia
- Alienation
- Altered Belief in Humanity
- Altered Belief in Spirituality
- Anger
- Amnesia
- Attention Deficit Disorder (ADD)
- Attention Deficit Hyperactivity Disorder (ADHD)
- Chronic Breakups
- Chronic Frustration
- Chronic Grief
- Chronic Pain
- Chronic Relationship Attempts
- Co-Dependency
- Damaged Goods Image
- Decreased Concentration
- Decreased Interest
- Depression
- Despair
- Disconnection from Community
- Disempowerment
- Disorganization
- Dissociative Symptoms
- Eating Disorders
- Educational Obstacles
- Emotional Dysregulation
- Emotional Pain
- Exaggerated Startle Response
- Explosive Outbursts
- Feelings of Failure
- Flashbacks
- Foreshortened Future

- Fragmented Memories
- Generalized Anxiety
- High-Risk Behaviors
- Homelessness
- Hopelessness
- Hyper-Sexualization
- Hypersomnia
- Hypervigilance
- Incarceration
- Insomnia
- Intolerance
- Intrusive Memories
- Irritability
- Isolation
- Lack of Life Skills
- Learning Disabilities
- Loss of Sexual Desire/Response
- Meaninglessness
- Nightmares
- Numbing
- Overly involved in Caretaking Behavior
- Panic Attacks
- Paranoia
- Passive Communication
- Phobias
- Physiological Hyperarousal
- Physiological Hypoarousal
- Psychomotor Agitation
- Rage
- Ruptured Relationships
- Sadness
- Self-Blame
- Self-Destructive Behaviors
- Self-Harming Behaviors
- Self-Hatred
- Self-Loathing
- Sexual Diseases
- Shame
- Shattered Assumptions
- Somatic Dysregulation
- Somatic Symptoms
- Stigmatization
- Substance Abuse
- Suicidal Attempts
- Suicidal Ideation
- Trust Issues
- Vocational Obstacles

We can assist clients to become aware of how symptoms have manifested by asking a set of questions:

- What are the symptoms you generally experience?
- How did the symptom(s) help you to survive, cope, deal with others, and deal with the environment?
- Which symptoms are about your body, about your thoughts, about your existence?
- What happens to you now when you feel these symptom(s)?
- How does feeling this way help you to survive your current environment or triggers?
- What would you like to feel about your body, about yourself and others, about your existence?

Window of Tolerance - Trauma/Anxiety Related Responses:
Widening the Comfort Zone for Increased Flexibility

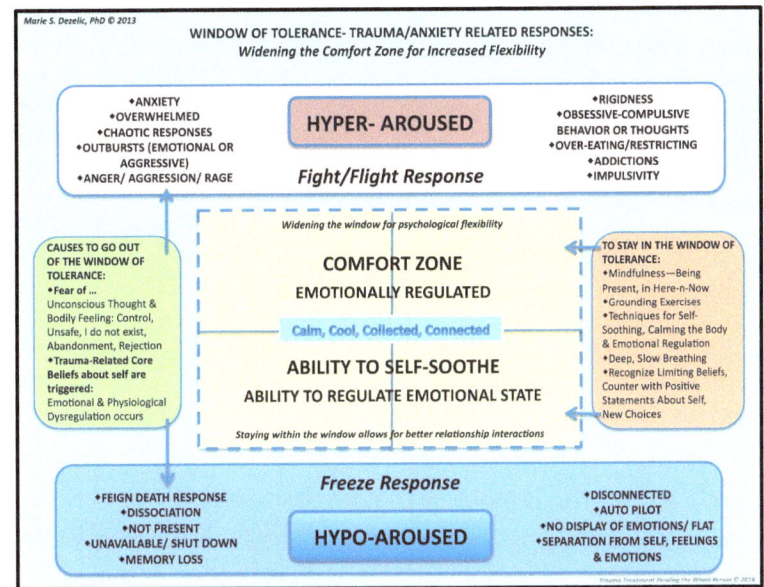

(Handout included in Section II)

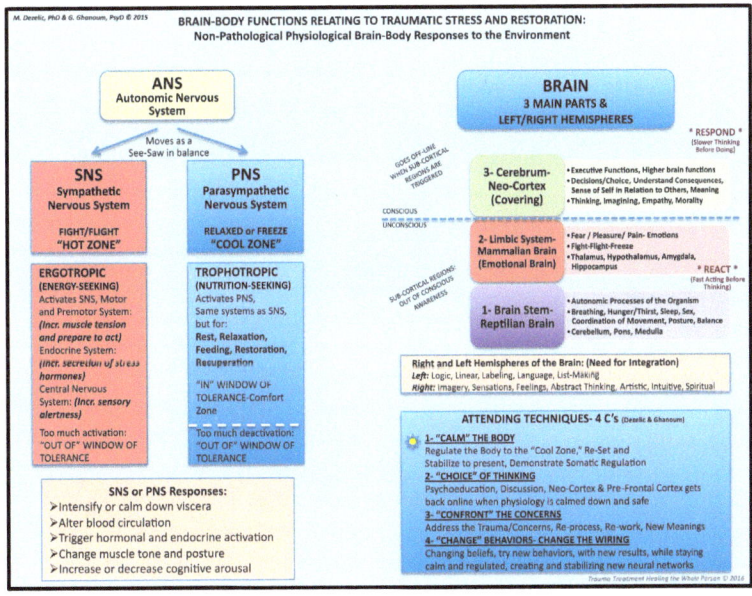

(Handout included in Section II)

"The Window of Tolerance" is a term coined by Dan Siegel that is now widely used in understanding normal brain/physiology reaction responses. It has also become part of trauma-informed treatment terminology, as well as a term used in many other areas of mental health. The Window of Tolerance refers to our unique zone of autonomic nervous system and limbic brain response (emotional arousal) that is optimal for our own personal comfort and well-being. Efforts are made to assist individuals to discover ways to widen their personal, unique Window of Tolerance, as well as to develop methods to stay in their Window of Tolerance via self-soothing and self-regulating behaviors.

When we "jump" out, are "catapulted" out, or feel "pushed" out of our Window of Tolerance on either the upper (hyper-aroused) or lower (hypo-aroused) sides of the window, the prefrontal cortex essentially "goes offline," with only subcortical brain regions (limbic system-emotional brain, and brain stem) staying active. This process removes our ability to "think through" our actions and possible consequences.

In order to get help, make sense of the situation, and talk through a problem (use any cognitive skills), we need to find a way back into our unique Window of Tolerance, that comfort zone where our physiology is regulated. We can help make this happen by using self-soothing and self-regulating techniques; that is, we can learn to calm the overactive parts of the brain and physiology. This process is called "bottom-up" therapy, first regulating the body before thinking and processing can occur. This will allow all regions of the brain (especially the prefrontal region) to get back online (activated), and will also cause our processing system to function appropriately. **Attending Techniques—4 C's,** offers a format to follow.

Visual representations (see client handouts) of our own unique Window of Tolerance and Brain-Body Functions (explanations of autonomic nervous system and brain regions) often help us to see what is happening within our nervous system and, therefore, help us better understand why disconnection in relationships can and does occur after we have experienced a traumatic event.

In intimate relationships between adults, and in interactions with children who are experiencing extreme distress, it is likely that one or both of them are out of their individual Windows of Tolerance, and are attempting to get their needs met by talking through a problem. Clinicians can help each person learn how to stay in or expand their personal Window of Tolerance, even when they are triggered emotionally or physiologically by the actions or behaviors of the other partner or by the event in their lives. It is also possible that couples, as well as parents with children, can learn to create matching Windows of Tolerance (attunement), where engagement can occur safely and comfortably.

Attending Techniques—4 C's

1) "CALM" THE BODY
- Regulate the Body to the "Cool Zone," Re-Set and Stabilize to present, Demonstrate Somatic Regulation

2) "CHOICE" OF THINKING
- Psychoeducation, Discussion, Neo-Cortex & Pre-Frontal Cortex gets back online when physiology is calmed down and safe

3) "CONFRONT" THE CONCERNS
- Address the Trauma/Concerns, Re-process, Re-work, New Meanings

4) "CHANGE" BEHAVIORS- CHANGE THE WIRING
- Changing beliefs, try new behaviors, with new results, while staying calm and regulated, creating and stabilizing new neural networks

The Body Holds the Memory, The Mind Acts it Out, Applying Logotherapy:
How Each Process Impacts our Internal Feeling and Outward Doing

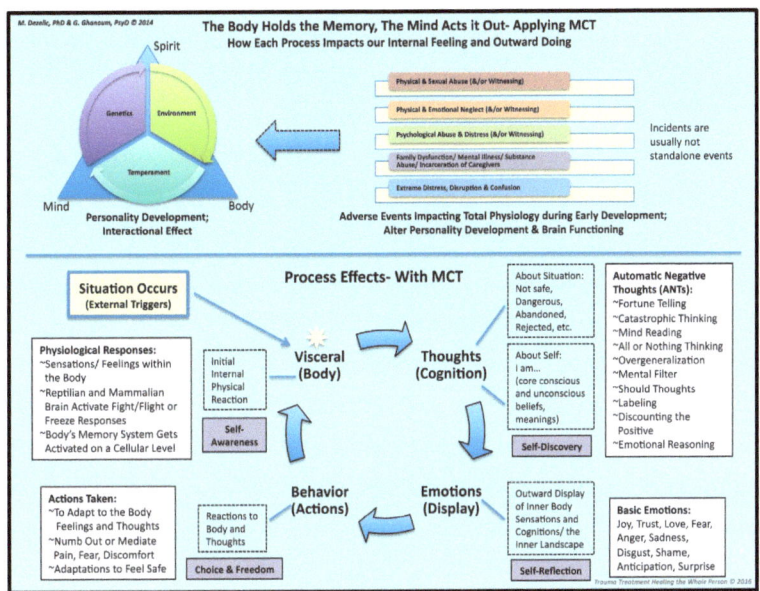

(Handout included in Section II)

Current instrumental trauma research, which focuses on the neurobiology of trauma's impact on the overall physiology, brain functioning, inner experience and display of behavioral symptoms, has shown how adverse events in early developmental years impact not only personality development, but also baseline brain functioning. These adverse conditions affect attachment style to initial caregivers, later attachment styles in interpersonal relationships, and symptomatology in childhood and later in adulthood. They can also result in clinical disorders. In no particular order of severity, the following is a list of the five categories of adverse events (van Der Kolk, 2014):

(1) Physical & Sexual Abuse (&/or Witnessing)
(2) Physical & Emotional Neglect (&/or Witnessing)
(3) Psychological Abuse & Distress (&/or Witnessing)
(4) Family Dysfunction/ Mental Illness/ Substance Abuse/ Incarceration of Caregivers
(5) Extreme Distress, Disruption & Confusion

These five adverse events impact the individual's developing personality structure:
Mind—Psyche (how we perceive, make sense of, and determine meaning of the situation)
Body—Soma (how the cellular tissue is recording information and how brain activity is being activated or de-activated)
Spirit—Noös—Unique Essence (how our inner meaning in life and motivation-thriving is affected).

These adverse events, which are often not stand alone happenings, impact our:
(1) Self-view
(2) Others-view
(3) World-view
(4) Overall meaning constructs, in terms of perceived sense of self and self-awareness
(5) Safety and security in our own bodies, with others, and within the world

It is helpful for all of us to understand these concepts even though not everyone will experience traumatic life experiences. That said, it is also likely that many individuals will experience traumatic events during childhood, adolescence or adulthood, and that traumatic events will impact these neurological systems, promote the expression of certain genes and pre-dispositions, as well as negatively affect the ongoing processes of physiological-body reactions, thoughts, emotions, and behaviors.

Trauma-informed therapies incorporate many levels/dimensions of the self, and often include the existential concepts in their treatment plan for core traumatic memories. Core traumatic memories generate physical sensations, images/pictures, and emotions that get disconnected and fragmented (cut off) from the individual's autobiographical timeline, and that have core existential meanings and beliefs attached to them. As these core existential meanings and beliefs are uncovered and discovered in each of the processes (physiological-body reactions, thoughts, emotions, and behaviors), reworking and reprocessing of them takes place on the Mind-Body-Spirit dimensions. Since all individuals go through this process to varying degrees, the effects of this re-working and re-processing will also include Logotherapeutic actions of self-awareness, self-discovery, self-reflection, choice and freedom, and can be applied not only to trauma and trauma-related disorders, but to other disorders or symptomatology.

Additionally, as Viktor Frankl always stated, Logotherapy & Existential Analysis can be used specifically and adjunctively, and can be a complementary method to use with other psychotherapeutic schools of thought. Some individuals have more difficulty recovering from trauma and can get stuck in certain physiological, cognitive, affective and behavioral responses, depending on their particular set of circumstances. Clinicians who use Logotherapy and Existential Analysis can assist clients to work through these areas to a greater or lesser degree, according to individual needs, tailoring treatment specifically to the client.

The Conceptual Pictograph—Client Handout: **The Body Holds the Memory, The Mind Acts it Out, Applying Logotherapy: How Each Process Impacts our Internal Feeling and Outward Doing** is a simple, one page snapshot of the adverse effects that traumatic or other negative events have on personality development.

This handout also shows how a **present or current situation triggers a process,** patterns that have been ingrained as an adapted coping style:

Situation Occurs (Event) impacts:
Visceral response (Body), impacts →
Thoughts (Cognitions), impacts →
Emotions (Display), impacts →
Behavior (Actions), impacts → more Visceral response

Within each of these areas, there are degrees of freedom to work on therapeutic changes:

Visceral: *Self-Awareness*
Thoughts: *Self-Discovery*
Emotions: *Self-Reflection*
Behavior: *Choice and Freedom*

Adapted coping styles should not necessarily be viewed in a negative light or seen as maladaptive. Someone's coping styles were often the only options available when they were initially set in place. However, in the present moment, they may no longer be serving the individual well, and may be interrupting social, interpersonal relationships, as well as damaging the sense of self, security, safety, and agency. With proper guidance, new discoveries, new understandings, and new choices can be made in the present, leading to meaningful and connected relationships, meaning in life, self-awareness, sense of inner security and safety, the will to meaning, and self-transcendence.

Trauma Treatment Foundational Phase-Work (TTFP) Model Integrative Trauma-Informed Treatment:
Core Elements For Stabilization, Recovery, & Reconnection

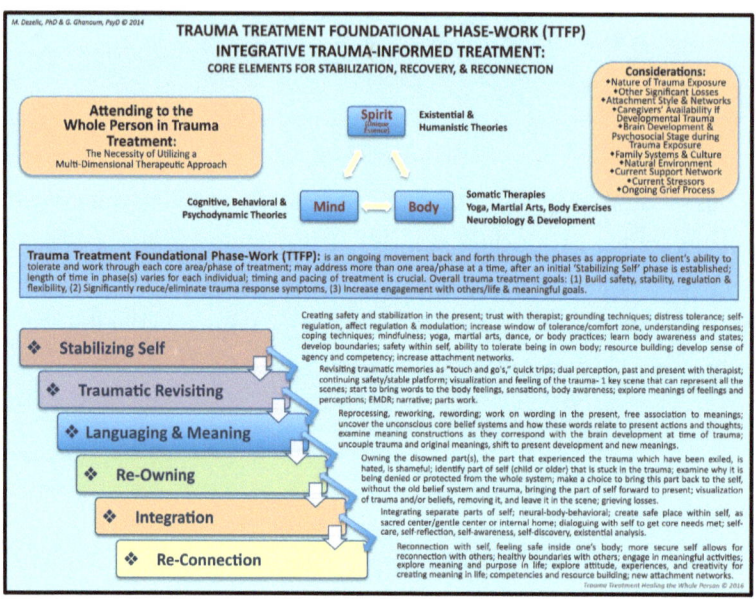

(Handout included in Section II)

Meaning in relation to self and the world, meaning in life, meaning in suffering, and meaningful engagement have long been addressed in trauma treatment both as general concepts and part of clinical treatment. This model specifically incorporates elements of Meaning-Centered Logotherapy & Existential Analysis, offering a clinical basis of existential topics relative to developmental trauma, PTSD, and trauma-and-stressor related disorders, in addition to core elements that trauma-informed treatment needs to include for recovery and healing.

According to SAMSHA (The Substance Abuse and Mental Health Services Administration), **Trauma-Informed Care (TIC)** is an approach that refers to the provider, program or organization's ability to: *Realize* the widespread impact of trauma, as well as understand pathways for recovery and facilitate healing; *Recognize* the signs and symptoms of trauma in clients, families, and staff; *Respond* to individuals by integrating knowledge about trauma into practices, policies, and procedures; actively resist **Re-traumatization** of clients. TIC is accomplished through the adherence to six key principles: *(1) Safety; (2) Trustworthiness and transparency; (3) Peer support; (4) Collaboration and mutuality; (5) Empowerment, voice and choice; (6) Cultural, historical, and gender issues;* while utilizing **Trauma-specific interventions** in treatment (samhsa.gov).

Trauma Treatment Foundational Phase-Work (TTFP) is an integrative trauma-informed treatment modality. The framework of trauma-informed treatment and therapeutic care combines the most recent, researched information available in the field of trauma treatment and development. It builds upon existing theories and strategies; however, this model utilizes a holistic and existential methodology, attending to the "Whole Person in Trauma Treatment," which necessitates a multi-dimensional therapeutic approach. Clinicians working in the trauma field understand that they must have a therapeutic toolbox full of treatment interventions, strategies, and skills, as trauma manifests itself in a variety of ways. Often, in addition to Post Traumatic Stress Disorder (PTSD), the manifestations occur as several diagnosable clinical disorders, including disorganization in early personality development and possibly ongoing social/relational interactions (referred to as personality disorders). Multiple disorders and symptoms are indications of traumatic experience that may occur as a result of developmental trauma, a one-time traumatic event, or chronic traumatic events in childhood, adolescence and/or adulthood. The chronic effects of trauma are often perpetuated by the ongoing symptoms and reaction cycles. One of the most important considerations clinicians should keep in mind is that the variety of maladaptive behaviors exhibited by trauma clients are actually coping strategies for survival and safety. These self-regulatory behaviors are means of sensory and affect management, are often self-soothing, and are aimed at a desired connection or disconnection with the outside world. If clinicians encourage trauma clients to remove these behaviors too quickly or do not help these clients replace them with healthier behaviors that they can tolerate, accept, and work with for self-regulation, the original coping behaviors will likely manifest in other unhealthy or dysfunctional ways or even increase in propensity.

Trauma Treatment Foundational Phase-Work (TTFP), Integrative Trauma-Informed Treatment, a treatment method developed by the authors, **Marie Dezelic and Gabriel Ghanoum,** is an ongoing "movement" back and forth through the phases, a movement that is determined by the ability of clients to tolerate and work through each core area/phase of treatment. Clinicians may address more than one area/phase at a time, after an initial "Stabilizing Self" phase is established for the client. Length of time in phase(s) varies for each individual; timing and pacing of treatment is crucial, as each individual is unique and needs to be guided and assisted rather than pushed to overcome new core areas. The overall trauma-informed treatment goals are: **(1) build safety, stability, self-regulation & flexibility, (2) significantly reduce and/or eliminate trauma response symptoms, (3) increase engagement with others, with life and with meaningful goals.**

Whole Person in Trauma Treatment

Trauma-informed Treatment addresses the Whole person: Mind, Body, and Spirit (Unique Essence—Existence). Trauma-informed treatment is not a specific theory; rather, it is a treatment style based on a range of theoretical and psychological models, incorporating several techniques, and addressing a variety of symptoms and issues. In doing so, there are several therapeutic theories that are utilized and combined throughout treatment. These theories include: **(1) Mind:** Cognitive, Behavioral, and Psychodynamic theories; **(2) Body:** Somatic therapies, Yoga, Martial Arts, Drama, Body Exercises, Neurobiology & Development; **(3) Spirit (Unique Existential Essence):** Existential and Humanistic theories. Attending to the whole person in trauma-informed treatment offers the possibility of true and lasting recovery, healing and engagement.

Considerations

There are several considerations that will impact how clients are able to tolerate each area/phase of treatment. Clinical judgment should be used in incorporating or adjusting to each of the considerations during the trauma treatment. These considerations include:

- Nature of Trauma Exposure
- Other Significant Losses
- Attachment Style & Networks
- Caregivers' Availability if Developmental Trauma
- Brain Development & Psychosocial Stage during Trauma Exposure
- Family Systems & Cultural Implications
- Natural Environment
- Current Support Network
- Current Stressors
- Ongoing Grief Process

Trauma Treatment Foundational Phase-Work (TTFP)
Integrative Trauma-Informed Treatment Model

It is important to complete the initial "Stabilizing Self" area/phase of treatment before moving on to the rest of the areas. This "Stabilizing Self" aspect will likely become an ongoing phase of treatment and care. Once clients learn to "be" and live in their own bodies, they can begin to develop an ability to tolerate and modulate physiological sensations and arousal. Most trauma therapists believe this must be done before any trauma processing work can be successful. Trauma-informed therapy, therefore, includes an element of "Traumatic Revisiting," offered through a variety of interventions and techniques. If this aspect is left out, it is not considered "trauma-informed therapy."

However, not all clients will be able to tolerate full trauma reprocessing, and will, therefore, only work on small parts of their traumatic events. The other areas/phases of this treatment model are likewise significant and can be worked through even if the "Traumatic Revisiting" phase is minimal or needs to be bypassed altogether. These areas/phases will help clients to increase the following: ***self-confidence, self-efficacy, agency, ability to tolerate and understand self and relationships with the world, and engagement with others and with positive, healthy activities.*** These areas/phases will also help clients to decrease the following: ***sense of shame, guilt, brokenness, loathing, anger, hatred, fear, confusion, distrust, chaotic dysregulation, and chronic maladaptive, harmful behaviors.***

Keep in mind that, although a positive later phase is reached, new changes to self, environment, and behaviors may trigger memories of other traumatic material that may not have surfaced until these areas/phases emerged. This will necessitate "Traumatic Revisiting" and working through the new trauma memories. This possibility is precisely why trauma treatment is an ongoing movement back and forth between the areas/phases.

Trauma-informed therapy, by its very nature, includes a considerable amount of grief work and processing within the areas/phases. As symptoms begin to shift or are removed, there will be a grief process revolving around several elements: ***Absence of or loss of connections to caregivers and other key figures, loss and changes of self, loss of time, missed opportunities, and loss of activities and choices in life.*** All of these lost possibilities are due to the trauma exposure and maintenance of symptoms.

The articles, books and workbooks with evidence-based practices that are listed in this manual have all aided in informing this model. These invaluable sources of information for informing treatment interventions, strategies, techniques, and concerns are resources that all trauma clinicians should have in their professional library. Each area/phase of the TTFP Treatment Model presented here can be expounded upon utilizing these mentioned resources. It is important for clinicians to receive training and supervision so that they will better understand core concepts in trauma theory and therapy before attempting to offer our model of trauma-informed treatment.

PHASES

"Stabilizing Self"

Creating safety and stabilization in the present; trust in the therapist; grounding techniques; distress tolerance; self-regulation, affect regulation & modulation; increasing window of tolerance/comfort zone, understanding responses; coping techniques; mindfulness practices; yoga, martial arts, dance, or body practices; body awareness and states; development of boundaries; safety within self, ability to tolerate being in our own body; resource building; development of a sense of agency and competency; increase in number of attachment networks.

"Traumatic Revisiting"

Revisiting traumatic memories as "touch and go's"—quick trips; experiencing dual perception—visiting past traumatic experience while staying grounded and present with therapist; continuing safety/stable platform; visualizing and evoking full physiological feelings about the traumatic event(s)—this may include recalling one key scene that can represent all of the scenes, or the earliest memory; starting to use words (bring language and meaning) to describe the body's feelings, sensations, and body awareness; exploring the meanings of feelings and perceptions; utilizing specific trauma processing approaches, such as: Eye Movement Desensitization Reprocessing (EMDR), Attachment-Focused EMDR, Narrative Therapies, Sand Tray and Sand Play Therapy, Internal Family Systems and working with "Parts" of self (Parts work), Trauma Incidence Reduction (TIR), Brainspotting (treatment where an eye position, a physiological subsystem holding emotional experience in memory form, that is related to energetic/emotional activation of traumatic issue is targeted and de-conditioned), Desensitization, or any other approaches that specifically target reprocessing of traumatic material.

"Languaging & Meaning"

"Languaging"—the process of making meaning and shaping experience and knowledge through the use of verbal language, with affective, cognitive, adaptive, and flexible behavior in social interaction; reprocessing, reworking, rewording; the examination, discovery, and changes of how words associated with emotions are being used in the present about self, others and the world; using free association to find meanings; uncovering the unconscious core belief systems and how these words relate to present actions and thoughts; examining meaning constructions (biological, personal, social/relational, and cultural) as they correspond with the brain development at the time of trauma; uncoupling the trauma and original meanings associated, by shifting to present development and new meanings.

"Re-Owning"

Owning and taking responsibility for the disowned part(s) of self, the part that experienced the trauma and has been exiled, buried away, locked away, repressed, is hated, disliked, is considered shameful, damaged goods, weak, inferior, or not worthy; identifying part(s) of self (child or older) stuck in the trauma; examining why this part is being denied or protected from being included in the whole system (one's integrated sense of self); making a conscious choice to be responsible for bringing the disowned part back to the present self, without the old belief system, meanings, and actual trauma (leaving the trauma in the past, but bringing the part that experienced the trauma into the present sense of self); visualizing the trauma and/or beliefs, removing it, and/or leaving it in the scene, while allowing the part of self (the one who experienced the trauma) to go forward toward the present; grieving all of the losses that the denied part(s) of self experienced due to the traumatic event(s).

"Integration"

Integrating or bringing together separate parts of self (this is actually accomplished through the development of new neural pathways that are integrated while one is incorporating new existential belief systems, languaging, and changing the view of self, others, and the world; old brain states can become deactivated; new neural pathways, physiological (body) patterns, and new behaviors develop—neural-body-behaviors; creating a safe place within self, as sacred center/gentle center or internal home (within one's own body); dialoguing with self to get core needs met; performing ongoing self-care, self-reflection, self-awareness, self-discovery, existential analysis.

"Re-Connection"

Reconnecting with self, feeling safe inside one's body; having a more secure self (ability to tolerate emotions and physical sensations) that will allow for reconnection and reengagement with others; developing healthy boundaries with others; engaging in meaningful activities; exploring and discovering meaning and purpose in life; exploring attitude, experiences, and creativity for finding meaning in life;

developing competencies, strengthening and building inner resources; discovering and creating new attachment networks and support.

Trauma Experience Through Meaning-Centered Therapy Exploration:
Bringing Awareness, Becoming Curious and Discovering the Mind-Body-Spirit

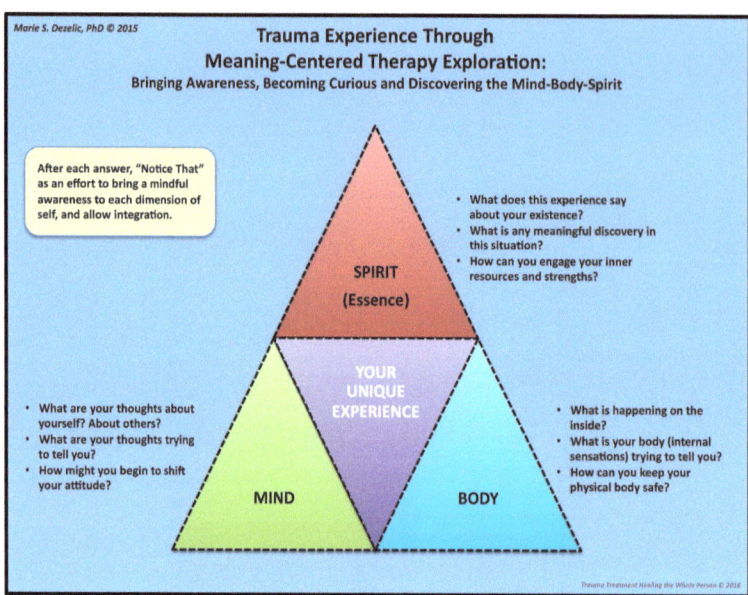

(Handout included in Section II)

We can begin to bring a focused awareness to the body, mind, and spirit by exploring each one of these areas with a set of questions. We can ask the client to notice each area, without judgment, without going into an explanation in that moment; we want clients to just notice the internal sensations, beliefs, thoughts, and discoveries related to the dimensions of body, mind, and spirit. After the exercise is over, we can ask clients to put a narrative around the experience, explore what is needed for continued safety and grounding, and/or how this experience has helped to make sense of physical, emotional, psychological, and deep "felt sense" sensations and understanding.

Unique Experience: Body-Mind-Spirit

Ask clients to discuss and explore a scene, a situation, or even this moment, that is emotionally charged (to deal with traumatic events), neutral or pleasant (to foster internal resourcing).

Ask clients a set of questions for each area of Body, Mind, and Spirit. After each answer, say "Notice That" as an effort to bring a mindful awareness to each dimension of self, and allow integration.

Body:
- What is happening on the inside?
- What is your body (internal sensations) trying to tell you?
- How can you keep your physical body safe?

Mind:
- What are your thoughts about yourself? About others?
- What are your thoughts trying to tell you?
- How might you begin to shift your attitude?

Spirit:
- What does this experience say about your existence?
- What is any meaningful discovery in this situation?
- How can you engage your inner resources and strengths?

Core Relational Wounds:
Initial Impact on Self-Concept and Identity
Secondary Impact on Relational Development

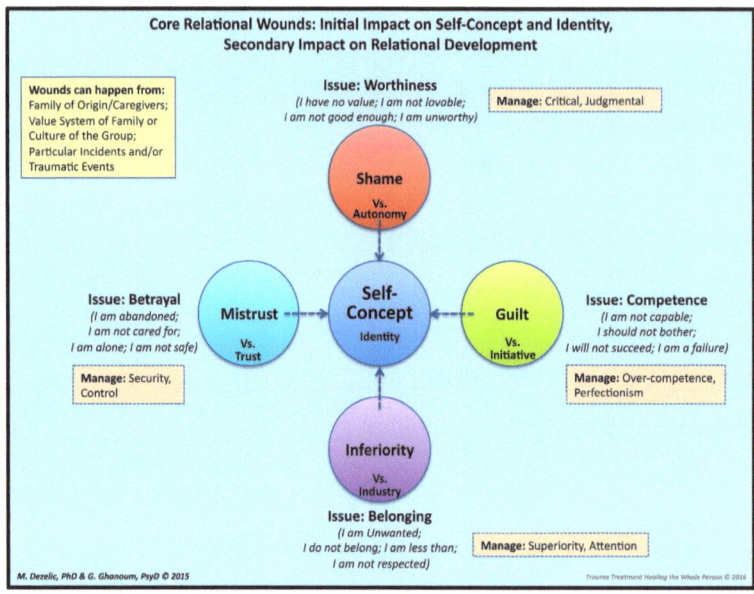

(Handout included in Section II)

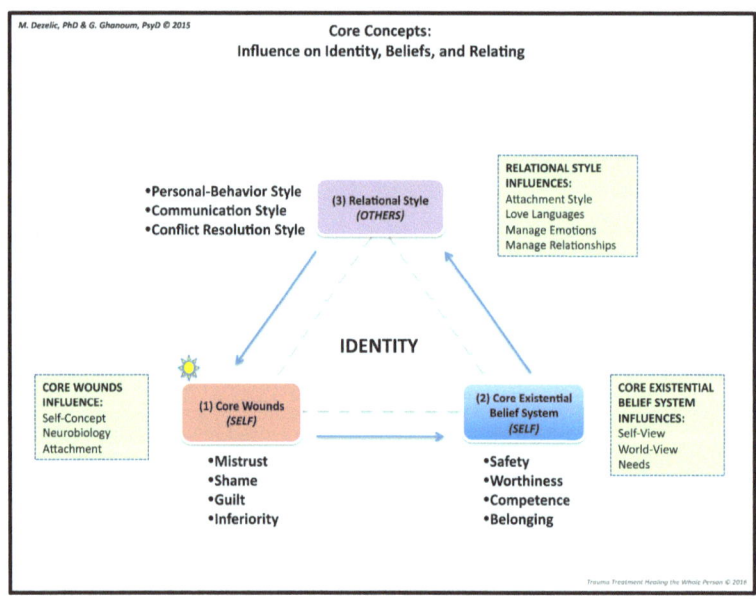

(Handout included in Section II)

"Core Wounds" occurring throughout the developmental stages of growth can negatively impact our self-concept and identity. They can simultaneously affect our attachment bonds, our belief systems, our understanding of and interactions in the world, in addition to our relationships as a whole.

These core wounds, which lie at the epicenter of uncomfortable, overwhelming or traumatic experiences, influence our "needs" (such as the need for: *love, closeness, affirmation, connection, acceptance, respect, loyalty, autonomy, separateness, freedom, space, etc.)* in life and in bonding relationships throughout self-development. These unmet Needs, reflecting Core Wounds often appear as unreasonable requests or demands as well as reactive responses. They can also manifest in approach or avoidance behaviors, and frequently trigger states of hyper or hypo arousal of our biological regulatory system.

Utilizing an Existential, Meaning-Centered approach and the principles of Internal Family Systems theory, therapists can assist clients to develop ways of establishing safe environments and secure attachments. Clients will become better able to validate their own unique experiences, develop a curiosity about their existence and place in the world, and learn to heal relational wounds, which have influenced their attachment styles and bonding as adults.

How do we identify Core Wounds? First it is important to determine their origin. Core Wounds can come from the on-going messages, overt or covert behaviors, and/or the inherent belief systems present in the cultural or value systems of caregivers. They can also arise from incidents that occurred in or out of school with peers and/or teachers. Overwhelming-traumatic events, such as sexual abuse, physical or other acts of violence, psychological abuse, witnessing abuse, parental neglect or inconsistent nurturing, can also precipitate the development of a core wound. Finally, one or both caregivers may suffer from mental illness or substance abuse problems or other environmental upsets. All of these events or factors can lead to the development of a Core Wound. These Core Wounds are known as "relational wounds," signifying that they happened in and within relationship to others. Relational wounds usually begin during our developmental years, when we do not have enough self-understanding, language development and capabilities, as well as abstract cognitive ability to understand that we are not the cause of problems that originate in our caregivers. It is true that we all gather information from the environment and those within it, and use this information to better understand and make sense of who we are in relation to the others or the group. Researchers on Child Development have shown that there are specific developmental milestones (psychosocial stages of development) that we all go through, and that the way we pass through them helps determine and build our self-concept—our identity, our sense of self. One such Developmental theory, developed by Erik Erikson, suggests that all children go through the following first four stages of development: Mistrust/Trust, Shame/Autonomy, Guilt/Initiative, and Inferiority/Industry.

CORE WOUNDS arise out of:
Mistrust vs. Trust
    Issue: Betrayal *(I am abandoned; I am not cared for; I am alone; I am not safe)*
    Manage: Security, Control (self and/or others)

Shame vs. Autonomy
    Issue: Worthiness *(I have no value; I am not lovable; I am not good enough; I am unworthy)*
    Manage: Critical, Judgmental (self and/or others)

Guilt vs. Initiative
    Issue: Competence *(I am not capable; I should not bother; I will not succeed; I am a failure)*
    Manage: Over-competence, Perfectionism (self and/or others)

Inferiority vs. Industry
    Issue: Belonging *(I am Unwanted; I do not belong; I am less than; I am not respected)*
    Manage: Superiority, Attention (self and/or others)

Core Wounds occur while our brains are developing and maturing (before 12 years of age). Depending on how old we are, we might or might not have access to language faculties, and might still be in what the cognitive developmental theorist, Jean Piaget, named the "concrete" thinking phase of cognitive development. In this stage, we take everything as truth because we do not have the ability to reason out that there might be other possibilities, or we are not developmentally ready to think in abstract ways. These early thoughts and understanding influence our existential beliefs (beliefs about our existence and the world), and managing styles (the way we manage ourselves and relationships). These existential thoughts and understanding build and shape our self-concept as we develop and grow; these early thoughts and understandings will fall out of conscious awareness; yet, they will become ingrained patterns of how we immediately appraise a situation, in reference to ourselves (self-referencing) and how we appraise others and the environment (environmental referencing). These appraisals will all eventually influence our behaviors.

It is possible that any problem/issue/trigger that we have today, links to one or more of the four Core Wound themes: Mistrust/Trust, Shame/Autonomy, Guilt/Initiative, and Inferiority/Industry. We might find ourselves internally saying any of the statements listed above relating to these Core Wounds. We may also say them to our partners, parents, children, co-workers, friends, and others. The way we manage the pain or discomfort of feeling these Core Wounds, is what holds us stuck in these managing patterns.

Courage and a willingness to be vulnerable allow us to understand our Core Wounds. This understanding will not only help us to work on healing from our wounds, but will also allow us to share our understanding with significant others. These "Core Wounds managing patterns" can become neural firing patterns, which will eventually be seen as "traits" or even ongoing "states" of being—that is, of personality development. These will affect our entire organism on a biological level as well as impact our existential well-being. When these patterns are related to deep trauma wounds, great care must be taken when attempting to help clients shift and heal them. This caution is necessary because, when it was originally deployed, the belief developed around the Core Wound, plus the managing style frequently served a vital survival purpose at the time. As an example, a client that was sexually abused as a child may have developed shame as a coping style, i.e., when they would feel shameful, they would somehow become smaller, less noticeable to others around them, allowing them to disappear from the radar of unwanted attention. As an adult, the client may still deploy shame as a way of retreating and withdrawing when the attention on them becomes too overwhelming and uncomfortable, even in circumstances unrelated to the original abuse.

When Getting Triggered Takes Over:
Taking a "Time Out" from the Situation to Take a "Time In" for Self-Discovery

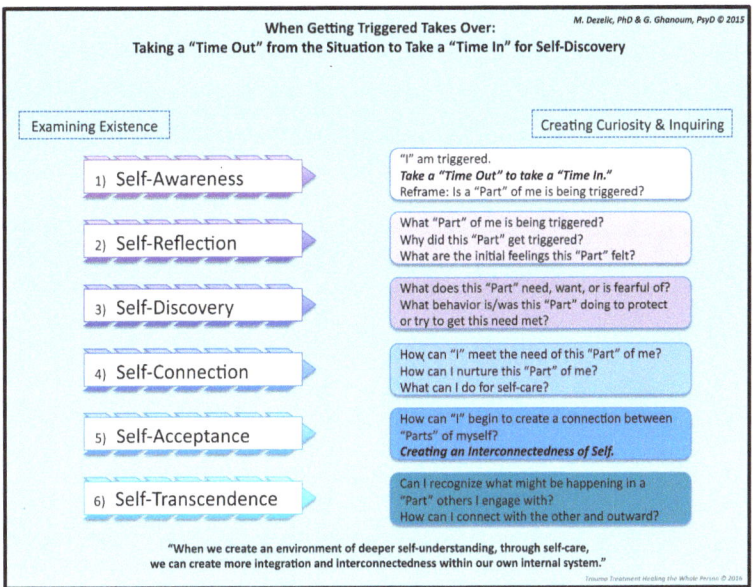

(Handout included in Section II)

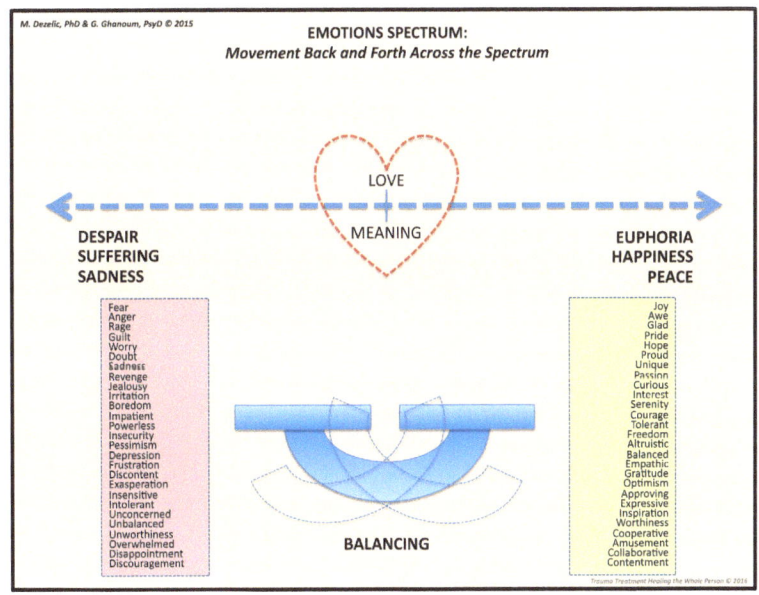

(Handout included in Section II)

Through Meaning-Centered Therapy combined with elements of Internal Family Systems Theory (IFS), or Parts Work, we can begin to examine our existence *(through Self-Awareness, Self-Reflection, Self-Discovery, Self-Connection, Self-Acceptance, and Self-Transcendence)* by creating an open space for curiosity and inquiry about specific areas. **When we create an environment of deeper self-understanding, through self-care, we can create more integration and interconnectedness within our own internal system.**

As we become more aware of our internal "states," inner dialogues, and existential beliefs, we can realize the impact of emotions on our mind, body, and spirit. If we look at a spectrum emotions ranging from despair, suffering, and sadness to euphoria, happiness, and peace, we can work on becoming more balanced rather than being pulled or hijacked by certain emotions related to internal states and circumstances. Experiencing the range of emotions is a natural part of human existence and the human experience; however, if we are stuck in certain patters and emotional states, we might experience more discomfort and distress, and can examine what might be underlying the emotion. Often, when we carry trauma imprints, we do not realize how this has affected our self-concept as well as emotional stability.

Examining Existence — Creating Curiosity and Inquiring

Self-Awareness

- "I" am triggered.
- ***Take a "Time Out" to take a "Time In."***
- Reframe: Is a "Part" of me is being triggered?

Self-Reflection

- What "Part" of me is being triggered?
- Why did this "Part" get triggered?
- What are the initial feelings this "Part" felt?

Self-Discovery

- What does this "Part" need, want, or is fearful of?
- What behavior is/was this "Part" doing to protect or try to get this need met?

Self-Connection

- How can "I" meet the need of this "Part" of me?
- How can I nurture this "Part" of me?
- What can I do for self-care?

Self-Acceptance

- How can "I" begin to create a connection between "Parts" of myself?
- ***Creating an Interconnectedness of Self.***

Self-Transcendence

- Can I recognize what might be happening in a "Part" of others I engage with?
- How can I connect with the other and outward?

Emotions Spectrum: Movement Back and Forth Across the Spectrum
Experiencing Meaning and Love

Despair — Suffering — Sadness (In no particular order)
- Fear
- Anger
- Rage
- Guilt
- Worry
- Doubt
- Sadness
- Revenge
- Jealousy
- Irritation
- Boredom
- Impatient
- Powerless
- Insecurity
- Pessimism
- Depression
- Frustration
- Discontent
- Exasperation
- Insensitive
- Intolerant
- Unconcerned
- Unbalanced
- Unworthiness
- Overwhelmed
- Disappointment
- Discouragement

Euphoria — Happiness — Peace (In no particular order)
- Joy
- Awe
- Glad
- Pride
- Hope
- Proud
- Unique
- Passion
- Curious
- Interest
- Serenity
- Courage
- Tolerant
- Freedom
- Altruistic
- Balanced
- Empathic
- Gratitude
- Optimism
- Approving
- Expressive
- Inspiration
- Worthiness
- Cooperative
- Amusement
- Collaborative
- Contentment

The Meaning-Action Triangle:
Becoming Existentially Aware

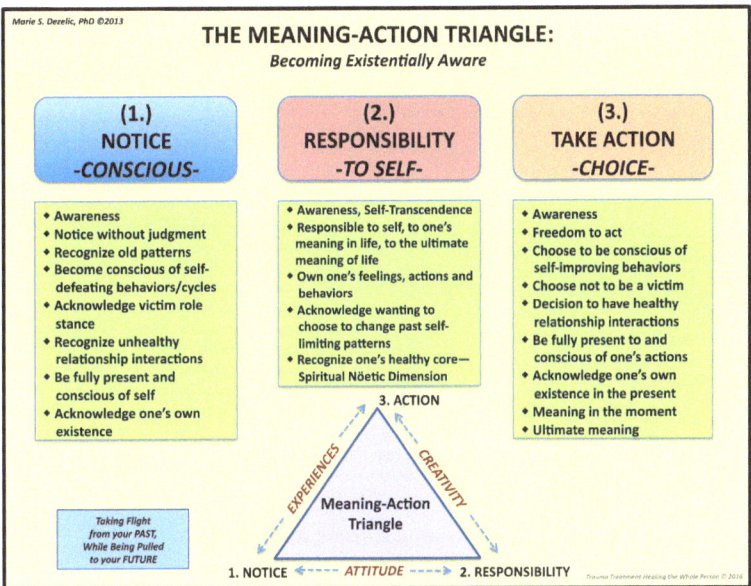

(Handout included in Section II)

How do we change the negative and potentially destructive patterns so that we can become "responders" who possess a mindful awareness, rather than being "reactors" to circumstances, who unconsciously or unwittingly engage in impulsive actions? The Meaning-Action Triangle composed of **(1) Becoming Conscious, (2) Becoming Responsible, (3) Taking Action** offers a Meaning-Centered process for shifting and making changes.

First, by **"Becoming Conscious"** of the Core Wounds and the significant purpose they served at an early developmental stage, we can begin to dig out the "splinters" (shards of left-over pieces of memory and disturbances). The process of beginning to dig out old splinters (Core Wounds) can be quite uncomfortable. When we touch on what really happened to us, it can be quite painful, and we will need to open up to a grief process. Secondly, by **"Becoming Responsible"** to and for our own existence, we can begin to have the courage to recognize our own Core Wounds, their sources, the current everyday triggers, and can begin to work on grieving and healing them ourselves. It will take time to grieve each wound, to grieve the hurt we experienced in a particular time period in life, and to grieve the time lost for other aspects of life. However, once we do this, we will be ready to move on with our lives. Removing the splinters brings about a feeling of relief and a freeing sensation—we break the bonds of old unconscious behavioral patterns within our system. Finally, by **"Taking Action,"** we empower our existential freedom and choice. Little by little, we can take new actions, shift our attitude, enhance our understanding, strengthen our existential beliefs, and change our behaviors. Because of the necessary, personal work we do through this process, we will become less frequently triggered by the same wounds (deep hurts), or, if triggered, these wounds become less painful, and thus more bearable.

Noögenic Activation Method:
LTEA Applied to the "Stages of Change" in Clinical Practice

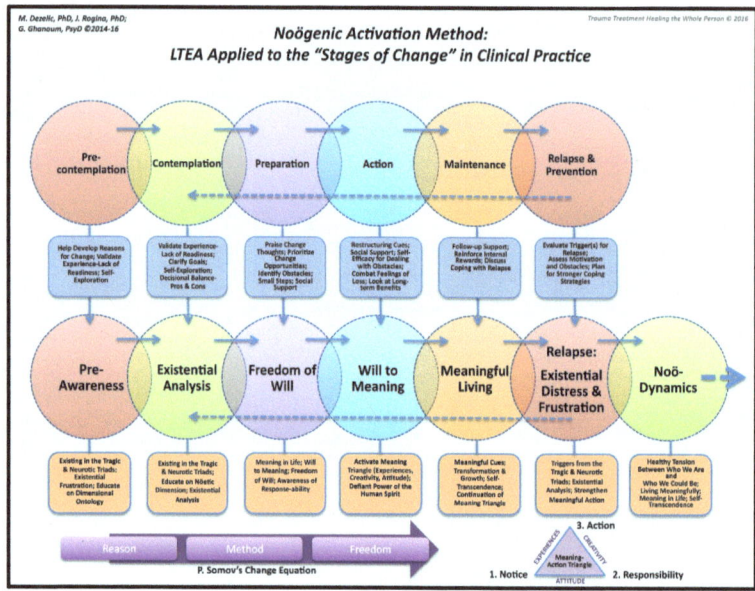

(Handout included in Section II)

In Trauma Treatment, as clients are making changes to existential beliefs, coping strategies and behaviors, it is helpful to examine changes through the lens of the "Stages of Change," while applying the understanding and techniques of the Meaning-Centered approach. In Pavel Somov's "Change Equation," expounded upon in *Choice Awareness Training: Logotherapy and Mindfulness Training for Treatment of Addictions* (2008), **changes in symptoms and behaviors can happen** when we recognize:

(1) a ***Reason-to-Change***—the internal motivation meaning-motivation to achieve a desired goal,
(2) a ***Method-to-Change***—the skillset to make ongoing and lasting changes by handling uncomfortable situations, emotionally challenging or physiological responses, and
(3) the ***Freedom-to-Change***—the existential, inner resource within our core being that we have to engage in order to find ourselves able, capable, and unrestricted of automaticity and vicious mindless patterns of behaviors (p. 7).

7-Step Noögenic Activation Method © Julius Rogina, PhD

Noögenic Activation is divided into two parts:

Part I:
(1) Assess the client for readiness to experience Noögenic Activation. This readiness should include an awareness of the Nöetic (Spiritual) Dimension.
(2) Invite the client to become aware of ways he or she already utilizes Noögenic (Spiritual) resources.
(3) Ask direct permission to engage the application of formal Noögenic Activation.

Part II:

Formal Noögenic Activation: All seven steps are integral to the process; sometimes the focus is "choices." Other times, the focus could be hope, forgiveness, gratefulness, compassion, freedom, meaning, etc.

- The **"7-Step Noögenic Activation Method"** can be combined and used daily as an **Appealing Technique** (guided meditation) in Noögenic (Spiritual) Training to ignite the **Defiant Power of the Spirit** and activate resources of the **Nöetic (Spiritual) Dimension.**
- And/or each of the 7 Steps can be explored within the context of the LTEA 7 Stages of Change

LTEA (Logotherapy & Existential Analysis) Stages of Change
LTEA adaptation and expansion of Prochaska and DiClemente's **"Stages of Change in the Transtheoretical Model (TTM)":**
(Dezelic & Ghanoum, 2015; Prochaska, J., Norcross, J. & DiClemente, C., 1994)

LTEA aspects and terminology are described in purple

- **Stage One: "Precontemplation"**
  *LTEA Stage One: *Possibly experiencing the Tragic and Neurotic Triads- Existential Frustration**
  People are not thinking seriously about changing and are not interested in any kind of help.
  - *"I don't want to."*
  LTEA Task: Educate on Dimensional Ontology

- **Stage Two: "Contemplation"**
  *LTEA Stage Two: *Possibly experiencing the Tragic and Neurotic Triad- Existential Frustration**
  People are more aware of the personal consequences of their bad habit and they spend time thinking about their problem. Although they are able to consider the possibility of changing, they tend to be ambivalent about it.
  - *"I may try."*
  LTEA Task: Educate on Nöetic Dimension

- **Stage Three: "Preparation/ Determination"**
  *LTEA Stage Three: *Freedom of Will**
  People have made a commitment to make a change. Their motivation for change is reflected by statements such as: "I've got to do something about this – this is serious. Something has to change. What can I do? What do I want to do?"
  -*"I will try."*
  LTEA Task: Explore Meaning in Life, Freedom of Will, Will to Meaning

- **Stage Four: "Action"**
  *LTEA Stage Four: *Will to Meaning**
  People believe they have the ability to change their behavior and are actively involved in taking steps to change their undesirable behaviors by using a variety of different skills.
  -*"I am making changes."*
  LTEA Task: Activate Meaning Triangle, Defiant Power of the Spirit

- **Stage Five: "Maintenance"**
  *LTEA Stage Five: *Meaningful Living**
  Maintenance involves being able to successfully avoid or overcome any temptations to return to the undesirable behaviors. The goal of the maintenance stage is to maintain or continue the new status quo. People in this stage tend to remind themselves of how much progress they have made.
  -*"I have made a new habit and choices."*
  LTEA Task: Explore Meaning, Transformation, Self-Transcendence

- **Stage Six: "Relapse"**
  *LTEA Stage Six: *Existential Distress & Frustration**
  Along the way to permanent cessation or stable reduction of undesirable behavior, most people experience relapse. In fact, it is much more common to have at least one relapse than have none at all. Relapse is often accompanied by feelings of discouragement and seeing oneself as a failure.
  -*"I went back to my old pattern."*
  LTEA Task: Explore Existential Despair & Frustration—Tragic & Neurotic Triads

- **Stage Seven:** (not in original "Stages of Change, TTM")
  *LTEA Stage Seven: *Noö-dynamics and Self-Transcendence**
  If maintenance is successful for a long period of time, we reach a point where we are able to work with our emotions and understand our own behaviors and view them in a new light. Self-Transcendence is manifested in the human spirit's ability to reach beyond the present problems and visualize how we want to be in order to actualize meaning possibilities. Noö-dynamics create a tension between who we are and who we could be.
  -*"I am responsible to my life, and am consistently making healthy choices."*
  LTEA Task: Explore Living Meaningfully, Meaning in Life, Existential Analysis, Self-Transcendence

Formal "7-Step Noögenic Activation Method":
(Clinicians can read the following statements with a slow-paced, relaxed voice and gentle tone.)

> 1. As I take a few deep breaths... I become aware of the healthy core within me (my human spirit).
>   *(Access to the Nöetic Dimension)*
>
> 2. I affirm the uniqueness that I am in this particular moment of my life with all my experiences, needs, wants and aspirations.
>   *(Recognize the Uniqueness of the individual)*
>
> 3. I affirm the reality of having choices: I choose flexibility over rigidity; I choose to tolerate uncertainty and resolve ambiguity; I choose to reduce my tendency to form self-harming interpretations about the meaning of my experiences; I choose to reduce emotional referencing and increase reality skills.
>   *(Choices)*
>
> 4. I am gradually making experiential shifts from passivity and/or excessive stimulation with increased referencing of my personal responsibility to myself and to others.
>   *(Responsibility to... not from)*
>
> 5. I continue to listen for meaningful possibilities with attentiveness for contextual cues, which are inviting me to appropriate action that will guide me into a hopeful future.
>   *(Will to Meaning)*
>
> 6. I choose specific actions, made in harmony with nöetic referencing and my personal values.
>   *(Freedom of Will)*
>
> 7. I remind myself that my thoughts, my feelings or my sensations, do not decide any action I take, I do! I experience meaning in every action I choose to take and I walk toward my ultimate meaning in life everyday!
>   *(Meaning in Life, Meaning in the Moment, Ultimate Meaning)*
>
> ***The Key to Meaningful Changes In Logotherapy & Existential Analysis (LTEA) is to:***
> *Explore with the patient/client the reality of nöetic resources as related to unique human qualities.
> *Help the patient/client to become aware of his/her unique nöetic qualities already in place.
> *Assist the patient/client to explore his/her values that support and guide towards activation of nöetic (spiritual) resources.
> *Encourage the patient/client to choose contextually his/her activities corresponding with resources and abilities.

The Trauma-Addiction Cycle:
How Life Behaviors are Used to Avoid/Receive Physiological and Psychological Responses

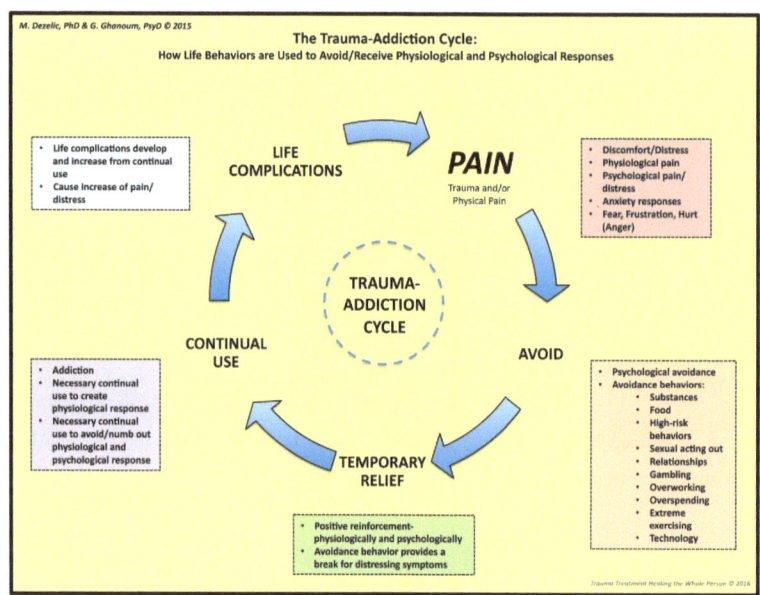

(Handout included in Section II)

In psychological terms, "Trauma" can be understood as any "overwhelming experience" that impacts our individual organism in a unique way. Trauma has a biological component that causes physiological changes in the brain and body system, as well as psychological-cognitive components, such as sensory imprints, thoughts, emotions, and feelings attached to the experience. These components are often not accessible to a natural, autobiographic narrative, and instead can be fragmented or distanced from comprehension and from our autobiographic narrative. For example, receiving a life-limiting medical diagnosis, and realizing that we will face death in the near future, can be an overwhelming or traumatic experience. Likewise, we may also have traumas from the past that are still causing distressing symptoms. Physical or psychological pain can be the result of distressing symptoms, past illnesses, or prior experiences. The severity of pain can be debilitating; therefore, we likely prefer to avoid it at all costs. Unfortunately, certain behaviors, including the use (and overuse) of pain medications or other "coping" drugs, become the easiest way to "manage" or lessen pain. In an effort to manage and decrease the distressing physiological and psychological symptoms of pain, we can become entangled in a deeper pattern that can lead to various addictions (the continual necessity of use to maintain a level of functioning). Clinicians need to keep in mind that this can easily happen with traumatized clients. It is therefore important to determine if a client has become addicted; and if so, exploration of addiction treatment strategies will become necessary.

"**The Trauma-Addiction Cycle: How Life Behaviors are Used to Avoid/Receive Physiological and Psychological Responses**" is a handout that clinicians can use to review the cycle of addiction and its effects, as well as to help clients understand where they are in this cycle should addictive behaviors be present and become problematic.

Trauma-Addiction Cycle

(1) PAIN (Trauma and/or Physical Pain): Coming from
- Discomfort/Distress
- Physiological pain
- Psychological pain/distress
- Anxiety responses
- Fear, Frustration, Hurt (Anger)

Leads to →

(2) AVOID: Avoidance behaviors
- Psychological Avoidance (desire to avoid dealing with the pain or underlying trauma, denial, repression, use of avoidance behaviors)
- Avoidance Behaviors:
    - Substance Abuse or Addiction
    - Food Addiction or obsession
    - High-Risk Behaviors
    - Sexual Acting Out
    - Relationship Difficulties
    - Gambling Addiction
    - Overworking (Workaholism)
    - Overspending
    - Extreme Exercising
    - Technology Addiction

Leads to →

(3) TEMPORARY RELIEF: Behaviors that provide temporary relief from Pain
- Positive reinforcement- physiologically and psychologically
- Avoidance behavior provides a break from distressing symptoms

Lead to →

(4) CONTINUAL USE: Of the temporary relief behaviors to avoid Pain
- Addiction
- Necessary continual use to create physiological response
- Necessary continual use to avoid/numb out physiological and psychological response

Leads to →

(5) LIFE COMPLICATIONS: That promote continual Pain
- Life complications (problems with family, friends, relationships, work, school, the law, physical abilities, cognitive abilities, etc.) develop and increase from continual use
- Cause increase of pain/distress

Meaning-Centered Grief Model:
An Existential Approach for Addressing the Lifelong Phase of Grief

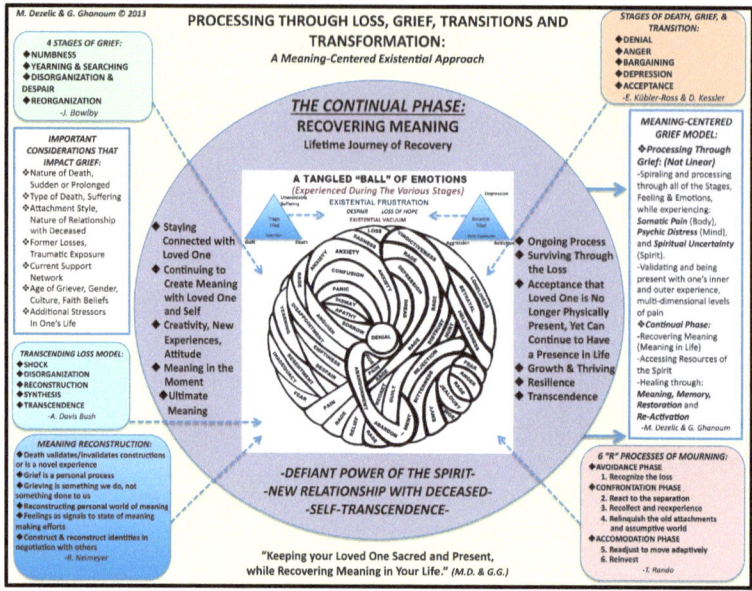

(Handout included in Section II)

The Meaning-Centered Grief Model, **"Processing Through Loss, Grief, Transitions and Transformation: A Meaning-Centered Existential Approach,"** based on Viktor Frankl's Logotherapy & Existential Analysis, is depicted in a "Conceptual Pictograph" to offer clinicians and grievers a guide to and an education about the ongoing process of grief. This model incorporates previous grief models, stresses important considerations that impact grief, and proposes a "Continual Phase" of grief—a lifelong journey of recovery and meaning-discovery. The Continual Phase encompasses key concepts from Viktor Frankl's Logotherapy & Existential Analysis, specifically, healing and recovery through the discovery of meaning and the ability to change our attitude in the face of unavoidable suffering.

Introduction

The Meaning-Centered Grief Model, developed by Marie Dezelic and Gabriel Ghanoum, the authors of this manual, is an existential approach for understanding the ongoing changes that typically occur during the grief process. The underpinnings of this Model are based on Viktor Frankl's Logotherapy & Existential Analysis (LTEA), a meaning-oriented theory and existential therapy (Dezelic, 2014; Frankl, 1978, 1986, 1988, 2000, 2004, 2006; Graber, 2004; Lukas, 2000). This new model combines the grief models and conceptualizations of theorists and clinicians John Bowlby, Elisabeth Kubler-Ross, Terese Rando, Robert Neimeyer, and Ashley Davis Bush (Bowlby, 1980; Davis Bush, 1997; Kubler-Ross, 1969; Kubler-Ross & Kessler, 2005; Neimeyer, 2006; Rando, 1993). The theoretical models of these theorists are part of the foundational processes and stages of grief and mourning that form the basis for the Meaning-Centered Grief Model. This new model expounds upon these previous theories to incorporate the ongoing lifelong grief phase (derived as a meaning-centered concept).

Grief, the process a bereaved individual goes through to mourn and assimilate any significant loss, such as the death of a spouse, child, any family member or friend, the loss of a parent or significant caregiver, the loss of a parent's everyday involvement due to divorce, a diagnosis of life-terminating illness, a significant trauma that changes one's life forever, even the loss of a one's home due to a natural disaster, is a unique and individualized process. We can certainly say that no two displays of grief are exactly the same. Since all of theories and models are, by their very nature, conceptual constructs, it is unlikely that one model alone will work for every individual. The more knowledge, understanding, language, and tools clinicians have, the greater the benefit that can be provided for clients who have entered into the unchartered territory of grief. Having various models and conceptualizations to draw information from offers clinicians a more comprehensive map and guide to follow when walking with the client in this new unknown world—life after the loss. This multi-faceted meaning-centered model builds upon the pre-existing stages and models, and moves toward an ongoing "lifetime phase" through an existential perspective.

Untangling the Ball of Emotions in Grief

The Meaning-Centered Grief Model, **"Processing Through Loss, Grief, Transitions and Transformation: A Meaning-Centered Existential Approach,"** is depicted in a *Conceptual Pictograph—Client Handout*. Conceptual Pictograph, a term coined by Marie Dezelic (Dezelic, 2014), is a visual display of information, and can be used as a concrete tool and handout that illustrates the concepts of any model. In our model, we have incorporated the well-known concept of the "Tangled Ball of Emotions," which is often used as a visual aid to help clinicians and clients understand how the many emotions, and layers of these emotions, are experienced (inwardly), and expressed (outwardly). We have conceptualized that the various models designed by pioneers in the field of Grief Work, Death and Dying apply to "untangling the ball of emotions in grief."

Viktor Frankl's depictions of the *Tragic Triad* and the *Neurotic Triad* (Dezelic, 2014; Dezelic & Ghanoum, 2015; Frankl, 1978, 1986, 1988, 2000, 2004, 2006; Graber, 2004; Lukas, 2000), also helps us to understand the tangled ball of emotions that is experienced and expressed. These two triads, and their components, are often preceptors to existential crises. They can manifest as despair or even as a sense of meaninglessness, what Frankl termed an existential vacuum. The *Tragic Triad—Unavoidable Suffering, Guilt, and Death,* and the *Neurotic Triad—Aggression, Depression, and Addiction,* have been included on the Conceptual Pictograph to help clinicians examine how these triads are experienced emotionally during the initial stages of grief.

"The Tragic Triad" and "The Neurotic Triad": Inner Experiences and Outer Expressions of Pain

In *The Tragic Triad (Unavoidable Pain, Guilt or Death)*, people in **despondency** experience **Unavoidable Pain:** Pain experienced from suffering which is unavoidable, such as in the case of a death of a loved one or an unavoidable trauma; **Guilt:** Responsibility, fault, or blame we may experience due to something we have done or have not done, or may have caused to happen, or in the case of survival where others have not also survived; and **Death:** The deep sadness, awareness or questioning we feel when we face the transitoriness of life after the death of someone.

In ***The Neurotic Triad (Depression, Aggression or Addiction),*** people in ***despair*** experience **Depression**: The feelings we experience in our inner world, and when we may have even lost our will to live; **Aggression**: An outward expression of violence precipitated by anger (possible fear, frustration, and deep hurt), and rage experienced internally; this aggression may be an effort to control others; or Aggression can even be turned inward—for example, the attempt to harm ourselves through self-mutilation or, at the extreme level, a suicide attempt—a way to extinguish our existence from this world completely. Finally we can experience **Addiction**: The attempt to numb or dull our pain and despair through substance abuse or a particular behavior (i.e., gambling, food, shopping, sex, exercise, self-mutilation, religiosity, etc.); addiction can also manifest itself as thrill-seeking behavior which is done in order to experience invincibility and appear larger-than-life, without regard to potential negative consequences (Dezelic, 2014; Dezelic & Ghanoum, 2015).

The initial stages of grief, and the inner experiences and outer expressions of pain as viewed through Frankl's Triads, can often lead to Existential Frustration, Despair and Loss of Hope. This in turn can lead to what Frankl calls an *Existential Vacuum*—an internal pulling force, an inner void, emptiness, boredom, apathy, struggle, and meaningless existence (Dezelic, 2014). It is the responsibility of clinicians to be actively present, to validate, to support, and to navigate through the internal emotional landscape and meaning constructs of their clients. These particular meaning constructs of grief are often expressed and experienced through the Tragic and Neurotic Triads (Lukas, 2000; Neimeyer, 2006, 2012; Rainer, 2013; Rando, 1993; Winokuer & Harris, 2012).

Important Considerations about Grief or Important Factors that Impact Grief

While it is true that we all experience grief in our own individual and unique way, nonetheless, we also share some similarities with each other. Because of this, it is helpful to have models that show the vast range of emotions, behaviors, cognitions and reactions to grief. There are several factors that can cause grief to be more or less difficult, more or less chronic, and more or less complicated. For example: If the griever experiences a traumatic death of a loved one/family member/friend due to suicide, homicide, or tragic accident; if someone has already experienced several losses and has not had time to recover from these losses prior to the current loss; if there is still unfinished business with the person who has passed, leaving no time for the survivor to heal from these issues; if the suffering of the person who has passed has been prolonged and/or traumatic; if the survivor does not have an adequate support network to help throughout the grief process. Once clinicians recognize the particular context in which their grieving clients are living, what emotional difficulties they are carrying into the grieving process, what might be preventing their progress, and why they may "stuck" in a particular area, they will be better prepared to provide optimal treatment.

Important life events or factors—Considerations to assess include:

- Nature of the Death
- Amount of Suffering
- Attachment to deceased
- Nature of Relationship with Deceased
- Other Significant and Former Losses
- Previous Traumatic Events or Exposure
- Current Support Network
- Age of Griever
- Gender
- Culture
- Faith or religious background
- Beliefs, values (about self, others, the world, life, and death)
- Additional Stressors

The following is an explanation of the factors listed above:

Nature of the Death

It is important to determine whether the death was **sudden,** as in the case of a tragic accident, was the result of suicide or homicide; or was **prolonged and expected,** as in the case of a terminal illness. These factors will have an effect on both grievers and the grief process. The **specific cause of death** creates an impact as well. A terminal illness, a tragic accident, death by suicide, homicide, or substance overdose, may all be experienced differently by loved ones, depending on the meaning constructs previously developed for each type of death. Several issues that may present themselves include whether grievers were provided the opportunity to "say goodbye;" what information was known about the condition or situation; what was seen and experienced by the grievers; and how any of these issues were integrated (Kubler-Ross & Kessler, 2005; Neimeyer, 2001; Rando, 1993).

Amount of Suffering

The grieving process can be affected by such things as having witnessed the prolonged or acute suffering of a loved one, or knowing that a loved one suffered during the last moments of life. However, if there was prolonged suffering before death, grievers may also feel relief that their loved one is no longer in pain. In the case of sudden deaths, grievers can sometimes take solace in the fact that there was no prolonged suffering (Kubler-Ross & Kessler, 2005; Rando, 1993).

Attachment & Nature of Relationship with Deceased

The Attachment style—*secure, anxious-ambivalent (preoccupied), avoidant (dismissive),* or ***disorganized (fearful-avoidant)***—will play a major role in how grief is experienced. Attachment styles refer to the various ways that primary caretakers form initial bonds with children. They are internal working models of attachment and safety with close childhood caregivers and, later in adulthood, in intimate relationships with others. Attachment styles were originally discussed in the Attachment Theory developed and researched by John Bowlby and Mary Ainsworth. It is important to understand the nature and style of our attachments, as well as our ability to soothe ourselves and regulate our emotions. This knowledge will help us better understand how we grieve and are affected by the loss of our attachment figures and other significant people in our lives. Below are brief descriptions of **Attachment styles:**

Secure Attachment: Individuals feel comfortable with close connections and intimacy. These same individuals can be independent and have an ability to explore the world. As babies, they feel connected to their caregivers, but are also able and willing to explore their environment with the comfort of knowing that their caregiver is the secure base. The other three attachment styles are referred to as ***Insecure Attachments.***

Anxious-Ambivalent Attachment (Preoccupied adult attachment): Individuals feel overly dependent on attachment figures for a sense of safety, security, and sense of self; they often seek high levels of connection, intimacy, and responsiveness from others, especially when they are agitated and need to regulate their emotions (they prefer to co-soothe). As babies, they feel anxious when away from their caregivers; however, they are ambivalent (mistrusting) that caregivers will be there to meet their needs.

Avoidant Attachment (Dismissive adult attachment): Individuals feel independent and desire ample independence in order to feel safe and secure, and exhibit distancing from others, especially when they are agitated and need to regulate their emotions (they prefer to self-soothe). As babies, they either feel smothered by the caregiver and prefer to have space, or feel the caregiver is not available, and therefore, learn to rely on themselves for soothing.

And finally, *Disorganized Attachment (Fearful-avoidant adult attachment):* Individuals have experienced trauma and losses during their early development years with caregivers or other relationships/people, (e.g., sexual abuse, physical abuse, severe neglect, abandonment, deaths, caregivers with mental illness, substance abuse, incarceration, etc.) This trauma disrupts normal development and safe attachment to adults. They exhibit all of the attachment styles, but not one consistently, and often need others to feel safe and secure. They are fearful of losing relationships, yet avoid getting too close or avoid becoming dependent on anyone. This avoidance is precipitated by their ultimate fear of losing the relationship completely. As babies, they feel anxious when away from their caregivers, are mistrusting of the caregivers ability to provide safety and security, are fearful the caregiver will abandon them, and avoid depending on the caregiver (they have a difficult time being soothed, whether co-soothing or self-soothing) (Johnson, 2008; Levine & Heller, 2010).

Grievers will likely use the same style they use to regulate emotions in addressing their grief; however, there may also be times in which their "usual" attachment style will no longer feel comfortable or offer safety. The nature of every relationship is different, and depending on whether this is a couple/partnership, a parent-child, sibling, relative, friend or other type of relationship, the closeness or lack thereof, impacts the intensity of the grief process (Bowlby, 1961, 1980; Rando, 1993).

Other Significant & Former Losses, Previous Traumatic Exposure

Other significant or former losses, or previous exposure to traumatic events, can impact the current grief process. If grievers have had several losses in the past, this fact can compound the traumatic response for the current grief, or, on the other hand, can lessen the impact of the current loss (provided that coping strategies have already been developed, or the prior losses have helped grievers to become comfortable with death). If grievers have already been exposed to traumatic events, this can either increase or decrease the impact of the current grief. Multiple deaths occurring at the same time, such as an accident in which several family members or friends are killed, or a terminal illness in which several people are diagnosed with the same illness, such as HIV/AIDS or Cancer, can have a greater impact. This is because grievers will probably need to process several losses within the same or close time frame. Loss of family pets can be as traumatic as the loss of family or friends, especially if the pet is part of grievers' support system, is viewed as a family member, and/or grievers have a strong attachment bond to the pet (Kubler-Ross & Kessler, 2005; Neimeyer, 2001; Rando, 1993).

Current Support Network

If grievers currently have a support network of family, friends and co-workers, this can help the grief process. The grief experience can be a very lonely time, as grievers may feel that no one understands their loss. Having outside support can offer some reprieve from the inner state of loneliness, despair and loss. If grievers do not have a support network established, this can exacerbate the feelings of loneliness and despair. Efforts should be taken to help grievers join a support group and begin to expand their social network. Additionally, it is important to recognize that the first few weeks after the death are often characterized by extra support from family and friends; however, this support often diminishes when grievers need it the most. Some of the more difficult stages of grief occur after the first few weeks. For example, an especially difficult time in the grief process is when grievers are starting to recognize that life will no longer be the same, and the deceased is no longer returning to them (Kubler-Ross & Kessler, 2005; Neimeyer, 2001, 2006; Rando, 1993).

Age of Griever, Gender, Culture, Faith or Religious Beliefs and Values

The age of grievers and their cognitive development impact the grieving process. The way that we grieve, and the manner with which we understand and integrate the death into our current life experience are important aspects of the grief process. For example, a child losing a parent or sibling will have a different impact on the grieving process than a parent losing a child, spouse, or parent. Likewise, usually men and women not only grieve differently, but also approach the process from a different set of acceptable gender roles. Additionally, there is a need for culturally sensitive grief clinicians. Cultural and religious practices can negatively impact or exacerbate the grief process by placing specific expectations on grievers; however, they can also bring peace and comfort through familiar rituals, ceremonies and additional support (Clements et al., 2003; Kubler-Ross & Kessler, 2005; Sunoo, 2002).

Additional Stressors

Additional current or ongoing stressors (e.g., relationship issues, work-related problems, financial difficulties, health related concerns, etc.) can add to feelings of helplessness, hopelessness, and/or despair. During the initial stages of grief, grievers often feel overwhelmed by their feelings, emotions, cognitions, and/or behaviors. Having additional stressors such as financial constraints, work-related problems, family relationship issues, additional losses, and personal medical complications/disabilities will only add to the experience of being overwhelmed, and can often exacerbate the grief response. All of these factors can lead up to a chronic or traumatic grief response.

"The Meaning-Centered Grief Model"

I. Processing Through Stages

This is the first phase of the "Meaning-Centered Grief Model." **Processing Through the Stages** refers to the manner of going through the many stages and constructs of the grief models (the feelings, emotions, cognitions, and behaviors—the inner and outer experiences of grief). These are the stages depicted by Bowlby, Davis Bush, Kubler-Ross, Neimeyer, and Rando, in the "Conceptual Pictograph" (Bowlby, 1980; Davis Bush, 1997; Kubler-Ross, 1969; Kubler-ross & Kessler, 2005; Neimeyer, 2006; Rando, 1993). The "Tangled Ball of Emotions" in the Pictograph illustrates the emotions, which become translated into thoughts and behaviors by the griever.

(1) Spiraling Through the Stages of Grief

First and foremost, it is important to recognize that grief is a NON-LINEAR PROCESS. The theorists of the models presented in the "Conceptual Pictograph" do not claim that all individuals will follow a linear pattern; rather, they propose an overall understanding of the entire grief construct and possibilities. Clinicians will usually see grievers spiraling through the stages described in the various models. Sometimes the movement is in a forward direction, sometimes in a backward direction, and frequently, there is jumping back and forth between the stages. Occasionally someone will even skip one or more stages. The *"Important Considerations That Impact Grief,"* (previously detailed above), will determine the pattern of this typical spiraling action. Throughout the various stages of grief, unique experiences of the griever will have a tri-part impact; that is, they will impact the **Body—Somatic pain,** the **Mind—Psychic distress,** and the **Spirit—***Spiritual uncertainty and questioning.*

(2) Validating and Being Present with the Griever

The role of clinicians, in addition to offering specific techniques, is to help alleviate distressing symptoms and thus allow grievers to move toward coping and healing. In addition, clinicians **validate the experience of grievers, and are fully present with them** as they reveal inner and outer experiences, and feel the multi-dimensional levels (somatic, psychic, and spiritual) of pain and distress. In many case, all grievers need is a therapist who is a non-anxious, supportive and validating presence that also demonstrates unconditional positive regard. Having our experiences validated and witnessed by another can be healing in itself. The opportunity to make sense of the overwhelming changes that the loss and grief is having in our life makes navigating the "newness" less stressful. Grief is often an unknown or uncharted territory and thus can produce a stress/traumatic response. Psychoeducation, aimed at defining and explaining the various stages of the grief cycle, is often helpful when navigating these unfamiliar waters. It is usually reassuring and comforting to know, not only what to expect, but also what others have gone through before us. Clinicians can offer grievers guidance and support, as well as various exercises and techniques that will help reduce distressing symptoms while movement is taking place between the stages depicted in the models. Grievers often feel comforted knowing that there is an experienced guide (someone with a "flashlight" in this dark and unknown place), and that there is the possibility of hope; hope not only for recovery from pain, but hope for a future filled with meaning in life once more.

II. The Continual Phase of Grief

The **Continual Phase of Grief,** the second phase of the "Meaning-Centered Grief Model," is not a finite stage; rather, it is an ongoing phase that continues throughout lifetimes of those who suffer bereavement or loss. Grievers continue to assimilate their loss, and reconnect to life and meaning-discovery possibilities. In essence, this continual phase of grief is an ongoing journey of recovery that continues throughout life; it is an *"overall, ongoing life phase"* that allows those who experience loss to (1) Recover Meaning, access (2) Resources of the Spirit—the unique essence of the individual, and work on (3) Healing through Meaning, Memory, Restoration and Re-activation.

(1) Recovering Meaning

Clinicians employ Meaning-oriented Logotherapy & Existential Analysis techniques to help grievers become aware that their **Will to Meaning** exists even if it has been covered by the debris of grief. They also learn that **Meaning in Life** has not ceased even though a tremendous loss has occurred. Grievers discover how to simultaneously hold their grief in the one hand, while accessing Meaning and Recovery in the other. **Recovering Meaning** does not signify that grievers will leave their grief behind and move on ("moving on" often holds grievers stuck in grief); rather, they will be able to honor their grief and be able to access Meaning and engagement in life simultaneously. They will continue to grow in spite of and through their grief process, while discovering an ongoing relationship with their loved one.

(2) Resources of the Spirit

Clinicians help grievers learn how to access the many ongoing **Resources of the Human Spirit** (What Viktor Frankl calls the Nöetic or Spiritual Dimension) so they can reactivate their meaning possibilities. Resources of the spirit include: *Spirit as the Healthy Core of the Individual; Self-Awareness and Discovery;*

Responsibility and Response-ability; Freedom To Act with Choice (Not Freedom From Something); Will To Discover Meaning; Goals and Purposes in Life; Creativity and Imagination; Personal Conscience (Beyond the Superego); Ideas and Ideals; Love (Beyond the Physical); Awareness of Mortality; Commitment to Tasks; Compassion and Forgiveness; and *Sense of Humor* (Dezelic, 2014; Graber, 2004; Rice et al., 2004).

(3) Healing through Meaning, Memory, Restoration, and Re-Activation

Through these four specific areas: **Meaning, Memory, Restoration,** and **Re-Activation,** clinicians assist and help move grievers toward healing of and recovery from the various levels of multi-dimensional pain.

(A) Meaning: Helping grievers discover the *Meaning of the Moment,* such as a creative act, loving someone, changing their attitude in the face of unavoidable pain. This allows grievers to act with purposeful living even though their loved one is no longer physically present to experience life with them. Clinicians can help grievers become aware of the meaning possibilities of each moment; find new *Meaning in Life* when their loved one is no longer physically present to experience life with them, yet can be present in memory and spirit; and recognize that the *Will to Meaning* exists even after the loss.

New meanings can be discovered through Viktor Frankl's *Meaning Triangle—Creativity, Experiences,* and *Attitudes.* The *Meaning Triangle* consists of **Creativity:** The unique creative gifts we offer the world through our innate gifts and talents, such as in the creative arts, work, career, raising children, deeds, and goals achieved; **Experiences:** The experiences internalized from encountering and loving or receiving love from others in relationships of all types (marital partners, loved ones, friends, work colleagues, and animals), and from our appreciation of the beauty of nature (being in nature) or art (creating art, or witnessing artistic endeavors and performances); **Attitudes:** The attitudinal values we can realize by taking a courageous or self-transcending stance toward an unavoidable situation or circumstance such as an act of fate (death of a loved one, our own mortality, life-threatening illness, etc.) (Dezelic, 2014). All of us, in the choices me make through our Personal Conscience are moving daily toward *Ultimate Meaning,* (sometimes called God/Divine, Supreme Being, The Universe, Higher Power), an overarching meaning in life, that is unknowable until the point of death or beyond. Grievers can begin to incorporate their relationship with the deceased loved one into their personal journey toward *Ultimate Meaning.*

(B) Memory: Memory brings grievers solace by helping them stay connected to the deceased loved one. For example, they can hold onto memories, revisit memories, or keep their loved one's memories alive through rituals, dreams, and spiritual presence. It is even possible to create new moments/memories with the deceased, such as sharing a current significant event with them by sensing their spiritual presence or by thinking of them during that time. For example, grievers can include their loved ones in the event by making mention of them, lighting a candle in their place, bringing a picture of them to the event, or any other way that will help them feel as if their loved one is also experiencing and is a part of this moment.

(C) Restoration: The feeling that we have been restored or returned to a place where we can continue to ***move through life, yet not "move away" from the deceased.*** There is a space where we can experience joy and happiness, while still maintaining the memory, sadness, and connection with the deceased. This joy and happiness does not replace the loved one; rather, it can happen while simultaneously holding the loved one close and present in our life.

(D) Re-Activation: The feeling that life has regained a spark, excitement and even passion. New Meaning is often discovered through becoming mindfully present and connected to life. This is experienced as moving *from Dis-Connection*, while in the throes of the painful grief, *to Re-Connection*, with an acceptance that the loved one, who is no longer physically present, can still be a major part of our ongoing life. At this time, the griever possibly takes up and carries out a current or new cause or project on behalf of or in memory of the loved one. The *"Transitoriness of Life,"* a recognition that death marks an end to a temporal existence, (Dezelic, 2014; Frankl, 2006; Graber, 2004) can open our eyes to the possibility of following through with old, unrealized dreams, and old or new goals to accomplish before our own death. It is important to recognize that "Acceptance" does not mean moving on from the loved one; rather, it is the ability to recognize that the death has occurred, that it was difficult to go through the loss and change, and that we can maintain a connection with our deceased loved one, even though the context of the connection has changed. From this perspective, acceptance is the ability to continue moving forward in life after the loss has occurred, with an awareness of *Will to Meaning* and *Meaning in Life*.

Overview of the Continual Phase of Grief—Recovering Meaning, a Lifetime Journey of Recovery
- Staying connected with the loved one
- Continuing to discover meaning with the loved one and with ourselves
- Creativity, new Experiences, and Attitude
- Meaning in the Moment
- Ultimate Meaning
- Ongoing Process
- Surviving through the loss
- Acceptance that the loved one is no longer present, yet can continue to have a presence in the griever's life
- The possibility of growth and thriving
- Resilience
- Transcendence
- Defiant Power of the Spirit
- New relationship with the deceased
- Self-Transcendence

Conclusion: Processing Through Loss, Grief, Transitions and Transformation

The Meaning-Centered Grief Model, "**Processing Through Loss, Grief, Transitions and Transformation: A Meaning-Centered Existential Approach,** is depicted in a "Conceptual Pictograph" to offer clinicians and grievers a format, a guide, a navigation tool, and an awareness of the ongoing process of *"Keeping your loved one sacred and present, while recovering Meaning in your life."* The **Continual Phase of Grief's** essence focuses on discovering new meaning and significance after the loss, and learning how to maintain a healthy relationship with our grief and with our deceased loved one. This new Grief Model incorporates previous well-known and researched grief theories and models. All these models can serve as building blocks of the Continual Phase of Grief. They show grievers how to continually navigate through the grief process and to accept that their lives are forever changed by the loss of a physical relationship with their deceased loved one (or other loss).

Addressing Anger:
A Multi-Dimensional Construct

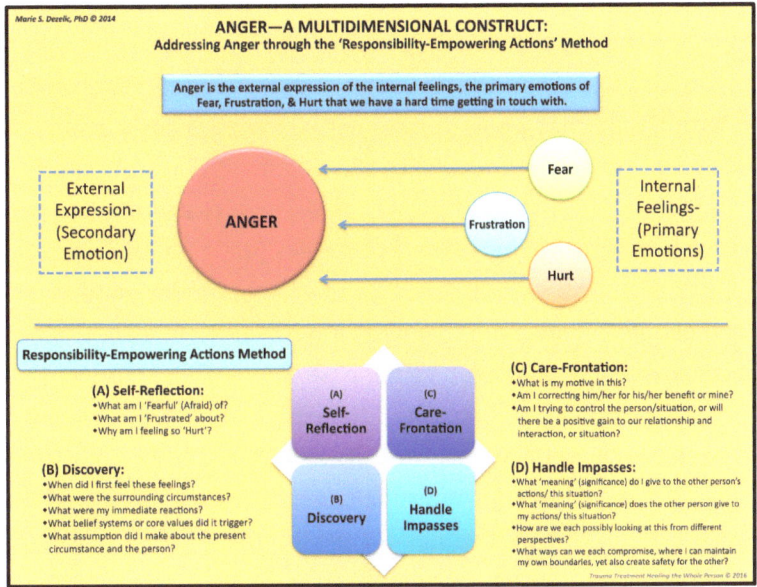

(Handout included in Section II)

Anger is usually the external expression of internal feelings (sensations and emotions), such as fear, frustration, and hurt (the primary emotions). We often have difficulty getting directly in touch with these internal feelings. Anger allows us to express the internal emotion experienced with energy (a fight response). It could be precipitated by intense sorrow, or fear, or loss, a sense of injustice or of unexpressed guilt. Guilt might also be the cause of anger directed at others, self, and a medical condition or traumatic situation; for example, guilt caused by deeds left undone. Anger might also be caused by a combination of fear, frustration, deep sadness and/or hurt that cannot be expressed or may not even be understood. Anger is viewed as a surface emotion that promotes agency (action); beneath it we might find unexpressed guilt (not being able to do something—agency thwarted), and at a further deeper level, a combination of fear, frustration, and/or hurt (deep sadness) toward an experience of a person or situation (e.g., a caregiver/perpetrator that sexually abused, physically abused, or neglected a child; fear that the abuse would continue, frustration of not being able to fight back and change the situation, and hurt that this person was causing harm to the child).

Clinicians often view anger as a secondary emotion, essentially providing an external "cover-up" for the primary emotions of (1) Fear, (2) Frustration, and/or (3) Hurt. At the existential level, the fear of non-existence is often the root of all difficult situations, and manifests as more fear and anxiety, or anger to fight against it. The primary emotions of fear, frustration and/or hurt are experienced internally (intrapsychically). At the deepest level, hiding these internal emotions can be viewed as a need to validate or protect our existence. However, we usually cannot maintain these difficult emotions within us as they cause us to suffer. We eventually want to move away from pain, and, while we may not be consciously aware of it, we can quickly, almost simultaneously, flip these primary emotions into the secondary emotion of anger, and send it outward (projection) onto an external target such as a family member, friend or other object. This anger directed at another person or situation allows us to create a safe distance (avoidance) from of our own inner feelings. It can also allow us to create a boundary that we did not have the "courage" to create without the power of anger (energizing action). Anger gives us the energy boost to do this boundary-making, partly because it makes us feel stronger or more empowered. We can "blame" (being in victim stance) our negative actions on the anger rather than take "responsibility" (personal choice) for those actions. Likewise, anger, and all of the behaviors associated with that emotion, gets reinforced when the boundary-making works. We often make the erroneous and even unconscious assumption that we must get angry (engage anger's energy) in order to create the boundary or get a need met. Getting in touch with the deeper feelings of fear, frustration, and/or hurt can sometimes make us feel more vulnerable. However, when are able to get in touch with our internal feelings on a regular basis, we begin to "discover" ourselves (become existentially aware) on a deeper, more intimate level, and can connect with others on a deeper, more intimate level. Vulnerability allows for a more authentic and genuine connection to ourselves (our own existence) and others.

Helping clients uncover what is happening beneath their anger, to discover the hidden existential messages and needs, begins a process of healing, and the possibility of handling unfinished business, even if that unfinished business is only with themselves. The "Responsibility-Empowering Actions Method" listed below, offers clinicians a pathway for assisting clients in recognizing the deeper emotions, what might be holding them stuck, as well as avenues for exploration. If the anger (as well as the deeper associated emotions) is directed toward a person who is no longer alive (such as a deceased parent/person), steps (C) and (D) of this process can be done as a role-play or simply talked about with the clinician.

One of the ways that anger can be prolonged is an inability or unwillingness to forgive a wrong. This state of non-forgiveness acts as a protective barrier against the deeper existential fear of non-existence, and consequently our need for human existence. The non-forgiveness state can block our healing potential. Clinicians can help clients recognize that discovering (1) their own anger state; that is, understanding the core wounds that have impacted their existence and recognizing their need to protect these wounds can then lead to (2) forgiveness. Forgiveness can be viewed as an internal action of letting go of deep hurts and wounds (whether forgiveness gets expressed externally or not), which can lead to true (3) existential healing. More on *Forgiveness* is addressed in the following section after *Anger*.

Pavel Somov (2013), in his book *Anger Management Jumpstart: A 4-Session Mindfulness Path to Compassion and Change*, defines anger as wanting to hold onto what no longer is, and that it can be the catalyst to look at what could be. Therefore, addressing anger opens us to the possibility for true healing, within ourselves, and with others.

Addressing Anger through the "Responsibility-Empowering Actions" will allow:
- A.) Self-Reflection: Engage in self-reflection or self-examination
- B.) Discovery: Discover or uncover our inner feelings and core wounds
- C.) Care-Frontation: Practice care-frontation (confronting a person or situation from a caring and compassionate stance rather than from an aggressive one)
- D.) Handle Impasses: Learn new strategies for handling difficult interpersonal situations

A.) Self-Reflection

If we pause for a moment when we feel extremely angry with a person or at a situation, we can begin the process of self-reflection, and ask ourselves these questions:

1) **What am I 'Fearful' (Afraid) of?** *(What is triggering my fear or anxiety?)*
2) **What am I 'Frustrated' about?** *(For example, what is causing me to feel frustrated at my inability to be successful at something?)*
3) **Why am I feeling so 'Hurt'?** *(What am I feeling hurt or emotionally distressed about?)*

Writing/journaling often allows deeper belief systems (core beliefs and values that are being challenged by the current interaction) to appear. The act of journaling/writing that uncovers deeper belief systems is often more beneficial than our immediate, superficial, quick verbal answers, sometimes called "surface thoughts."

B.) Discovery

Through the process of discovery and further exploration, we can explore and attempt to uncover areas of discomfort within us. We will often find that the root of uncomfortable feelings (sensations and emotions) stems back to childhood (the feeling is stuck in the unconscious—out of conscious awareness), a time in which some need did not get met by caregivers or peers, or a time when a violation was made. Even if this is not the case, and it is about a current need not being met by a partner, family member, co-worker, or friend in the present circumstance, the same path for change (positive growth opportunities) can be taken. While Logotherapists do not usually go into great depth to uncover early childhood experiences, there are times when it is important for therapists to address some of these past experiences in order to facilitate the process of healing from these traumas and to help clients move on with their lives; likewise, it is often a necessity in situations where an individual has had developmental trauma.

Begin to examine the following questions:
1) **When did I first experience (feel) these feelings?**
2) **What were the surrounding circumstances?**
3) **What were my immediate reactions?**
4) **What belief systems or core values did these feelings trigger?**
5) **What assumption did I make about the present circumstance and/or about the person?**

C. Care-Frontation

Healthy actions can begin when we are willing to make choices for ourselves (responsibility), rather than allowing ourselves to be controlled by our emotions (victim stance and/or unaware). We can begin "care-fronting," a term that combines the two words, "care" and "front." In Care-fronting we approach or challenge the person/situation that is causing us distress, but we do so from a benign perspective rather than from an aggressive stance. This allows us to do the following: Take more responsibility for our actions and our needs; create healthy boundaries for ourselves; and be "responsive" (conscious and aware, engagement of prefrontal cortex) rather than "reactive" (emotionally hijacked by our limbic system). When we use "I" language rather than "you" language, we are better able to maintain a sense of responsibility to ourselves and to others as well. It is also better not to assume that we understand what other people mean by their words or actions. Our assumptions about others or situations can be completely wrong, especially since we view the world and events through our own unique lenses and meaning constructs that we have developed over our lifetime. Thus it is important to ask for clarification about meaning and motivation; to refrain from quick assumptions and to avoid assigning blame.

We can ask ourselves:
1) What is my motive?
2) Am I correcting others to benefit myself or them?
3) Am I trying to control others or the situation? Or am I seeking something positive for our relationship, the interaction, or the situation?

D. Handle Impasses

It is important to handle impasses that arise with people we care about so that we can stay in contact with them and thus maintain the relationships. When a subject matter generates a lot of emotion for each person, and when there is the feeling of being misunderstood or even not heard at all, this can result in an "existential block" (two different meanings and significance that are equally powerful for each person). When we are open to dealing with an existential block, then we are able to be vulnerable and are willing to share our personal experience, as well as what meanings (significance) we derived in that experience or set of experiences. This willingness to share allows for the possibility of compromise between the two people; otherwise, what often happens is that neither person wants to budge from a feeling of safety (perceived safety) and move toward an unknown and uncomfortable territory where fear, frustration and/or hurt might get triggered. The more we practice authentic, non-blaming disclosure, the more likely it is that we will develop an authentic and caring relationship.

Explore:
1) What "meaning" (significance) do I give to the other person's actions/this situation?
2) What "meaning" (significance) does the other person give to my actions/this situation?
3) How are we each possibly looking at this from different perspectives?

4) What ways can we each compromise, where I can maintain my own boundaries, yet also create safety for the other (in order that we can create a compromise and collaborate with each other)?

The process of moving through the "Responsibility-Empowering Actions" Method helps us engage in self-discovery and develop self-awareness, improves our ability to handle future, similar situations, and allows us to experience a gentle acceptance of the situation, and, most importantly, of ourselves—self-acceptance.

Forgiveness- ACCESS Model:
How to Release Blocked or Stuck Energy and Move Toward Existential Healing

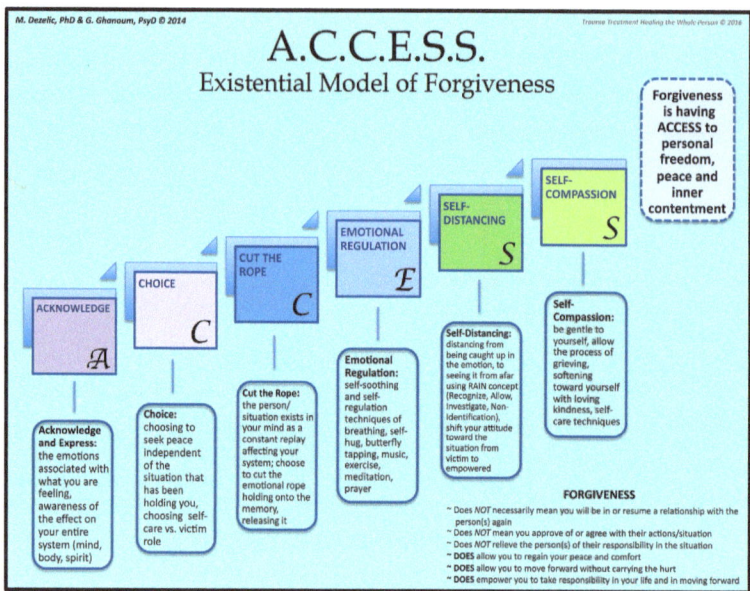

(Handout included in Section II)

There is a significant amount of literature and research on the topic of forgiveness. For example, much has been written on what forgiveness is, what it entails, why it is important, and why we find it difficult to do. How do we practice the art of forgiveness? We believe it is important for clinicians to become familiar with all aspects and challenges of forgiveness so that they can discover ways this process could prove beneficial to clients who have suffered relational trauma (trauma caused by people). Many clients are holding onto anger, and possibly also holding on to deeper existential guilt, regrets, hurts, core wounds, and unfulfilled dreams, some or all of which can block access to their nöetic (spiritual) core, and to their spiritual well-being and healing. An existential approach to the therapeutic process is one way to address the topic of forgiveness with clients, especially as it relates to our personal existence and healing.

ACCESS is a model that we have developed for clinicians to use when helping clients move toward forgiveness. The acronym **ACCESS** stands for the following six actions:

    A = Acknowledge
    C = Choice
    C = Cut the Rope
    E = Emotional Regulation
    S = Self-Distancing
    S = Self-Compassion

The acronym is also used as a metaphor to help us gain "access" to (a pathway into) and take steps toward our own personal existential space of peace, contentment, and healing. Clinicians can use the ACCESS model as a guide for assisting clients in each of these six key action areas. When clients are able to follow the ACCESS Model, they move closer to letting go of what they have been protecting and holding onto for a long time, sometimes for decades. In essence, they become able to release blocked or stuck energy and move toward their existential emotional and bodily healing.

The very act of forgiveness can be both emotionally charged and cathartic for clients. Grieving will often occur, as the non-forgiveness state has likely blocked their ability to lead a healthy and fulfilling life. Because of this, clients will often need to grieve opportunities for positive life experiences that were not realized and were lost when they were unable to heal the hurt or wound. Clinicians can tailor the aspects of the ACCESS model to what clients can handle and where they are willing to go, always keeping in mind that safety and self-regulation is of paramount importance to clients. Throughout the entire therapeutic process, it is vital that clinicians help clients engage in adaptive self-soothing behaviors, regulate their heightened emotional states, and maintain connection with others. It is helpful for clients to recognize that forgiveness is about them, it is not about the person they are forgiving. The act of forgiveness brings an internal healing process, and is a personal choice, not a mandated action.

What Forgiveness is Not

- Forgiveness is not reconciliation. It does *NOT* necessarily mean we will be in, or wish to resume a relationship with the person we are forgiving; for many reasons, one or both parties may not want to reconcile the relationship
- Forgiveness does *NOT* mean we condone, approve of, or agree with the other person's actions/situation
- Forgiveness does *NOT* relieve the person(s) who are forgiven of their responsibility in the situation

What Forgiveness Can Do

- Forgiveness DOES allow us to regain our peace and comfort
- Forgiveness DOES allow us to move forward without carrying the hurt
- Forgiveness DOES empower us to take responsibility for and move forward with our lives

THE ACCESS MODEL
Having ACCESS to Personal Peace and Inner Contentment

1. Acknowledge and Express: Acknowledging and expressing the emotions associated with what we are feeling, an awareness of the effect that our hurt and "unforgiveness" is having on our entire system (mind, body, spirit).
- *Self-Reflection, Self-Awareness, and Self-Discovery of what the emotions represent; validation of our existence and situation.*

2. Choice: Choosing to seek peace independent of the situation that has been holding us hostage; self-care versus victim role.
- *Freedom to make conscious Choices; courage to go where it is difficult (our deepest hurts and pain).*

3. Cut the Emotional Rope: Choosing to cut and release the rope (the metaphoric tie) that is holding us to the memory of the hurt. When this happens, the constant memory of the hurt that the person/situation caused no longer exists in our mind as a constant replay on repeat, negatively affecting our entire system. What does the rope that is tied to the situation represent? If we cut the rope, what would happen to us? The use of imagery can help us to recognize the fact that part of our existence is held (tethered) (in memory) to the person or issue on the other side of the rope.
- *We have the Choice to accept (learn how to be with, not agree with) what has happened, and what we are letting go of; cut the tie that holds us stuck to our past hurts/traumas.*

4. Emotional Regulation: Self-soothing and self-regulation techniques such as diaphragmatic breathing, self-hugging, butterfly tapping (crossing arms over chest and bilateral tapping on shoulders), listening to music, taking a shower (water therapy of any sort, pool, Jacuzzi, bath), exercising, and meditating.
- *Self-Regulation and Self-Soothing helps to regulate the autonomic nervous system and helps us feel calm and cared for; clinicians can explore different methods that work for each individual.*

5. Self-Distancing: Distancing ourselves from the emotion will help us avoid getting caught up in the emotion. We can use the Buddhist RAIN concept: **Recognize-** what we are feeling; **Allow-** the emotion without labeling it as good or bad or labeling ourselves; **Investigate-** what the emotion is trying to tell us without judgment; **Non-Identification-** observing the emotion from afar frees us from "being" in the emotion (Brach, 2013). Self-distancing from the emotion in a non-judgmental stance will help move us from a victim stance to one of empowerment and strength.

- *Through the reduction of responding from our reactive, emotionally hijacked brain (limbic system response) to responding to the feelings and emotions with Self-Care (prefrontal cortex response), we can learn to move away from a reactive, almost knee-jerk emotional response to a response that has both elements of self-care and self-regulation. This shift will allow us to both recognize and respond to our feelings in a healthier way so we can better understand and process them.*

6. Self-Compassion: Being gentle with ourselves; allowing the process of grieving to occur but also treating ourselves with loving kindness.

- *Opening up to the inner space of "being" without judgment and also honoring our Dignity and worthiness helps develop a compassionate stance toward ourselves.*

Part IV
Meaning Discovery & Exploration Interventions

Sources of Discovering Meaning in Life & Adversity:
Through Meaning-Centered Therapy

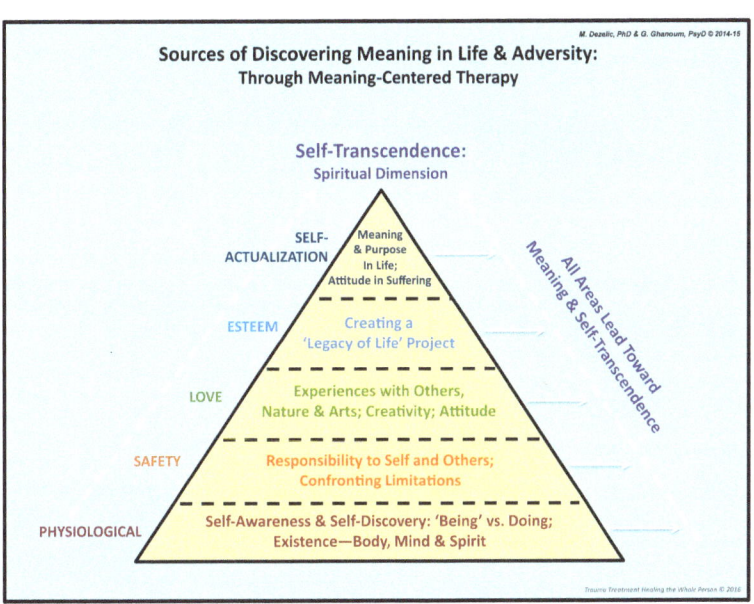

(Handout included in Section II)

While Viktor Frankl and Abraham Maslow had some differences in their understanding of the importance of or even the need for a psychological model based on our Hierarchy of Needs, they both emphasized the importance of ascertaining ways we can discover meaning by giving of ourselves to others and the world. In fact, although Frankl disagreed with Maslow about the importance of **Self-Actualization**, instead maintaining that **Self-Transcendence** was how we discover meaning and purpose; nevertheless, toward the end of his life, Maslow began talking about self-transcendence as a way to self-actualize, and therefore, seemed to be moving in Frankl's direction.

Regardless of the differences Maslow had with Frankl, his Hierarchy of Needs model coupled with Frankl's meaning-centered concepts can be useful ways to assist clients to discover areas of meaning when faced with unavoidable situations, trauma, tragedy, and/or illness. Both theories are able to assist in self-discovery through shifting focus to "Being" and "Becoming," rather than paying attention to what was lost, has changed, or what limits clients in any way as a result of their current circumstances. The "needs in life" can be processed and addressed with clients, while simultaneously working on *Meaning in Trauma and Adversity.* Although Maslow's model was depicted in the hierarchy format, we want to make clear that lower areas on the triangle do not need to be met or progressed through in order to reach self-transcendence; rather, all of the meaning-discovery opportunities lead toward self-transcendence and a new way of looking at life (a shift in attitude).

Sources of Discovering Meaning in Life & Adversity

- **Physiological:** Self-awareness and self-discovery—"being" vs. doing; existence—body, mind, and spirit
    - *Allows us to discover the essence of our being as well as our roles in life*

- **Safety:** Responsibility to self and others; confronting limitations
    - *Allows us to take ownership of our lives and create boundaries for safety*

- **Love:** Experiences with others (giving and receiving love and appreciation from others and relationships), and appreciating the beauty of nature and arts; creativity (experiencing our unique essence through our creative outputs); attitude (experiencing profound shifts through the new attitudes we take)
    - *Allows us to experience meaningful love with others, the world, and creative projects*

- **Esteem:** Creating a "Legacy of Life" (Meaning-Legacy Project) project
    - *Allows us to experience our many meaningful engagements, significant moments, and the accomplishments of our entire life as depicted in our unique life review project*

- **Self-Actualization:** Meaning and purpose in life; attitude in suffering
    - *Allows us to discover, choose and experience our own unique purpose and meaning in life (an existence on purpose with purpose)*

~ All areas lead toward the discovery of meaning and self-transcendence

Meaning Exploration Topics:
"Meaning-Legacy Project"

(Handout included in Section II)

"Life, Death, Suffering, Love, and Work" are general topics that assist clients in discovering and uncovering a new awareness and recognition of meaning in the past and present moments, as well as meaningful opportunities and possibilities that are still available for future moments. Discovering meaning in these aspects of life will enhance their sense of integrity, their dignity and their belief in the worthiness of life and existence.

"Life, Death, Suffering, Love, and Work" can be explored with clients in counseling sessions, or as part of a **"Logo-Legacy Project"** or **"Meaning-Legacy Project"**—a compilation of logos (Meaning) as a legacy of our life. To create a memento of clients' Meaningful Life, clinicians can write down or record the answers to questions; clients can also transcribe their answers, make a video as a documentary, or find other creative ways to keep track of their responses. If clients do not have living family members, clinicians can act as witnesses of their lives and acknowledge the meaningful contributions they have made, and that they will continue to make.

"Logo-Legacy Project" – "Meaning-Legacy Project"

Clinicians can say: I am going to read you some questions to think about; imagine you are asking these questions of yourself.

- **Meaning of Life:**
    - What is the "Meaning of Life" for me?
    - What situations/circumstances, experiences, creativity, and attitudes throughout life have brought me meaning, purpose, and significance?
    - When have I discovered "after the fact" Meaning regarding a situation that appeared meaningless, difficult, or even traumatic/tragic?
    - What is my concept or understanding of an Ultimate Meaning of life?
    - When have I said *"yes to life"* despite any and all inherent difficulties of the human condition?
    - What brings me Meaning in Life right now?
    - What would I like to do or see that would bring me Meaning in Life now, and in the coming days?
    - What is one statement I would want to share with others about the Meaning of Life?

- **Meaning of Suffering:**
    - What is the "Meaning of Suffering" for me?
    - How have I experienced Suffering throughout my life?
    - How have I responded to this Suffering that is in line with or against how I want to live my life?
    - How has Suffering influenced my possibilities for growth?
    - What has Suffering taught me about life?
    - What has Suffering taught me about myself?
    - How does Suffering influence my life right now?
    - How do I want to live my life going forward in the face of Suffering?
    - What is one statement I would want to share with others about the Meaning of Suffering?

- **Meaning of Death:**
    - What is the "Meaning of Death" for me?
    - How has Death impacted my life?
    - What are my beliefs about Death?
    - How has the knowledge of my life-limiting illness and eventual Death impacted the way I want to live right now?
    - Have I realized or discovered any opportunities to make a positive difference in my own life and that of others within this limited time on earth?

- What would a Meaningful Death look like for me?
- What brings me Meaning in the Face of Death right now?
- What is one statement I would want to share with others about the Meaning of Death?

- **Meaning of Love:**
    - What is the "Meaning of Love" for me?
    - How have I experienced Love throughout my life?
    - How have I responded to different types of Love throughout my life?
    - How has Love influenced my life by facilitating growth possibilities?
    - How has my Love facilitated the possibility of growth in others?
    - What has Love taught me about life?
    - What has Love taught me about myself?
    - How does Love influence my life right now?
    - Moving forward, how do I want to show and experience love in my life?
    - What is one statement I would want to share with others about the Meaning of Love?

- **Meaning of Work:**
    - What is the "Meaning of Work" for me?
    - How have I experienced Work throughout my life?
    - How have I responded to different types of Work throughout my life?
    - How has Work influenced my life by facilitating possibilities for growth?
    - How has my Work facilitated growth in others?
    - What has Work taught me about life?
    - What has Work taught me about myself?
    - How does Work influence my life right now?
    - What meaningful Work experiences will I always remember?
    - How has Work influenced my personal creativity, experiences, and attitude in life?
    - What is one statement I would want to share with others about the Meaning of Work?

Additional topics:

- **Meaning of Spirit**
    - What is my understanding of the "Meaning of Spirit"?
    - How have I experienced Spirit, (or spiritual or religious practice) throughout my life?
    - How has Spirit, my essence, facilitated possibilities for growth?
    - How has Spirit, my essence, facilitated the possibility for growth in others?
    - What has Spirit, spiritual or religious practice, taught me about life?
    - What has Spirit, spiritual or religious practice, taught me about myself?
    - How does Spirit, spiritual or religious practice, influence my life right now?

- How has Spirit, spiritual or religious practice, changed for me because of my current illness/difficulty/situation?
- What Spiritually-transformative experiences will I always remember?
- What is one statement I want to share with others about the Meaning of Spirit?

- **Meaning of Peace**
  - What is the "Meaning of Peace" for me?
  - How have I experienced Peace throughout my life?
  - How has Peace influenced my life by facilitating growth possibilities?
  - How has my state of Peacefulness facilitated the possibility for growth in others?
  - What has Peace taught me about life?
  - What has Peace taught me about myself?
  - How does Peace influence my life right now?
  - How has Peace changed for me because of my current illness/circumstance/situation?
  - What Peaceful experiences will I always remember?
  - What is one statement I would want to share with others about the Meaning of Peace?

- **Meaning of Laughter**
  - What is the "Meaning of Laughter" for me?
  - How have I experienced Laughter throughout my life?
  - How has Laughter helped me get through difficult moments?
  - How has my Laughter influenced other people's lives by facilitating possibilities for others to get through difficult moments and by helping them grow?
  - What has Laughter taught me about life?
  - What has Laughter taught me about myself?
  - How does Laughter influence my life right now?
  - How has Laughter changed for me in light of my current illness/circumstance/situation?
  - What Laughter experiences will I always remember?
  - What is one statement I would want to share with others about the Meaning of Laughter?

- **Meaning of Happiness**
  - What is the "Meaning of Happiness" for me?
  - How have I experienced Happiness throughout my life?
  - How has Happiness influenced my life and helped me get through difficult moments?
  - How has my Happiness helped others get through difficult moments?
  - What has Happiness taught me about life?
  - What has Happiness taught me about myself?
  - How does Happiness influence my life right now?

- How has Happiness changed in light of my current illness?
- What Happiness experiences will I always remember?
- What is one statement I would want to share with others about the Meaning of Happiness?

- **Final Thoughts**
    - What meaningful discovery has come to my awareness as a result of working on my life's legacy through this Meaning–Legacy Project?
    - Are there any final thoughts that I may have that were not covered by these questions?
    - Is there anything I want to do differently in my life going forward as a result of working on this project?

The Meaning of Life, Suffering, Death, Love, and Work topics were inspired by Viktor Frankl's existential analysis themes. The Meaning of Spirit, Peace, and Laughter topics were inspired by Lexie Brockway Potamkin's book series: *What is Spirit, What is Peace, What is Laughter, What is Death, What is Love*. Frankl believed that happiness cannot be pursued directly, and that when we try to directly pursue it, we are bound to fail; however, happiness ensues as a byproduct of discovering meaning or doing the next right thing.

Mind-Body-Spirit Rejuvenation Method:
Simple Techniques for Stress Reduction & Healthy Living
(Dezelic & Ghanoum, 2015)

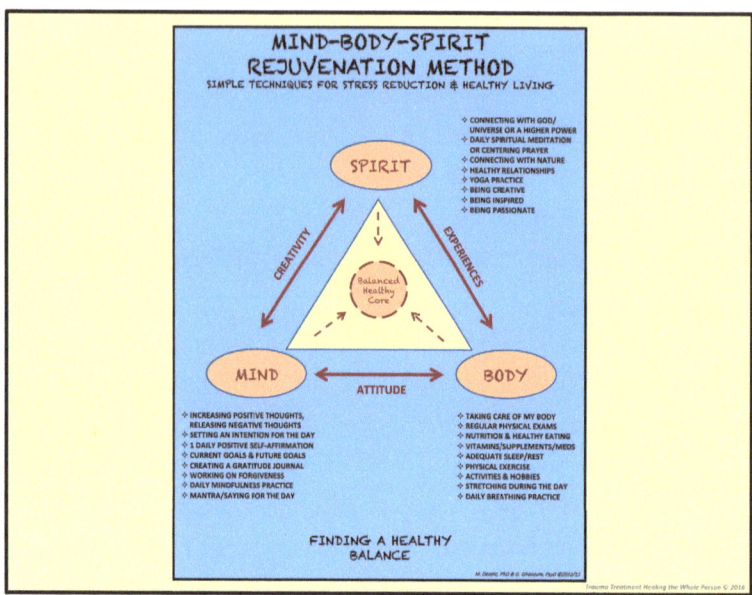

(Handout included in Section II)

Our overall health is affected by our physical, psychological and emotional well-being. There can be no question that our attitude and state of mind can have a profound impact on our physical health. Our bodies are aware of how much energy we spend "fighting" off negative or painful experiences, rather than spending time "nurturing" ourselves. When we nurture our mind, body, and spirit, we can experience growth, overall health, and healing, all of which naturally fosters physical improvement (Siegel & Sander, 2009). When we make a decision to take care of all aspects of ourselves—our minds, bodies, and spirits, we can improve our well-being, our connection to ourselves and others, and therefore, improve our overall Quality of Life.

The **"Mind-Body-Spirit Rejuvenation Method: Simple Techniques for Stress Reduction & Healthy Living"** Conceptual Pictograph—Client Handout embodies this sentiment of improving our overall Quality of Life. This handout provides clients and their families with ways to increase their well-being and satisfaction in life. Additionally, this information can help clinicians and caregivers increase their own well-being, promote collaborative compassion, and reduce compassion fatigue and the overall stress that often results from the responsibility of caring for clients or family members.

Through the *Mind-Body-Spirit Harmony* perspective, we view ourselves as a WHOLE of three inseparable and integrated parts. As Viktor Frankl described in his mind, body, and spirit dimensional ontology (Dezelic, 2014; Dezelic & Ghanoum, 2015; Frankl 1978, 1986, 1988, 2000, 2004, 2006; Graber, 2004), human beings are comprised of **Mind**—the conceptual thinking part of ourselves, otherwise known as our psyche, which governs our physiology, cognitions and behaviors; **Body**—the physical and physiological part of ourselves, which in biological terms is the living and breathing organism; and **Spirit**— the essence of ourselves, which is comprised of our particular uniqueness in this world and lifetime, our exclusive existence (in a non-religious sense yet compatible with the philosophy inherent in most religious and faith belief systems).

Creating a healthier lifestyle will automatically lead to less stress in our daily lives; less stress will lead to less psychological and physiological issues, and/or spiritual/existential distress. This healthier lifestyle will allow us to be energized, and free to follow creative and meaningful pursuits. By balancing these three dimensions of ourselves—the Mind-Body-Spirit, we create a triangular effect of energy movement. We call this movement the **Mind-Body-Spirit Rejuvenation Method.** We feel more rejuvenated in all of our dimensions, which ultimately can result in a healthier lifestyle.

The Mind-Body-Spirit Rejuvenation Method promotes

- Healthier Lifestyle → Less Stress
- Less Stress → fewer Psychological and Physiological Issues, and less Spiritual/Existential Distress; More Energy to Follow Creative and Meaningful Pursuits
- Balance the Triangle of Mind-Body-Spirit → Rejuvenation Method
- Rejuvenation Method → Healthier Lifestyle → ... (repeat)

By learning and then utilizing a few simple exercises, we can start to develop a new shift in our lives, create a healthier lifestyle, and begin to feel rejuvenated. We will no longer feel energetically depleted, fatigued, irritable, depressed, or anxious. Chronic pain will be less intense or may even disappear, and our overall stress level will begin to diminish. The Mind-Body-Spirit Rejuvenation Method is an easy-to-follow format; the end result will be a **Balanced Healthy Core**, an internal sense of well-being originating within ourselves.

As we begin to balance our mind, body and spirit, we will notice the emergence of a new triangle: **The Meaning Triangle** composed of **Creativity, Experiences,** and **Attitude.** These three areas offer opportunities and possibilities for a more engaged, meaningful and meaning-filled life. The three areas of meaning *(Creativity, Experiences, Attitude)* have an interactional effect with the three dimensions of our being *(Mind, Body, and Spirit)* thus producing positive outcomes. We begin to become more engaged in the specific areas of meaning as a byproduct of a balanced and healthy system.

The Meaning Triangle, described by Frankl as the three areas where we have the capacity and choice to create, experience and find meaning and purpose in life, includes Creativity, Experiences, and Attitudes.

The Meaning Triangle

- *Creativity:* The creative gifts we offer the world through our innate gifts and talents; we can also express this creativity through meaningful work, deeds, and accomplishments.
- *Experiences:* The meaningful moments we have through encountering others in relationships of all kinds, and from nature, the arts, culture or religion.

- ***Attitudes:*** The courageous and self-transcending attitudinal values we realize by taking a stance toward a situation or circumstance that is out of our control.

The **Mind-Body-Spirit Rejuvenation Method** techniques are described using common, familiar terms and ideas; however, they are creatively combined in a distinct and tangible layout. When we can visualize the goals that we are working on and are using specific exercises to achieve those goals, the task becomes that much easier to follow and accomplish. Goals that are too general or broad, such as "wanting to become healthy," are often difficult to reach, as there are no concrete objectives. Having a clear method to follow gives us a direction and a purpose.

We can begin each day using The Mind-Body-Spirit Rejuvenation Method. Keep the handout readily available, and choose a specific time each day to read through the directives. This action promotes brain-memory integration and can actually create new neural pathways.

Suggested ways to use ***The Mind-Body-Spirit Rejuvenation Method*** are listed below:

Daily "Check-In" Method

- Pick one or several items under each dimension, (Mind, Body, Spirit), and work on them throughout the day. It is usually easier to begin with one task from each area. This helps prevent us from feeling overwhelmed. Be careful not to choose an impossibly, difficult task.
- In the evening, we can review our goals to see how well we followed through with our chosen tasks.
    - Congratulate ourselves for the efforts that we have made.
    - Do not be hard on ourselves because we did not complete some tasks; we can simply try to take note of them and possibly attempt them the next day, or move on to a different, more favorable task.
- Try new tasks once we have mastered or have a continued practice with other tasks.
- We can disregard any tasks that make us feel nervous, afraid or uncomfortable.
- If we *Check-In with Ourselves* a few times per day, it is best to pick the most opportune times, (e.g. after waking up, lunch break, coffee break, prior to or after work/school/social hobbies, before going to bed).
- We need to remember to have fun! This is about feeling good, being energized, building our self-esteem, recognizing our choices, being creative, and creating new, healthy patterns.

Overview of the *Mind-Body-Spirit Rejuvenation Method*

MIND

- INCREASING POSITIVE THOUGHTS, RELEASING NEGATIVE THOUGHTS
- SETTING AN INTENTION FOR THE DAY
- ONE DAILY POSITIVE SELF-AFFIRMATION
- CURRENT GOALS & FUTURE GOALS
- GRATITUDE JOURNAL
- FORGIVENESS
- MINDFULNESS PRACTICE
- MANTRA/SAYING FOR THE DAY

BODY

- TAKING CARE OF MY BODY
- REGULAR PHYSICAL EXAMS
- NUTRITION
- VITAMINS/SUPPLEMENTS/MEDICATIONS
- ADEQUATE SLEEP/REST
- PHYSICAL EXERCISE
- ACTIVITIES & HOBBIES
- STRETCHING DURING THE DAY
- DAILY BREATHING PRACTICE

SPIRIT

- CONNECTING WITH GOD/UNIVERSE OR A HIGHER POWER
- DAILY SPIRITUAL MEDITATION OR CENTERING PRAYER
- CONNECTING WITH NATURE
- HEALTHY RELATIONSHIPS
- YOGA PRACTICE
- BEING CREATIVE
- BEING INSPIRED
- BEING PASSIONATE

MEANING TRIANGLE

- CREATIVITY—utilizing our creativity, having creative pursuits
- EXPERIENCES—with others, nature, animals, the arts
- ATTITUDE—that we can choose to have in difficult or unalterable situations

Adjustments: Clinicians can help clients decide which, if any, exercises are not applicable, and also help them substitute other more appropriate ones. They can also adjust exercises to best fit the capability of their clients, (i.e., a client may not be able to do a full, body movement yoga practice, but may be able to do a sitting yoga practice; a client may not be able to go outside, but can watch a nature or travel program to engage in the same feelings). Focus can be on specific topics under each of the Mind, Body, or Spirit areas, or on expanded topics that allow for client-specific applications and adaptations, preferences, and needs.

Having a healthy balance of various methods for taking care of ourselves allows us to experience and appreciate life more fully, take better care of ourselves and our loved ones, find new purposes, create new goals, experience hope, discover meaning, and feel rejuvenated. The resources for positive health and healthy, stress-free living exist within ourselves; it is merely up to us to capitalize on the assets we have available at our fingertips—our Mind, Body, and Spirit. Clients often experience a reduction of stress-related symptoms, and overall improvement in Quality of Life. ***Finding a Healthy Balance in life begins with me!***

Appealing Technique:
"Accessing the Defiant Power of the Spirit" Guided Meditation
(Dezelic, 2014; Dezelic & Ghanoum, 2015)

Whether practiced alone or with a guide, one way to achieve relaxation is through guided meditation practices. Mediation helps us access inner resources such as our *Defiant Power of the Human Spirit.* This often gives us the ability to discover Meaning, even in the face of death.

The Appealing Technique, a guided form of meditation, gently draws attention to and accesses the **Defiant Power of the Human Spirit.** This technique can be used with clients and their family members. Clinicians may want to include the Appealing Technique in their own contemplative practices as another way to reduce compassion fatigue and increase their spiritual well-being.

The Appealing Technique is useful in both individual and group therapy sessions. It can be scheduled once a week or whenever clinicians determine that their clients need to strengthen access to their **Defiant Power of the Human Spirit** and the **Nöetic Dimension.**

Suggestions for ways to implement the Appealing Technique

- Make a recording of your voice guiding clients through the **Appealing Technique** that can be used by clients when they are outside of therapy and in need of reinforcement.
- Any revised version of the **Appealing Technique** can be designed based on the specific population and the specific areas clients are addressing.
    - For **"Your Spirit States…"** clinicians can substitute additional phrases that their clients have stated they would like to strengthen for themselves.

Important Note: *Special consideration should be taken with actively suicidal or suicidal prone clients; this technique is not recommended for actively psychotic clients; clients should be under supervised medical and/or psychiatric care.*

Appealing Technique:
"Accessing the Defiant Power of the Spirit"
(Marie S. Dezelic, PhD © 2014)

The use of the Appealing Technique, an "appeal" to the client's spiritual dimension, is a guided meditation and autogenic training approach which encourages clients to connect with their inner resources, as well as to develop and strengthen a sense of inner calmness.

Preparation:
Ask client(s) to lie down or sit back in a comfortable position, with their back supported, placing their hands gently in their lap or on their abdomen, and to close their eyes when they feel comfortable.

You may have soft music (meditation music) or the sound of gentle running water playing in the background.

Proceed in a slow, softly spoken, gentle voice; taking slow pauses between sentences. *Any words in bold and italic should be emphasized.*

Therapist to client(s):
As you place your body in a comfortable position, begin to gently close your eyes, allowing your body to relax and quiet down. Begin to take deep, full breaths, allowing your breath as you exhale through your mouth or nose, to wash over your body in warm soothing waves. Notice any noises happening around you, and let them fade gently into the distance. Feel any tension throughout your body begin to slowly soften and dissipate as your warm breaths wash over your body. I will begin to slowly count backward from 10 to 1, and as I get closer to 1, your body will be feeling more and more relaxed, and all tension will be released from your body.

10 – 9 – 8 – 7 – 6 – 5 – 4 – 3 – 2 – 1… (tone of voice in a decrescendo). You are now in a state of deep and gentle relaxation. Your body is resting quietly while your spirit, the essence of you, is ever present.

As you take notice of the different parts of your body, you notice them getting more and more relaxed. Your head and neck have become completely relaxed; all tension has left this area… Your shoulders and both of your arms have become completely relaxed; all tension has left this area… Your chest and stomach area have become completely relaxed; all tension has left this area… Your hips and pelvis area have become completely relaxed; all tension has left this area… Your legs have become completely relaxed; all tension has left this area… Your entire body feels relaxed and calm. Nothing disturbs you now, you are completely relaxed. If any tension, thoughts, images or feelings arise, whatever they may be, simply notice them as if they are engulfed in a soft, puffy cloud, and let them gently pass by, paying no attention to them and offering no judgment as they pass and dissipate in the distance. You are completely relaxed.

As your body is resting gently and quietly, and feeling complete calmness and safety, your spirit is ever present. Your spirit states: *I have willpower, I am strong, I am able, I am well.* Again, as your body is resting quietly and feeling complete calmness and safety, your spirit is ever present. Your spirit states: *I have willpower, I am strong, I am able, I am well.*

A color of your choice comes to mind, for which when you see this particular color of yours, you become **empowered, resilient, full of strength, wellbeing and joy.** Picture this color all around you like flowing scarves in the wind of your soft and soothing breath. See this color vividly, which awakens your spirit, and your spirit states: *I have willpower, I am strong, I am able, I am well.*

Now allow your attention to drift back to your resting and calm body. Your color has gradually permeated the air around you and you are now able to breathe this color in and out, which washes over your body in gentle waves as you exhale. As you breathe your color in and out, you are feeling **empowered, resilient, full of strength, wellbeing and joy.** See and feel that your resilient spirit allows your body to feel calm, at peace, and full of joy. Your body and your spirit alike state: *I have willpower, I am strong, I am able, I am well.*

Now as I count forward from 1 to 10, climbing from the deeply relaxed state of wellbeing to the awake consciousness of 10, notice that your body and spirit bring with it the thoughts and feelings of: *I have willpower, I am strong, I am able, I am well.* As we climb toward 10, notice your body beginning to wake up slowing, so that when we arrive to 10, you open your eyes, feeling fully awake and alive, and are filled with the thoughts and feelings of: *I have willpower, I am strong, I am able, I am well.*

Let us begin our soft and gentle climb to becoming fully awake and conscious in this room…
1 – 2 – 3 – 4 – 5 – 6 – 7 – 8 – 9 – 10! (tone of voice in a crescendo). Gently open your eyes, move your arms and fingers, your legs and toes, head and neck around. Recall your thoughts and feelings from the combined sense of your body and spirit of: *I have willpower, I am strong, I am able, I am well.* Carry with you for the rest of the day: *I have willpower, I am strong, I am able, I am well.*

This concludes the Appealing Technique session. Ask client(s) to describe how they are feeling and what they will take away with them from this exercise for the day. Ask client(s) to recall their color, and to begin to notice it throughout the day.

Peaceful and Comforting Place Meditation:
Relaxation for Stressful-Anxious Moments

Clients often have ongoing physiological and emotional dysregulation, and experience chronic distress, all of which can produce highly stressful states. For example, difficult moments of any type can result in increased stress and strain on the physical system and precipitate anxiety-emotional responses. It is helpful for clinicians to have a "**Peaceful and Comforting Place" meditation** practice available to help clients experience comfort, relaxation, a sense of safety, and positive states of well-being. States of relaxation can improve treatment outcomes, and help clients feel less anxious and more at peace with themselves and their surroundings. The "Peaceful and Comforting Place" meditation can be used to address a specific response to a frightening or uncomfortable situation, or at the beginning and/or end of counseling sessions.

Note: The words *"Peaceful and Comforting"* can be exchanged with words that are more comfortable for each client, or additional words can be added, thereby making the "Place" a unique and safe place for the client to imagine in order to reduce stress and anxiety.

"Peaceful and Comforting Place" Meditation:
Relaxation for Stressful-Anxious Moments
M. Dezelic, PhD © 2015

I invite you to start breathing gently and relaxed, slowing your in breath and lengthening your out breath to your comfort level. As you exhale your breaths, see your body getting more and more relaxed, feel the muscles of your body releasing tension with every out breath, your overall sense of self feeling more and more relaxed. Gently close your eyes if you feel comfortable to do so.

Bring up in your mind's eye a place that we will call your "Peaceful and Comforting Place." This place can be a real place that you have been to before, or an imaginary place. It can have people, animals, or whatever you would like to see there, or it can be free of all people and things. An example of a place might be on a warm beach with gentle waves, a green grassy open area, an area full of trees and soft fallen leaves, a snowy mountain top, an area in the sky among the clouds, with family members, special people you love, or spiritual guides that are loving, caring, protective, and wise. Let your imagination take you to the most Safe and Comforting place you can think of, that brings you peace of mind, peace of heart, and peace of spirit.

As you sit here thinking about your special "Peaceful and Comforting Place," think about all of your senses. Try to *see* the colors and sights, beautiful and vibrant, or gentle and subtle. Try to *smell* the aromas, fragrant and vibrant, or gentle and subtle. Try to *hear* the sounds, if any, such as a gentle wind blowing, water moving, birds chirping, leaves crunching, music playing, people talking, kids laughing. Try to capture *taste*, if anything, such as a drink, or the salty, fresh or crisp air. Try to *touch* things around you, with your hands or feet, or feel the air on your body, warm and pleasant, or cool and inviting. With your essence, your spiritual dimension, invoke your entire mind, body, and spirit to feel comforted... safe... cared for... at ease... relaxed... peaceful... fulfilled... loved... healed... in harmony... and whatever else your mind, body, and spirit want to experience, in this special "Peaceful and Comforting Place" of yours.

Continue taking gentle and relaxing breaths, taking in your entire experience of this special and unique "Peaceful and Comforting Place" of yours, feeling your physical body, your mind, and your spirit free of any tension, anxiety, or discomforts from your illness or emotions, and being completely relaxed and safe. Breathe in this state of relaxation, and exhale any and all discomforts, until they seem to have faded away off in the distance. Know that you can come back to your Safe and Comforting Place whenever you need to relax, feel rejuvenated, let go of stressors, get comforted, feel utterly safe and secure, and feel your mind, body, and spirit in perfect harmony.

As you breathe in and out, start to bring a gentle awareness to your fingers and arms, to your feet and legs, to your muscles in your face and neck, your stomach, your back, your entire body. Start to wiggle your fingers and your toes, and gently open your eyes if they have been closed, bringing your full mind-body-spirit experience with you to the present. Feel yourself in the room, move your body a bit more, and try to yawn.

Remember that you can access your "Peaceful and Comforting Place," as well as your mind, body, and spirit relaxation and wellness, whenever you might need to or want to, for this is your unique and special place.

Seek & Find Meaning Every Day:
A Daily Method of Observation, Mindfulness Practice

Taking the time daily to nurture a mindfulness meditation, or prayer practice, allows us to become more compassionate and connected healthcare providers; we are better equipped to handle and be present with the ongoing suffering of others, as well as our own experience of the suffering with our clients.

The following 5 methods that incorporate soothing breathing practices, mindfulness, existential awareness, and meaningful or meaning-centered self-discovery can be used as a daily guide.

"Seek and Find Meaning Every Day" by practicing the following

1. **BECOME AWARE OF YOUR PRESENCE AND ESSENCE**

   - Begin each morning by focusing on your breath of life, bringing awareness to the "in breath" (inhalation) and the "out breath" (exhalation), feeling your entire body—muscles, organs, tissues, cells, skin, get invigorated and awake with the flowing oxygen.
   - Bring an awareness to your life; begin to recognize that you are alive, saying to yourself: I am alive today, and I am given the gift of this day to contemplate, connect, contribute, and make a difference in the world.
   - Lift your hands up and open them for the energy of this day (and/or to God/Universe/Higher Power/Your own Spirit or Connection to others on this earth).
   - Take in a breath of compassion and exhale any criticism, judgment, guilt or shame you have for yourself or others.
   - Recognize the preciousness of your existence with love, tenderness, compassion and peace.

2. **START THE DAY WITH GRATITUDE & GIVE THANKS DURING THE DAY**

   - Gratitude moment: We can give thanks for specific things (at least 3 new things every morning); this sets a positive tone for the day, regardless of the difficulties that will be encountered. We can begin to develop an "attitude of gratitude."
   - Throughout the day, we can begin to pay attention to 3 significant areas in our life: Creativity, Experiences, and Attitude *(The Meaning Triangle),* and how we experience significant moments derived from each. These three areas inspire Meaning in Life.
   - We can discover, pay attention to, and give thanks for Meaning nuggets—small positive aspects of life that we have been a part of or have encountered, (creativity, experiences, attitude, people, messages, or any other positive aspects) throughout the day.

3. **GIVE OURSELVES PERMISSION TO ACCEPT OUR HUMANNESS AND OUR EMOTIONS**

- Give ourselves permission to feel all of our emotions. This allows us to fully experience human existence.
- Take a reflective moment to check-in with ourselves, to discover what our emotions are trying to tell us. Our emotions do not need to be avoided or repressed; even the ones we recognize or think are negative. Possibilities of what we feel with each emotion:
    - *Sadness:* Letting go of pain, memories, beliefs and expectations; working through changes and transitions
    - *Anger:* Needing to put a safe boundary between ourselves and perceived violation; protection of existence
    - *Fear:* Needing to protect ourselves from possible danger or violation
    - *Frustration:* Needing to stand up and speak out against something, someone, a violation
    - *Guilt:* Feeling as if we should have or could have made a different decision or followed a different path
    - *Compassion:* Having empathy for ourselves or others (step into the other person's shoes or personal story)
    - *Joy/Happiness:* Feeling pleasure and elatedness
    - *Peace:* Feeling an inner calm, comfort, and contentment
- Throughout each day, review our emotional responses as we encounter other people and/or circumstances. Notice if a common theme emerges; that is, if we continue to experience the same emotion.
- Take a moment of quiet reflection to review what the particular emotion may be showing us about our life, our existence and/or the current situation.
- Remind ourselves that we are not our emotions, that instead, we have emotions, and that our emotions are only signals for us to elicit an action; allow our emotions to pass through us, noticing that we actually experience many emotions throughout the day.

4. **EVERY EVENING, REFLECT ON ONE SIGNIFICANT FEATURE OF THE DAY**

- Pick an aspect from the Meaning nuggets or one of the significant emotions we experienced.
- Become open to self-discovery:
    - Positive aspect of our day: This positive significant feature of our day is an opportunity to give thanks (gratitude), to help us grow, transcend and add meaning to our life.
- Negative aspect of our day: This negative significant feature of our day can provide us with the opportunity to trust our own intuition or guidance, to discover meaning, and transformation, so that we do not stay stuck in the negativity.

- Practice Self-Forgiveness and Other-Forgiveness, Self-Compassion and Other-Compassion through the help of a breath practice focusing on the following:
    - Let me release myself of the hurt and anger I may be carrying toward myself, others *(Name)*, and situations *(Describe)*. Let me practice kindness, gentleness, and compassion toward myself and others.

5. **LOOK FORWARD TO TOMORROW**
    - Evening "breath of life" practice: Noticing and bringing a focused awareness to our breath as it comes in and out of our body, and fills us with life.
    - Emotional check-in: Notice if we are holding onto any emotions. Gently release these emotions as we exhale our breath.
    - Review of the day: Despite the tragic aspects of the human condition and difficulties we encountered, what was meaningful about our day?
    - Gratitude Moment for the day: Give thanks for our breath, for our unique existence, for our three Meaning Nuggets. End our day on the Gratitude Moment practice because it sets the intention for a gentle and comfortable sleep, and a positive wakeup to the new day.

REACH Beyond the Limitations:
Sources of Meaning in Life
(Dezelic & Ghanoum, 2015)

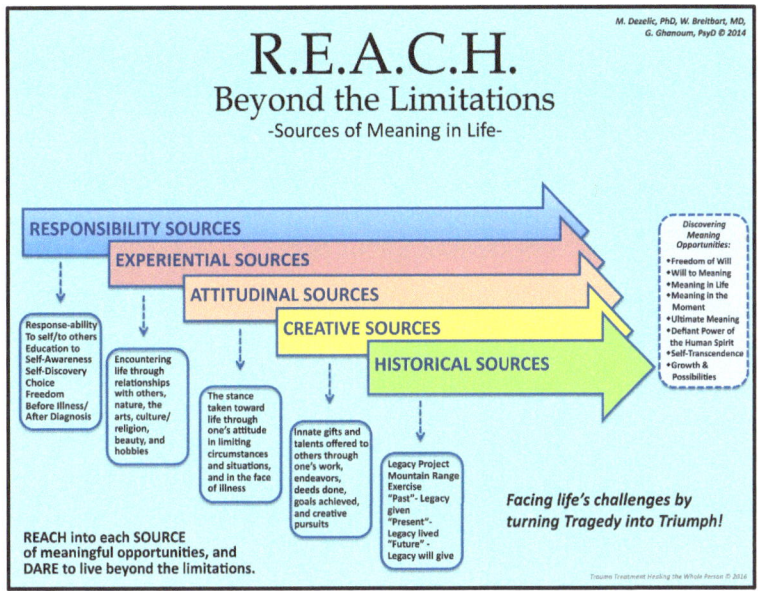

(Handout included in Section II)

The **"REACH Beyond the Limitations: Sources of Meaning in Life"** Conceptual Pictograph—Client Handout, was designed by M. Dezelic, PhD, W. Breitbart, MD, and G. Ghanoum, PsyD, based on Dr. William Breitbart's work and clinical research with randomized controlled trials of his Meaning-centered group psychotherapy (MCGP) and Individual meaning-centered psychotherapy (IMCP) (Breitbart et al., 2010; Breitbart et al., 2012; Breitbart et al., 2015).

The key concepts of Viktor Frankl's Logotherapy and Existential Analysis (LTEA): meaning in life, responsibility to life, and the spiritual aspects of the human being, inspired the applications and novel exercises in Breitbart's psychotherapeutic work with people in the advanced stages of cancer. Many who are diagnosed with cancer seek guidance and support in addressing the following issues: Sustaining meaning in life despite their life-limiting diagnosis; finding hope in the face of death; understanding their cancer diagnosis and progression; and facing or coming to terms with their impending death.

The particular interventions developed and rigorously tested by Breitbart and his colleagues at the Department of Psychiatry & Behavioral Sciences at Memorial Sloan-Kettering Cancer Center in New York City, NY, USA are designed for eight sessions of group psychotherapy and seven sessions of individual psychotherapy. These interventions utilize a mixture of didactics, discussion and experiential exercises that focus on particular themes related to meaning in life and advanced cancer. The themes of the REACH components: Responsibility, Experiential values, Attitudinal values, Creative values, and Historical values, are also part of each group or individual psychotherapy session. Clients are assigned readings and homework that are specific to each session's theme. These assignments are then utilized in the sessions, with the goal of motivating clients to discover meaning and purpose in life in the face of terminal illness and impending death.

Breitbart's manualized treatment workbooks for Meaning-centered group psychotherapy (MCGP) and Individual meaning-centered psychotherapy (IMCP) informed by his clinical research, are entitled: ***Meaning-Centered Group Psychotherapy for Clients with Advanced Cancer: A Treatment Manual*** (Breitbart & Poppito, 2014a); and ***Individual Meaning-Centered Psychotherapy for Clients with Advanced Cancer: A Treatment Manual*** (Breitbart & Poppito, 2014b).

The **"REACH Beyond the Limitations: Sources of Meaning in Life"** Conceptual Pictograph—Client Handout is applicable for anyone searching for ways to discover meaning in their lives, despite or because of traumas, tragedies, illnesses, and difficult life circumstances.

Clinicians can explain to clients that they can ***"REACH into each source of meaningful opportunities, and dare to live beyond any and all limitations."***

Explore each area of ***Meaning*** in the **REACH** acronym:

R = Responsibility
E = Experiential Sources
A = Attitudinal Sources
C = Creative Sources
H = Historical Sources

After examining the REACH sources of meaning listed above, clients may discover a way to ***"Face life's challenges by turning tragedy into triumph."*** *Clinicians can assist clients to explore* the following questions regarding their traumatic experience and the use of meaning-centered therapy:

- ***"How"*** have I grown from the experience?
- ***"What"*** have I taken away and learned from the difficulties in life?
- ***"Where"*** do I see new possibilities in the face of setbacks?
- ***"When"*** will I actualize the new possibilities?
- ***"Who"*** is making a difference in my life and am I making a difference in someone's life?

Connect—Create—Convey:
Living Life with Meaning and Purpose
(Dezelic & Ghanoum, 2015)

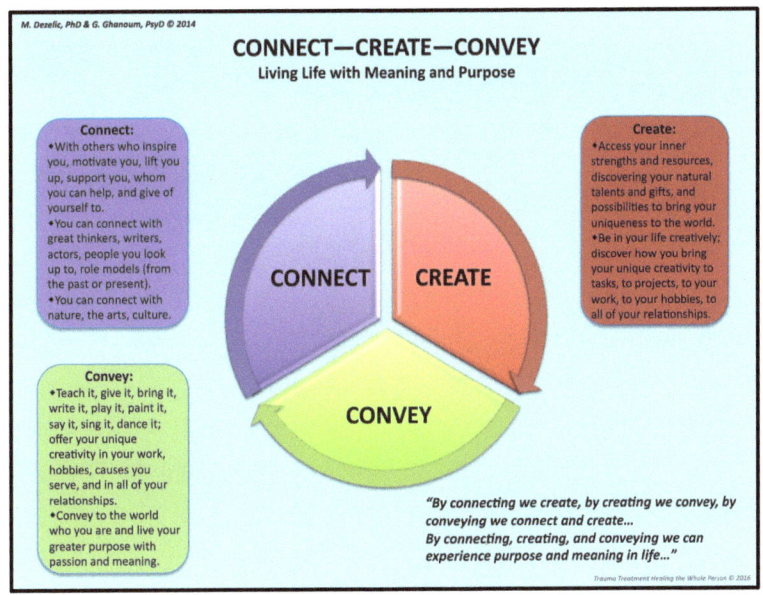

(Handout included in Section II)

It is worthwhile to express and give in whatever way we can to humanity, and thereby experience self-transcendence. We can share our unique gifts and talents with others rather than keeping them inside and hidden from the world. This act of sharing helps us uncover meaning, and is a part of our experience with others; it can be the expression of our purpose or just of ourselves, as we discover Meaning in our life.

One person's Purpose and Meaning may be to teach; another's may be the experience of being an amazing friend, mother, father, partner, pillar in the community, etc. One person may be an inventor or innovator of some sort, and another's purpose may be to bring communities together, or another's may be to assist in the creation or accomplishment of something significant in the world, thus being a part of a greater team. All are equally important and powerfully connecting roles.

We have the freedom to be response-able to life's demands; that is, we have the freedom to be "responsible," to transcend self and give to others and the world through our own unique and creative gifts and talents. We can connect with others, as we are biologically wired to do, and we can connect to life with our greater purpose. We can choose to connect with people who bring meaning in our lives and inspire us; and we can convey our uniqueness, share with others in a multitude of meaningful ways, and also discover personal Meaning through Self-Transcendence: the sharing of our gifts and talents with others and the world.

Connect—Create—Convey

1) With our support network – those people, past or present who promoted or are promoting positive growth, motivation and support.

2) With our particular resources, strengths, and talents or new areas of interests.

3) With our particular unique pathways that we utilize to express ourselves in the world.

Connect with

- Those who inspire, motivate and lift us up.
- Those who may benefit from our help, love or support.
- Those role models from the past or present, such as great thinkers, philosophers, authors, actors, leaders, or other people we look up to and admire.
- The beauty of nature, the arts, culture.

Create

- Access our inner strengths and resources; discover our natural talents and gifts, and possibilities in order to bring our uniqueness to the world.
- Be in our life creatively; examine how we bring our unique creativity to tasks, to projects, to our work, to our hobbies, to all of our relationships.

Convey

- Teach it, give it, bring it, write it, play it, paint it, say it, sing it, dance it; offer our unique creativity in our work, hobbies, causes we serve, and in all of our relationships.
- Convey to the world who we are and live our greater purpose with passion and Meaning.

"By connecting we create, by creating we convey, by conveying we connect and create...
By connecting, creating, and conveying we can experience purpose and meaning in life..."

Part V
Conclusion

Meaning-Centered Therapy in Trauma Treatment:
Healing and Lasting Recovery

Trauma is an overwhelming bio-psycho-social-spiritual event that causes a variety of ongoing disruptive responses and symptoms to develop within the biological and psychological domains, all of which can have significant impacts in the social and spiritual domains. Although from a Meaning-Centered Logotherapy & Existential Analysis perspective, our human spirit cannot be damaged, when we are exposed to trauma, we may experience existential angst and/or frustration, and can also find ourselves questioning meaning, self, others, life, and God/Universe. When any of these symptoms occur in the biological, psychological, or social domains, the spiritual dimension often becomes blocked due to our overactive and overwhelming symptomatology.

If we think of the word "**TRAUMA**" as an Acronym: ***T = Triggers are threat, R = Reactive responses, A = Alienation & isolation, U = Unsafe and uncertain, M = Memory distortion and fragmented pieces, A = Autonomic nervous system dysregulation,*** we can easily recognize the bio-psycho-social-spiritual impacts that result from trauma and are able to understand the necessity for having a therapeutic treatment approach that addresses all aspects of the mind, body, and spirit.

Trauma Treatment Foundational Phase-Work (TTFP) is an integrative trauma-informed treatment modality designed by the authors, Dezelic & Ghanoum. The framework of this trauma-informed treatment and therapeutic care combines and integrates the most recent, researched information available in the field of trauma treatment and development. Building upon existing theories and strategies, while addressing core trauma treatment reprocessing methods, this model utilizes a holistic and existential methodology, attending to the "Whole Person in Trauma Treatment," all of which necessitates a multi-dimensional therapeutic approach. TTFP focuses on Viktor Frankl's Logotherapy & Existential Analysis as a key component in trauma treatment.

Clinicians who follow the TTFP model described in this manual will develop an understanding of treatment interventions, strategies, and skills that are designed to attend to the mind, body, and spirit, as well as intended to address meaning in life and meaning in suffering. Because trauma manifests itself in a variety of ways, clinicians need to expand their repertoire of techniques and methods. Discovering meaning, even in the face of trauma, can provide a pathway toward healing the mind and body, and will enable us to access our healthy Human Spirit. According to Viktor Frankl and Meaning-Centered Logotherapy, the Human Spirit is incapable neither of becoming sick nor in need of healing. Existential crisis originates in the Spiritual Dimension, when it becomes blocked, but the dimension itself is not neurotic or sick. Offering the insight, as Frankl purported, that we are Spiritual Beings with a Soma (Body) and Psyche (Mind), and that the Human Spirit remains whole, intact, and healthy can be very reassuring and comforting to someone who is coping with the after effects of trauma.

This manual provides clinicians with the core elements for trauma treatment: stabilization, recovery, and reconnection. These core elements reduce or eliminate trauma symptoms, and help clinicians promote healing through the use of Meaning-Centered Therapy and Logotherapy & Existential Analysis, by understanding trauma elements and the Trauma Treatment Foundational Phase-Work (TTFP) Model, and through integrating specific Meaning-Centered Interventions for meaning discovery and exploration. The original conceptual pictographs—client handouts, for clinicians and clients – that are provided in this manual, offer an additional psychoeducational tool, as well as a specific method of treatment for use with clients.

Trauma disrupts safety and healthy engagement in life, and can interfere with the discovery of meaning in life. Clinicians who follow the Trauma Treatment Foundational Phase-Work (TTFP) Model, a trauma treatment approach incorporating specific Meaning-Centered aspects, are better able to guide clients to safety. They can do this by utilizing trauma and meaning-oriented interventions that are specifically designed to help their clients reconnect with life, discover meaning in life, and fulfill meaningful goals. Clinicians who follow the **TTFP Model** described in this manual will be better able to help their clients heal from trauma and realize that ***Meaning in Life can be rediscovered when trauma aspects are healed.***

Epilogue ..... *by Dr. Brent Potter*

Afterthoughts...

Within the pages of this comprehensive and practical text, you have undoubtedly learned about the trauma treatment model and the array of phenomena it covers: anger, forgiveness, core wounds, current social support, grief, loss, triggers, memories, hope, and resilience. A guiding thread running throughout this fine book is *forgiveness,* which by definition, is an act of faith and the penultimate gesture of presence, of letting go. A "letting go" is never simply an act on the part of an individually existing subject, but a letting go "in the service of" or "for the purpose of." Said differently forgiveness, letting go, has intentionality and necessarily implies an *Other,* whether that be what may lie "out there" or for the sake of the process itself. This is by no means a progressive idea of our contemporary era; rather, it is a tried and true medicine from antiquity. The ancient Greeks gave expression to the notion of *aphiemi* (ἀφίημι). As is usually the case, the single Greek word offers an anatomy of the notion: to send away, to send forth, to let go / le be, to permit, allow, not to hinder, to leave, go away from one, to divorce, to leave so that what is left may remain (Thayer & Smith, 1999). Clearly, the phenomenon of letting go is not a simple action, but wields an array of varying meanings and purposes. Within the varying meanings and purposes, there seems to be a common element of faith. "To let go" is to release certitude as well as the various means by which one seeks certitude; it is an act of faith. Forgiveness, it seems, requires a releasement in the service of allowing the larger process of healing and wholeness to do its work.

Openness to mystery and releasement to the things themselves, a kind of faith in Being, constitutes meditative thinking. It is a reflective faith and openness that "contemplates the meaning which reigns in everything there is" (Heidegger, 1966, p. 46). The centrality of meditative thinking is clear:

> At times it requires a greater effort. It demands more practice. It is in need of more deliberate care than any other genuine craft. But it must also be able to bide its time, to await as does the farmer, whether the seed will come up and ripen. (p. 47)

Viktor Frankl had a great affinity for the great thinker, Martin Heidegger. Apparently, Frankl even had a framed letter from Heidegger hanging on the wall. What is the highest form of thinking and doing? Heidegger responded by saying it was *meditative thinking*—openness to mystery and releasement to the things themselves. The psychoanalytic mystic, Wilfred Bion, said the psychoanalytic attitude is *Faith*, going as far as to use a capital "F." In some ways, Bionian Faith is an amplification of Freud's notions of evenly hovering attention and being steady, yet engaged with the client. Faith, like meditative thinking, requires a certain silence, an unknowing. Bion approached his clinical work without memory, expectation, understanding, or desire. Maybe Faith and meditative thinking are ideals, something to shoot for, like Carl Jung's notion of individuation or Nietzsche's *Übermensch*. In any case, Faith seems to be not only a pre-given, latent or expressed, but is also linked with growth of intuitive capacities. Eigen (2014) notes that intuition can, at times, be beyond ordinary sensory perception—more of an open "space" or capacity. Intuition and attention go together, since the more attention is paid to experience, the more one understands. As Heidegger pointed out, the face that a human being turns towards Being is the face that Being reflects back. It takes faith to express, to communicate oneself. Sometimes it takes even more faith to wait and let further processes develop—faith, meditative thinking, and patience go together. Sometimes action circumvents more mature existential growth and, sometimes, it adds to more existential-psychological possibilities (Potter, 2015, pp. 107-108).

As Frankl frequently pointed out, all of Creation (Being) is saturated with meaning and so is every moment of human existence. The task of the human pilgrimage, in his estimation, is to engage our unique capacity to understand our meaning and purpose in life. Frankl is clear and unambiguous that our freedom to choose how we take up our circumstances is critical to this process of discovery. It is often a mistaken interpretation of Frankl that he asserted that humans are supremely free to choose their meaning and purpose, life and circumstances. This would be the position of, perhaps, Jean-Paul Sartre. Frankl distances himself from Sartre and the notion that we have a vast region of freedom. Instead, he maintained that often our freedom is small, but precious. This small, interpretive "as" of experience – to take something "as" something – is our most fundamental freedom and the one that cannot be stripped from us. In any event, it is the inherent and ever outflowing meaning of the universe and this indispensable capacity for choice that are at play in Frankl's four overlapping dimensions of discovering meaning. First, there is the dimension of the creative that includes, but is not limited to, one's career and raising children. Second, is the dimension of social nexus of relationships in which we love and are loved. This region includes the aesthetic capacity to love and see the beauty in nature, others, and art. Third, is the capacity to encounter unavoidable suffering inherent in human life including suffering and, invariably, death. Finally, there is the region of our being embodied and psychological. Within this dimension, lies what Frankl calls the nöetic or spiritual.

As with Bion's use of the word "faith" and with Heidegger's use of the word "meditative," Frankl's use of the word "spiritual" or "nöetic" is not necessarily religious. If one chooses to take them up within some religious frame, that is one's choice, but a religious perspective is certainly not the context in which they are presented. Faith (inherent in forgiveness) is often faith in the midst of trauma. We are linked together by faith and also linked by catastrophe. The human discovery of meaning and purpose is necessary and remains all through life. We may not realize it clearly, but it lives "inside" us, part of an indistinguishable tension of faith-trauma that feeds a sense of living. Trauma and forgiveness are "designed" into life. Frankl's psychology accents that the very quality of being an emotional, meaning- and-purpose discovering being has catastrophic aspects and effects. Human existence has very destructive as well as exceptionally creative potentialities. The question of whether humankind can learn to live with its destructiveness is an open question for Frankl. It can go either way; Frankl leaves room open for the possibility of a dramatic turn down the wrong road or the positive possibility of recovering from the destructiveness already wrought. In any event, forgiveness in face of trauma is a point of entry. Faith is an extraordinary nucleus in the depths of our affective life, an emotional nucleus. This nucleus centers a complex patterning of human experience—trauma, existential shattering, dying, discovering, choosing, and (hopefully) emerging anew.

Aside from the countless concrete skills and easy to understand concepts made available in this excellent book, Dezelic and Ghanoum unpack a theory in which forgiveness is a porthole to healing. What a beautiful thing it is to realize that the age-old remedy for traumas, from the everyday to the catastrophic, is *aphiemi* (letting go) and forgiveness (faith in the Other / process). We have the ability to choose how to take up our circumstances, no matter how small or overwhelming those circumstances may be. There is a dignity and serenity to this sensibility. As my friend once said, "No matter who or what is to blame, I am responsible."

Frankl's sensibility and wisdom saturate the pages of Dr. Marie Dezelic and Dr. Gabriel Ghanoum's *Trauma Treatment - Healing the Whole Person*. It serves as a *point d'entrée* into open heart, into welcoming and embracing the healing power of *aphiemi* and forgiveness. Not only does healing occur by these means but, as one is disburdened, one is then free to discover evermore unfolding meanings inherent in this fascinating and often traumatic human journey. Coming through the whirlwind often affords an increased sensitivity to the struggle and pain of others. Moreover, self-transcendence often affords a greater sense of humor, levity, compassion, and an increased capacity for forgiveness. As done previously, Dezelic and Ghanoum have generously provided a manual that is true to Frankl's vision while also being practical and wieldy enough to be applicable to individual or group work. This book will undoubtedly serve as an invaluable guide to hope, healing, and self-transcendence for anyone willing to pick it up and engage in the work.

Brent Potter, PhD
Adult Psychotherapist & Child Mental Health Specialist
Spokane Tribe of Indians, Wellpinit, WA, USA
Author of *Elements of Reparation: Truth, Faith, & Transformation
in the Works of Heidegger, Bion, & Beyond; and Elements of Self-Destruction*
Co-Author of *Borderline Personality Disorder:
New Perspectives on an Overused and Stigmatizing Diagnosis*

References
Eigen, M. (2014). *Faith*. London: Karnac.
Heidegger, M. (1966). *Discourse on Thinking*. New York: Harper & Row.
Potter, B. (2015). *Elements of Reparation: Truth, Faith, & Transformation in the Works of Heidegger, Bion,
    & Beyond.* London: Karnac.
Thayer, J. & Smith. (1999). *The NAS New Testament Greek Lexicon* [online]. Available:
    http://www.biblestudytools.com/lexicons/greek/nas/aphiemi.html

Into the Light

A trail of breadcrumbs had been laid,
To help you navigate your way from the depths of this darkened cave.
I would toss them two steps ahead as we twisted and turned through the untraveled paths.

In the darkness, I sat on the floor with you and I held your hands.
We felt the cold, hard dirt beneath us, and I told you it would be okay.
I cried your tears for you, the ones you had never cried before.
And through my tears, you finally allowed yours to let go.
I helped you to use those tears differently now.
We allowed the grace of natural waters to wash away the soiled handprints of those days,
And let them be absorbed by the earth forever more.

You followed me.
I had walked these dark passageways before.
As we walked along the way... we talked, we laughed,
And we played those childhood games stolen from your hands.
We found a way to smile and to keep warm when it seemed an impossible task.
And soon we made our way through the frightened, frozen, musty, closed-up past.

We stepped into the sunlight, and suddenly felt alive.
Emerging as if renewed, but simultaneously totally anew.
You stopped and turned me around to face you,
To try and see what you could not make out in the blackness of the night.
And there you saw the mirror of my heart in my eyes,
Reflecting back only your beauty and Divine Light.
You found the breadcrumbs in your pocket,
And a clear path in front of you...

-M. Dezelic, 2016

II.
MEANING-CENTERED THERAPY & TRAUMA TREATMENT FOUNDATIONAL PHASE-WORK (TTFP) APPLICATIONS

"CLINICIAN & CLIENT HANDOUTS" IN COLOR

MY NOTES...

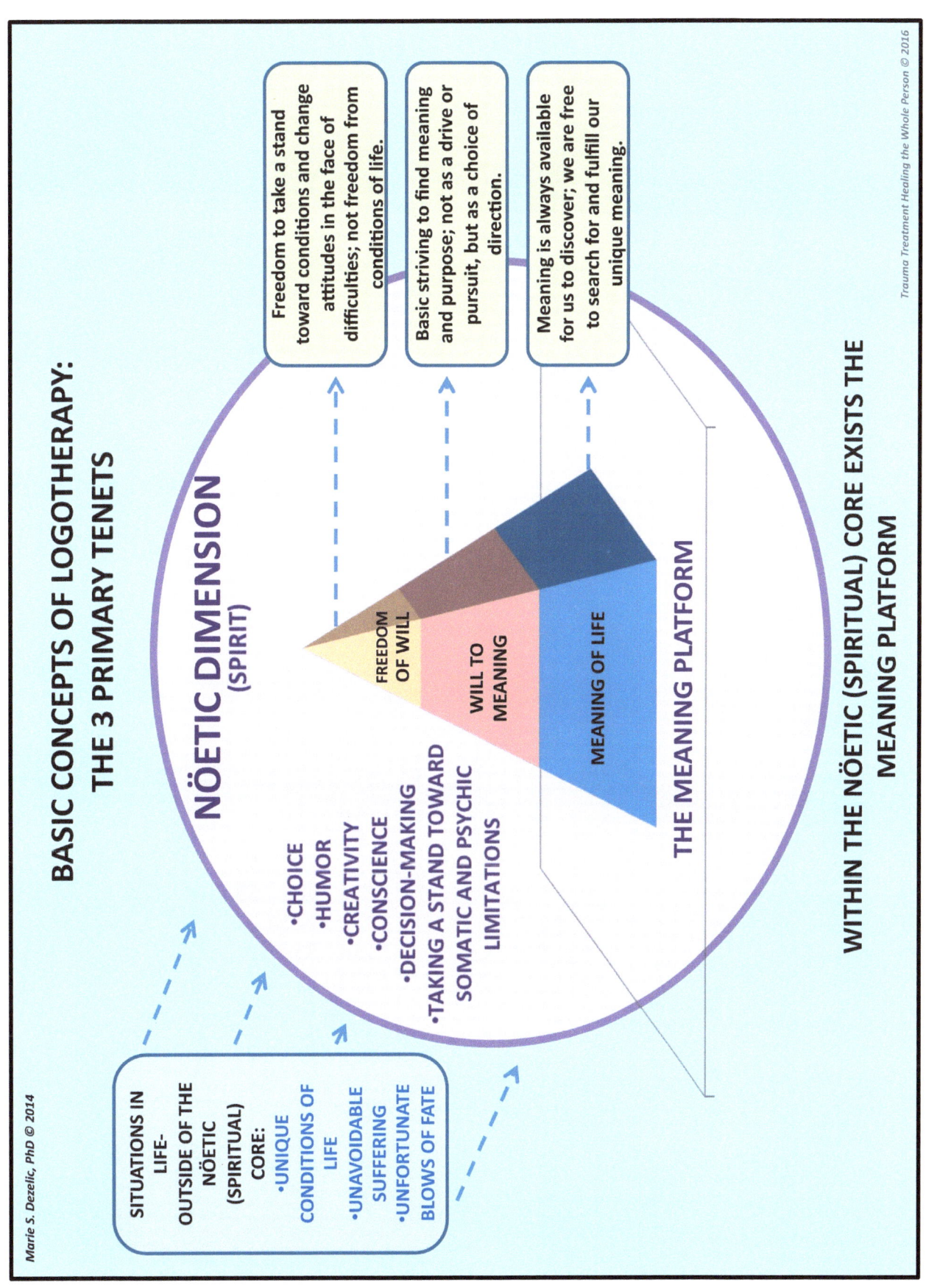

MY NOTES...

DISCOVERING MEANING IN LIFE

Marie S. Dezelic, PhD © 2014

MEANING OF THE MOMENT
- Can be found and fulfilled; opportunities to act with purposeful living, and to be aware of the meaning possibilities of each moment.

ULTIMATE MEANING
- Can basically never be attained; like the horizon, we walk toward it, always seeing it in the near distance but never reaching it.

What creative gifts have I offered to others through my innate gifts and talents in my work, deeds done, goals achieved, that held meaning for me?
- CREATIVITY

What experiences have I received from encountering others in relationships of all kinds, from nature, culture or religion, that were deeply meaningful?
- EXPERIENCES

What attitudinal values have I realized by taking a stance toward a situation or circumstance, that was courageous or self-transcending?
- ATTITUDES

MEANING TRIANGLE
FINDING MEANING & PURPOSE

- ATTITUDES
- EXPERIENCES
- CREATIVITY

FINDING MEANING IN LIFE BY:

1. What I give to life through my CREATIVITY.
2. What I receive from life through EXPERIENCES.
3. The stance I take toward life through my ATTITUDE.

GUIDEPOSTS TO SOURCES OF MEANING
(Opportunities and Areas to Discover Meaning in Life)

1. **SELF DISCOVERY**
   - WHO AM I
   - WHAT DO I WANT TO BECOME
2. **CHOICE**
   - CHANGE SITUATION
   - CHANGE ATTITUDE
3. **UNIQUENESS**
   - CREATIVITY
   - PERSONAL RELATIONSHIPS
4. **RESPONSIBILITY**
   - FREEDOM
   - FATE
5. **SELF-TRANSCENDENCE**
   - TOWARD A PERSON
   - TOWARD A CAUSE

MY NOTES...

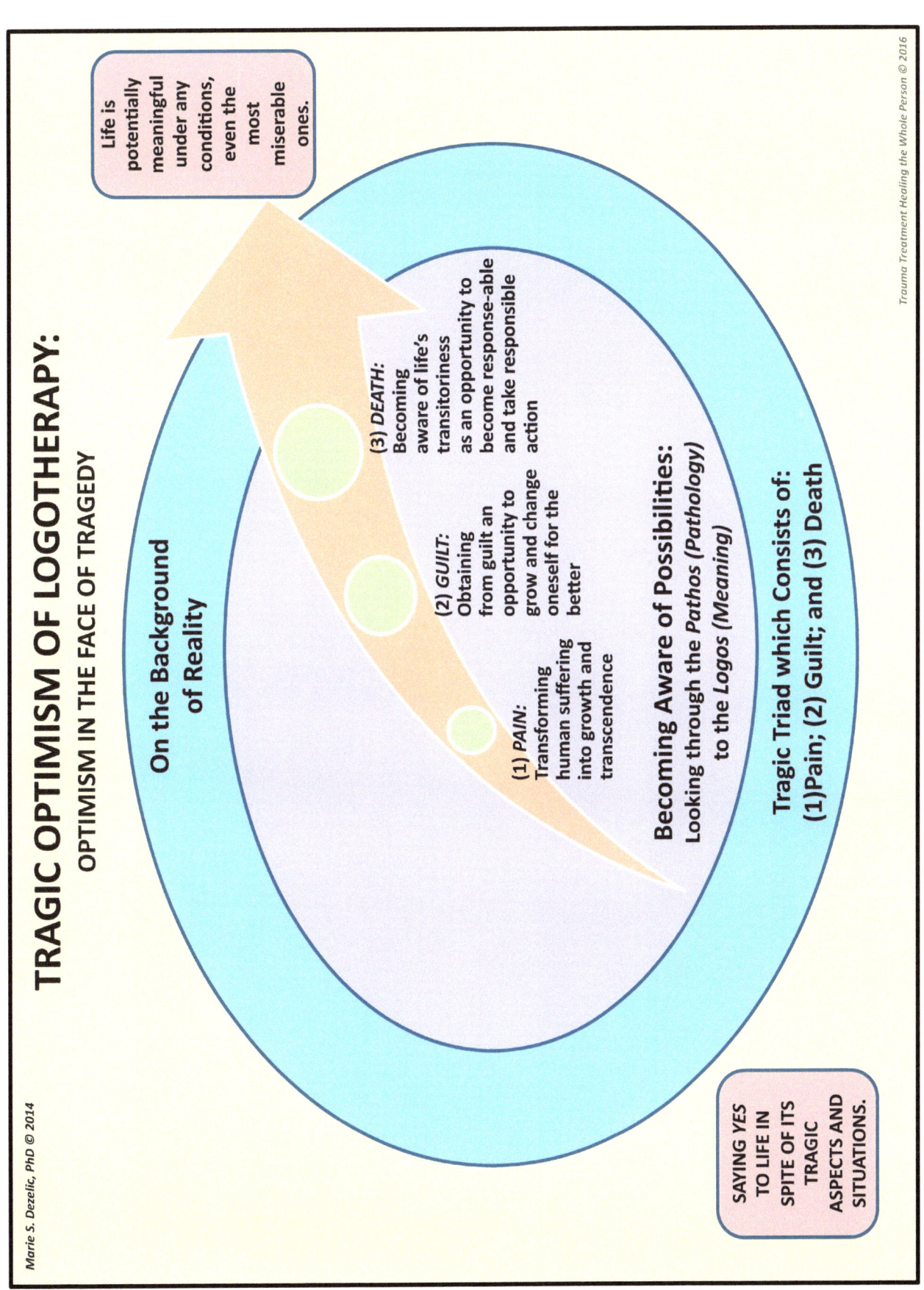

MY NOTES...

TRAUMA TREATMENT - HEALING THE WHOLE PERSON

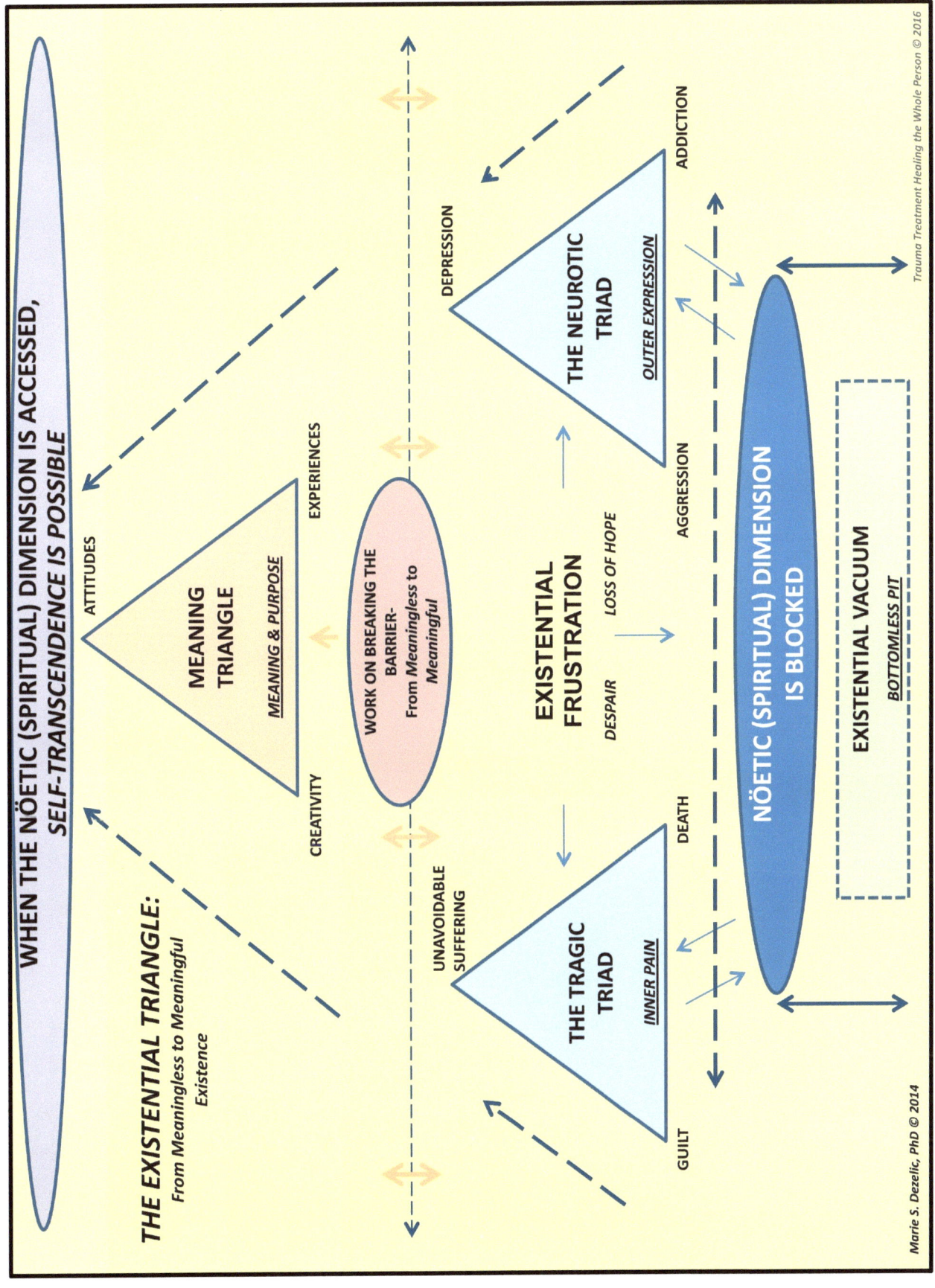

133

MY NOTES…

METHODOLOGY OF LOGOTHERAPY:
ELICITING WISDOM AND MEANING INHERENTLY HIDDEN WITHIN THE SPIRIT OF EACH SEEKER

Marie S. Dezelic, PhD © 2014

SOCRATIC (MAIEUTIC) DIALOGUE
A conversation that enables the birth of a latent idea, where the therapist acts as a midwife to help the patient give birth to new ideas; maieutic questioning awakens an innate knowledge into new attitudes, choices, and actions during the meaningful encounter.
• **Encounter, Meaning, Creativity, Self-Transcendence**

PARADOXICAL INTENTION
Having the patient try to do, or wish to have happen, precisely that which he/she fears; the effect is to disarm the anticipatory anxiety which accounts for much of the feedback mechanism that initiate and perpetuate the neurotic condition.
• **Self-Distancing, Humor, Self-Transcendence**

DEREFLECTION
Used when a problem is caused for the patient by too much reflection (hyperreflection), or by too much attention to solving the problem (hyperintention); consists of putting a stop to pathological hyperreflection and turning the mind to other thoughts or actions.
• **Self-Distancing, Self-Transcendence**

MEDICINE CHEST
Therapist makes the patient aware of the tremendous and often untapped resources of health within their healthy core- the spiritual dimension; activates will to find meaning, orientation toward goals, freedom to make decisions, creativity, imagination, love beyond physical.
• **Defiant Power of the Human Spirit**

Methodology & Outcome:

MODIFICATION OF ATTITUDES
Therapist facilitates and awakens attitudinal changes when the patient is in despair or finds him/herself in a situation that cannot be changed, i.e. unfortunate blows of fate, tragedies; each moment presents a unique opportunity in which we can respond to and discover meaning.
• **Attitudinal Change, Meaning, Self-Transcendence**

COMPLEMENTARY METHODS:
- ACT AS IF
- ALTERNATIVE LISTS
- APPEALING TECHNIQUE
- ART THERAPY
- DREAMS
- GUIDED FANTASIES/ IMAGERY
- IDENTIFICATION WITH OBJECTS
- IMPROVISATIONS
- JOURNAL WRITING
- LIFE MAPS
- LIST MAKING- (Good/Bad Consequences)
- LOGOANALYSIS: 7-STEP/ 10-STEP
- LOGOANCHOR TECHNIQUE
- LOGODRAMA
- LOGOHOOK
- METAPHORS
- MOUNTAIN RANGE
- MOVIE EXPERIENCE
- NOÖGENIC ACTIVATION
- POSITIVE SELF-TALK
- SCULPTING
- STORIES/ PARABLES

Trauma Treatment Healing the Whole Person © 2016

MY NOTES...

Meaning-Centered Therapy

Integrative Meaning-Centered, Existential and Humanistic Treatment Concepts

Meaning – *Meaning in life, Meaning in the Moment, Will to Meaning, and Meaning Triangle—Creativity, Experiences, and Attitude* create *Hope* and foster *Resilience*.

Personal-Existential Responsibility – Freedom to take ownership to one's own life through Becoming Conscious *(Aware)*, Becoming Responsible *(Response-Able)*, and *Taking New Actions (Choice)*; building *Resource* capacity.

Education – Learning about each aspect of *Mind-Body-Spirit, Responsibility, Neurobiology, Trauma Triggers* and *Responses, Tools, Freedom, Choice, Meaning/Engagement* in life.

Self Awareness – Through personal responsibility and education, *Making Choices* that support safety, well-being, boundaries, and trauma recovery; uncovering and discovering *Inner Strengths* and *Resources*.

Support – *Safe Environment, Safety* with others, *Connection* with others, *Reciprocity, Self-Transcendence*- going beyond oneself through giving, collaboration, community, and serving.

Treatment – *Collaborative* and *Guiding* approach, address experiences of *Human Existence* and the *Human Condition*, unconditional *Acceptance*, specialized *Trained* clinician, ongoing *Support*.

MY NOTES...

DARE
Existential Therapy
-Live Life in Each Moment & 'REACH' Beyond Limitations-

M. Dezelic, PhD, W. Breitbart, MD, & G. Ghanoum, PsyD © 2014

D: Dialectics
- Holding opposing dialectical and paradoxical internal states, feelings, emotions, circumstances, recognition of before and after diagnosis.
- Focus on becoming comfortable with interoceptive and emotional states.
- Notice, recognize belief systems, understand meaning held within each state.

A: Attitude
- Acknowledging and validating the dialectical positions; accepting to hold the dialectical positions without self-judgment.
- Education to awareness of the freedom of choice in choosing one's attitude in suffering and life-limiting circumstances.

R: Resources
- Discover and focus on inner human strengths as resources to health, and the balance between difficult or limiting experiences and meaning.
- Response-ability: respond (pre-frontal cortex activation) versus react (limbic system activation) to experiences and emotions, allows for self-distancing.

E: Encounter
- Encounter, Engage, Experience: the situation, the person, or the emotion, from an emotionally balanced place, allowing it without being consumed by it.
- Evaluate options, make choices from a stance of freedom in one's attitude.
- Engage in new experiences, activating meaning and self-transcendence.

DARE Existential Therapy Focuses on:
- Developing a sense of mindful awareness, and a compassionate stance toward oneself without judgment, through self-distancing and self-transcendence, with a focus on becoming existentially aware while holding dialectical positions in the face of difficult or life-limiting conditions.
- Particular emphasis on the 'Meaning-Action Triangle' 1) Noticing; 2) Responsibility; 3) Action

MY NOTES...

Existential Therapeutic Process
Logotherapy & Existential Analysis

➤ *Recognize strengths and weaknesses, and utilize both for growth*

➤ *Facilitate a greater understanding of the human condition and the experiences within it from the personal context*

➤ *Uncover and discover inner strengths and resources to live passionate, fulfilling and meaningful lives*

➤ *Live authentically, heal from traumatic experiences, and have personal and relational growth*

"When we are no longer able to change a situation, we are challenged to change ourselves."

(Viktor Frankl)

MY NOTES...

Existential Therapeutic Process
Logotherapy & Existential Analysis

M. Dezelic, PhD & G. Ghanoum, PsyD © 2014

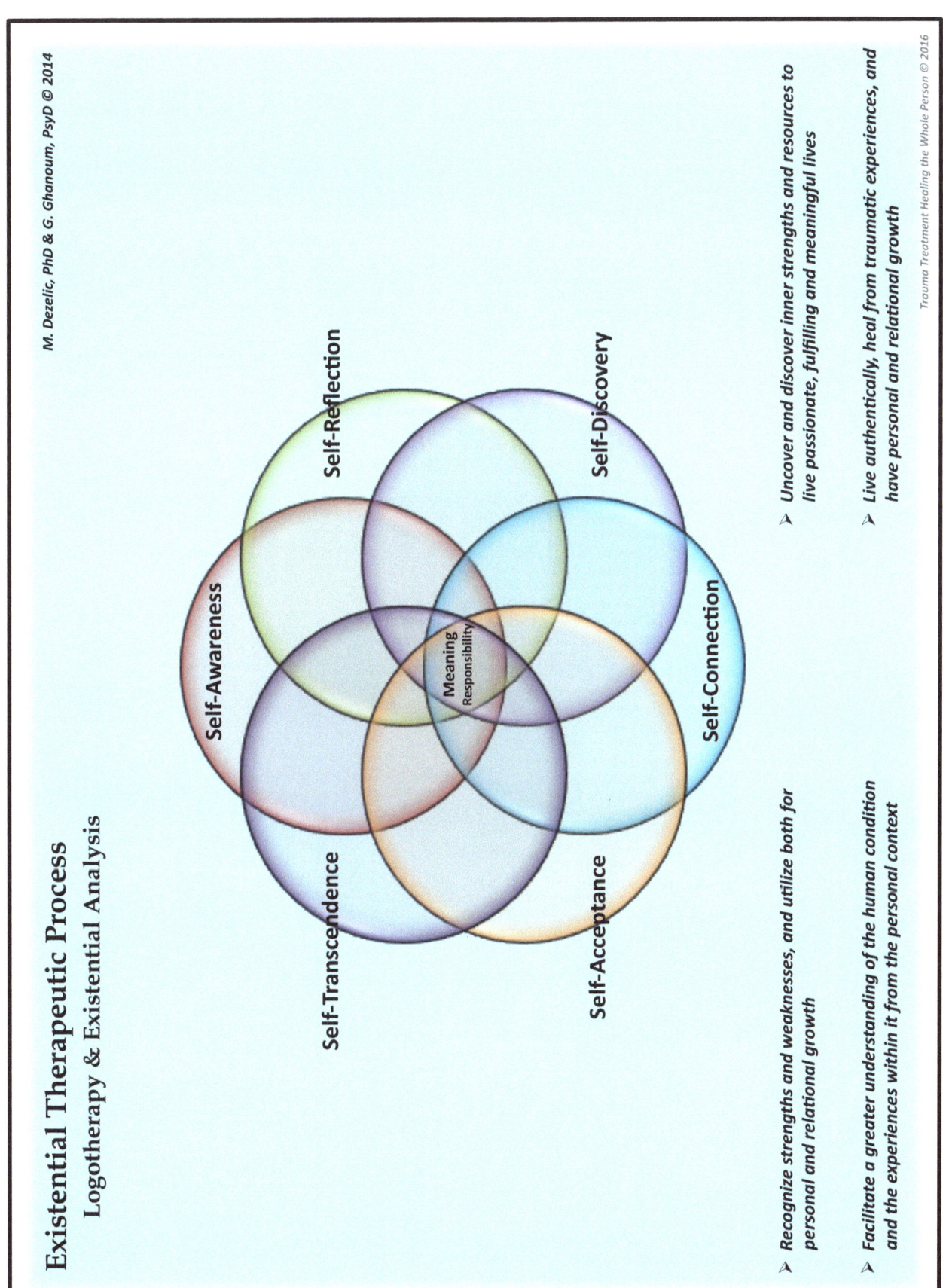

- Recognize strengths and weaknesses, and utilize both for personal and relational growth
- Facilitate a greater understanding of the human condition and the experiences within it from the personal context
- Uncover and discover inner strengths and resources to live passionate, fulfilling and meaningful lives
- Live authentically, heal from traumatic experiences, and have personal and relational growth

MY NOTES...

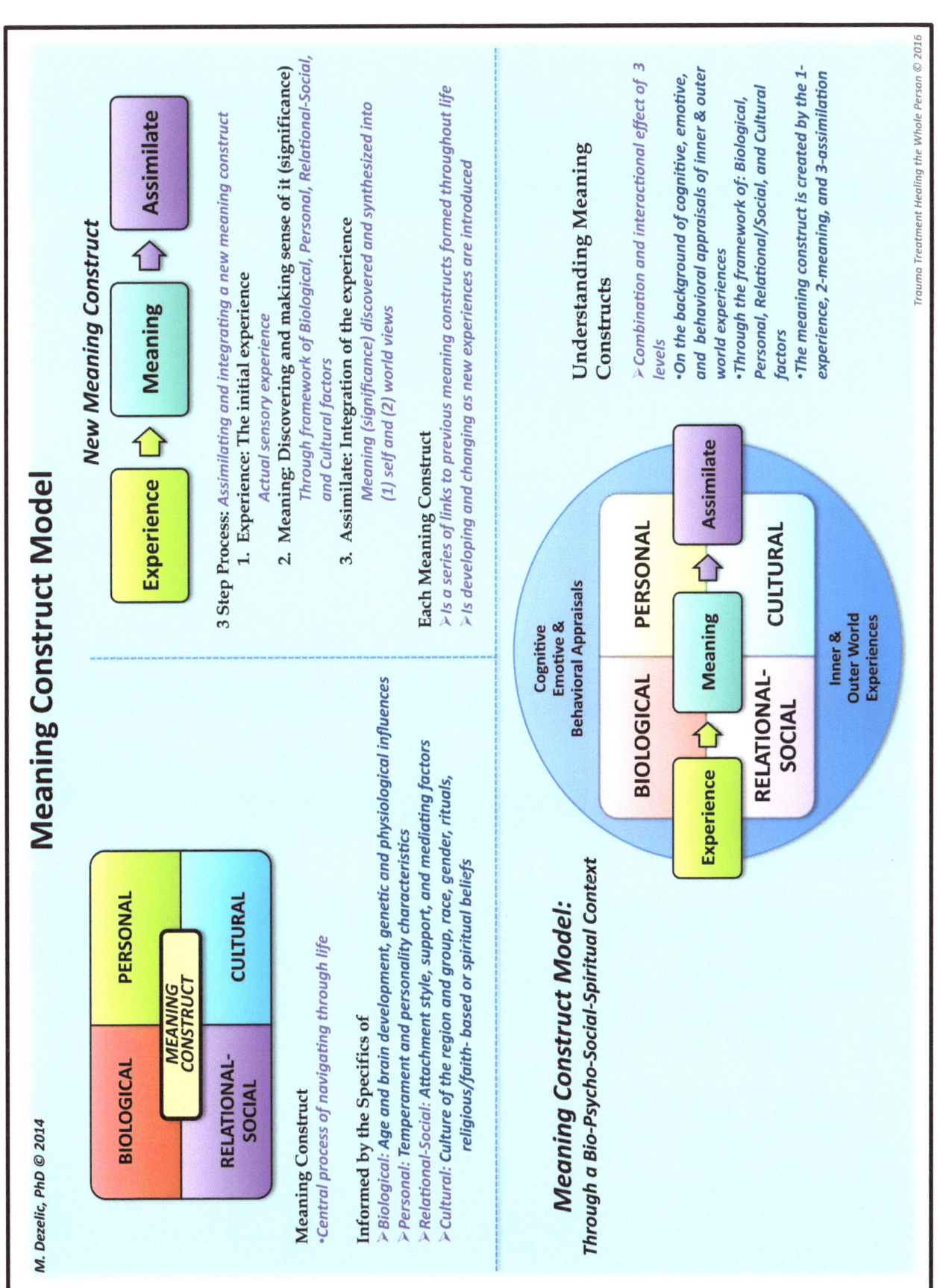

MY NOTES...

MY NOTES...

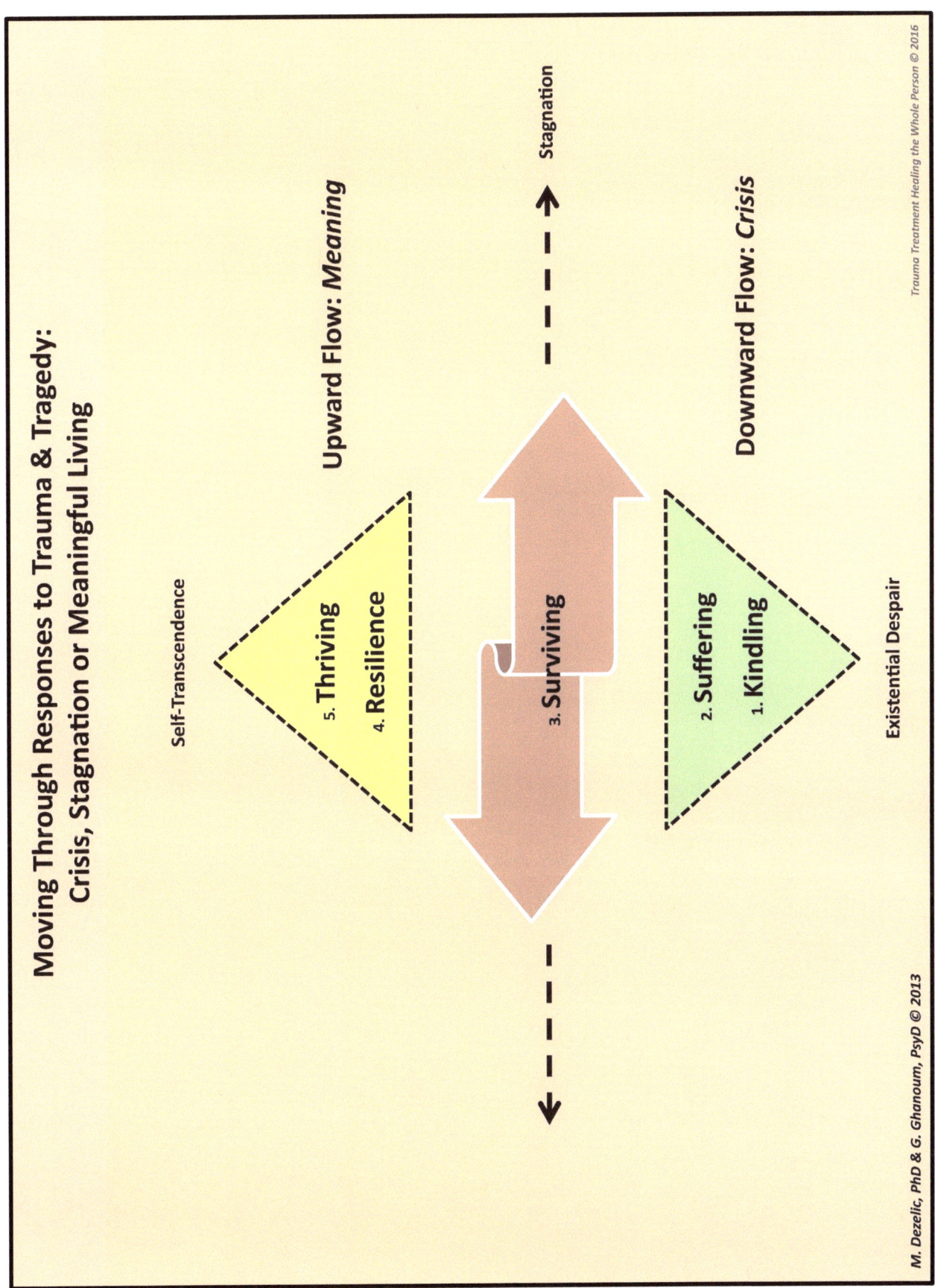

MY NOTES...

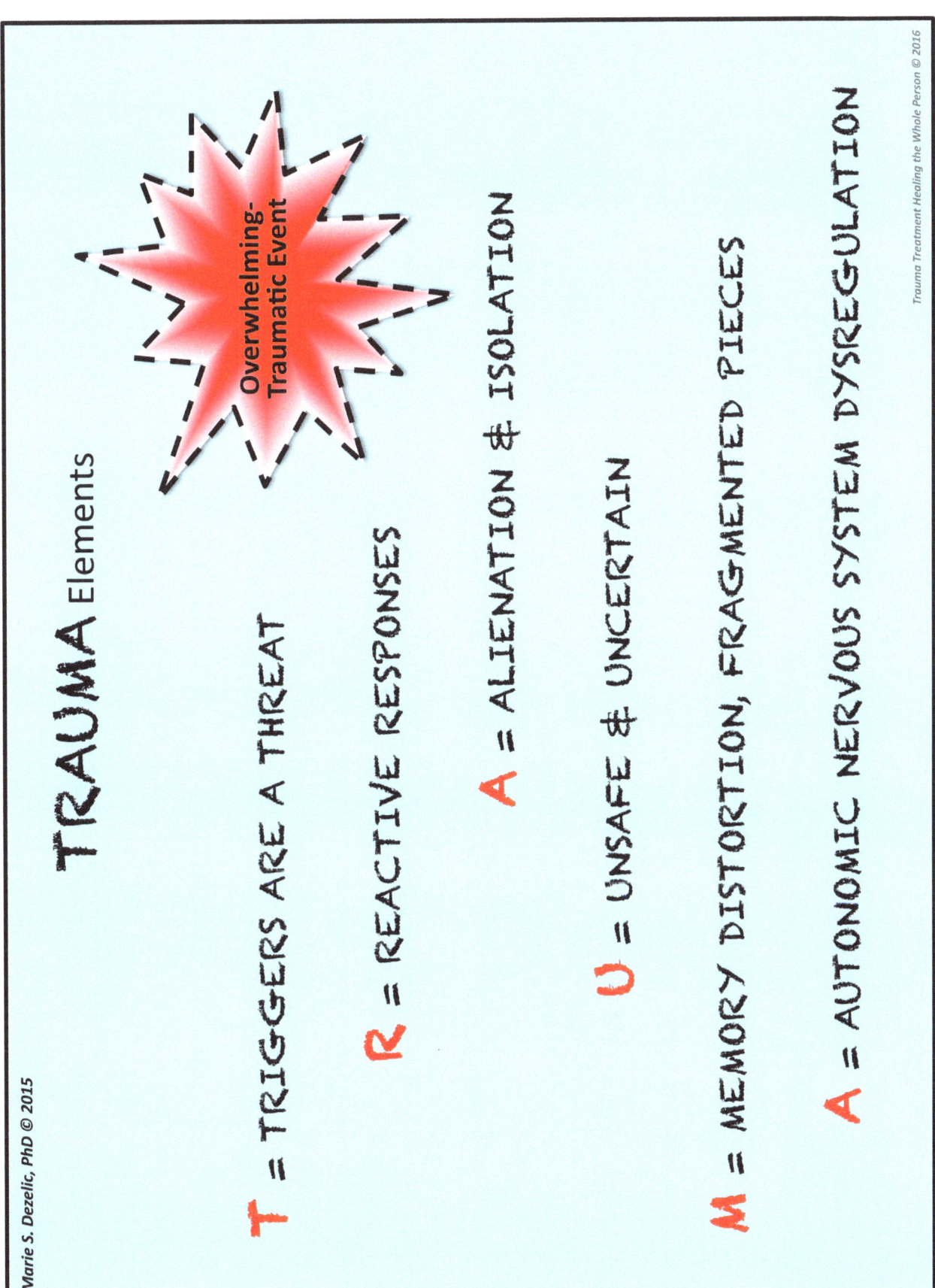

MY NOTES...

TRAUMA Definitions

- A "wound."
- Physical or psychological injury.
- Extremely distressing or disturbing experience.
- A deeply emotional upset.
- Extremely overwhelming experience to the body, mind, and spirit.
- Altered psychological or behavioral state resulting from an overwhelming or disorganizing experience.
- Inability to integrate an emotional experience that threatened one's life, bodily integrity or psychological capacities.
- Inability to tolerate physiological and psychological symptoms.
- Unique to the person experiencing it.

M. Dezelic, PhD & G. Ghanoum, PsyD © 2015

TRAUMA Experience
Fragmented... in disarray

~ Past, Present, and Future become entangled

~ The symptoms tell us the "story"

~ Trauma is saved as feelings, images, emotions, sensations

~ Trauma survivors usually don't have the words (or right words) to tell the story

MY NOTES...

TRAUMA Elements
Trauma Affects Each Person Differently

Marie S. Dezelic, PhD © 2015

Traumatic Event(s)

Psychological Impacts

Emotional Impacts

- Sadness
- Depression
- Decreased Interest
- Irritability
- Chronic Frustration
- Intolerance
- Hopelessness
- Despair
- Anger
- Rage
- Foreshortened Future
- Altered Belief in Humanity
- Altered Belief in Spirituality
- Meaninglessness
- Shame
- Self-Loathing
- Self-Blame
- Self-Hatred
- Shattered Assumptions
- Damaged Goods
- Aggressive Communication
- Passive Communication

Spiritual-Existential Impacts

- Numbing
- Insomnia
- Hypersomnia
- Nightmares
- Amnesia
- Decreased Concentration
- Physiological Hyperarousal
- Physiological Hypoarousal
- Psychomotor Agitation
- Somatic Dysregulation
- Exaggerated Startle Response
- Hypervigilance
- Emotional Pain

Physiological Impacts

- Stigmatization
- Intrusive Memories
- Flashbacks
- Fragmented Memories
- Disorganization
- Paranoia
- Explosive Outbursts
- Somatic Symptoms
- Chronic Pain
- Hyper-Sexualization
- Loss of Sexual Desire/Response
- Sexual Diseases

Social-Relationship Impacts

Practical Impacts

- Isolation
- Alienation
- Disempowerment
- Disconnection from Community
- Chronic Relationship Attempts
- Ruptured Relationships
- Chronic Breakups
- Trust Issues
- Co-Dependency
- Overly Caretaking
- Emotional Dysregulation
- Homelessness
- Incarceration

- Lack of Life Skills
- Vocational Obstacles
- Educational Obstacles
- Learning Disabilities
- Attention Deficit Disorder
- Attention Deficit Hyperactivity
- Panic Attacks
- Phobias
- Agoraphobia
- Chronic Grief
- Substance Abuse
- Generalized Anxiety
- Eating Disorders
- Addictive Behaviors
- Dissociative Symptoms
- Alexithymia
- Self-Harming Behaviors
- Self-Destructive Behaviors
- High-Risk Behaviors
- Suicidal Ideation
- Suicidal Attempts
- Feel Like Failure

Trauma Treatment Healing the Whole Person © 2016

MY NOTES...

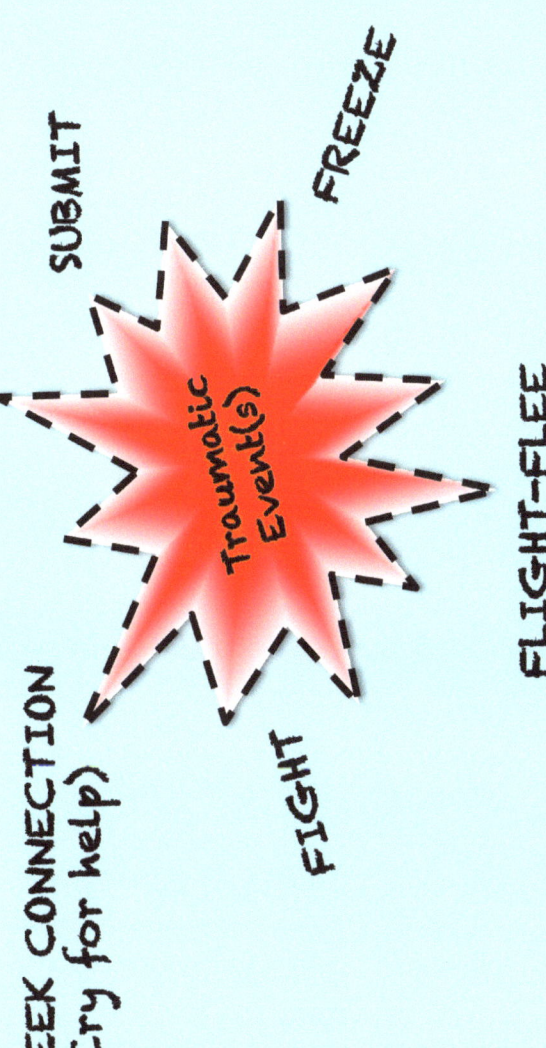

MY NOTES...

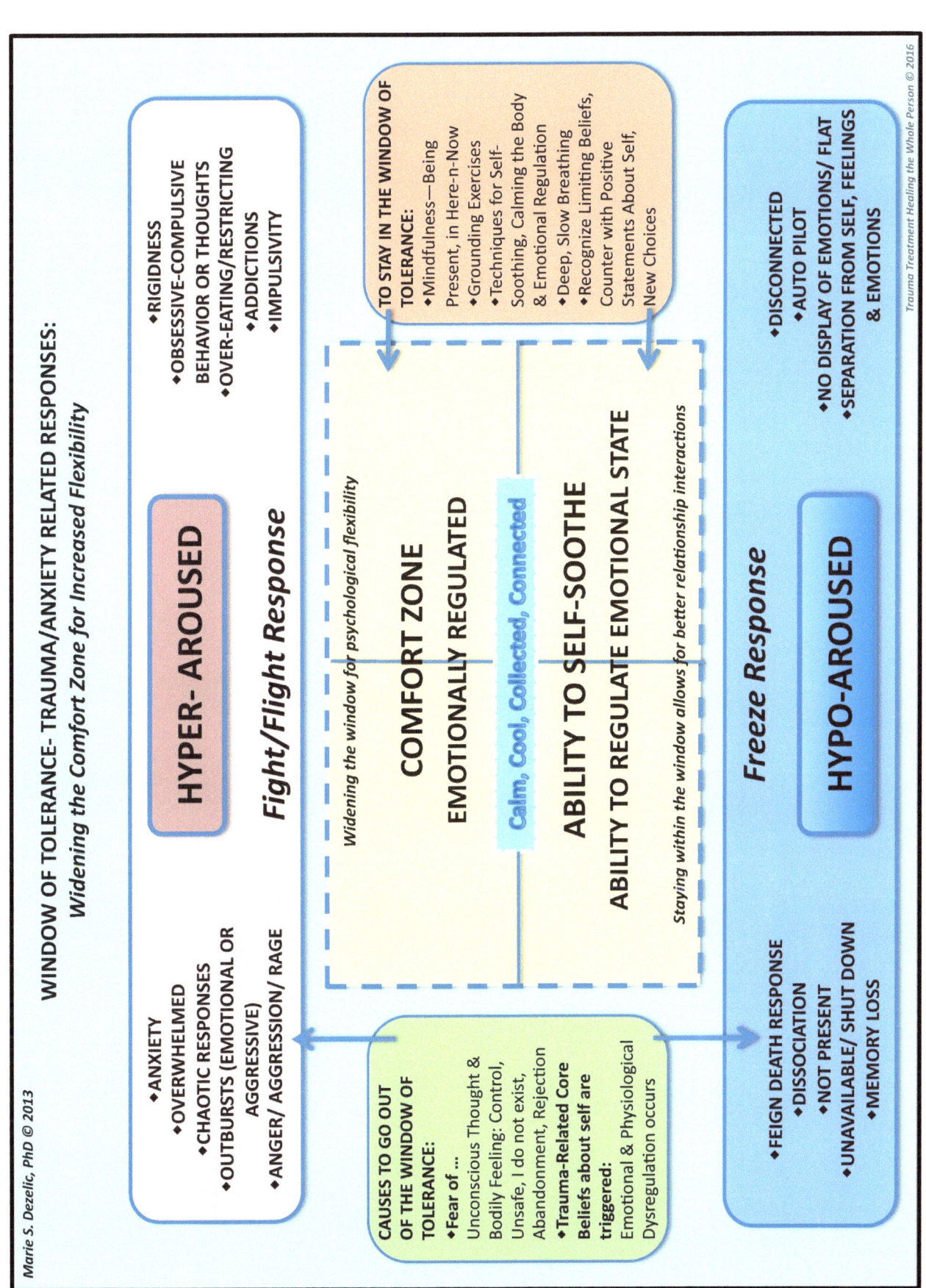

MY NOTES...

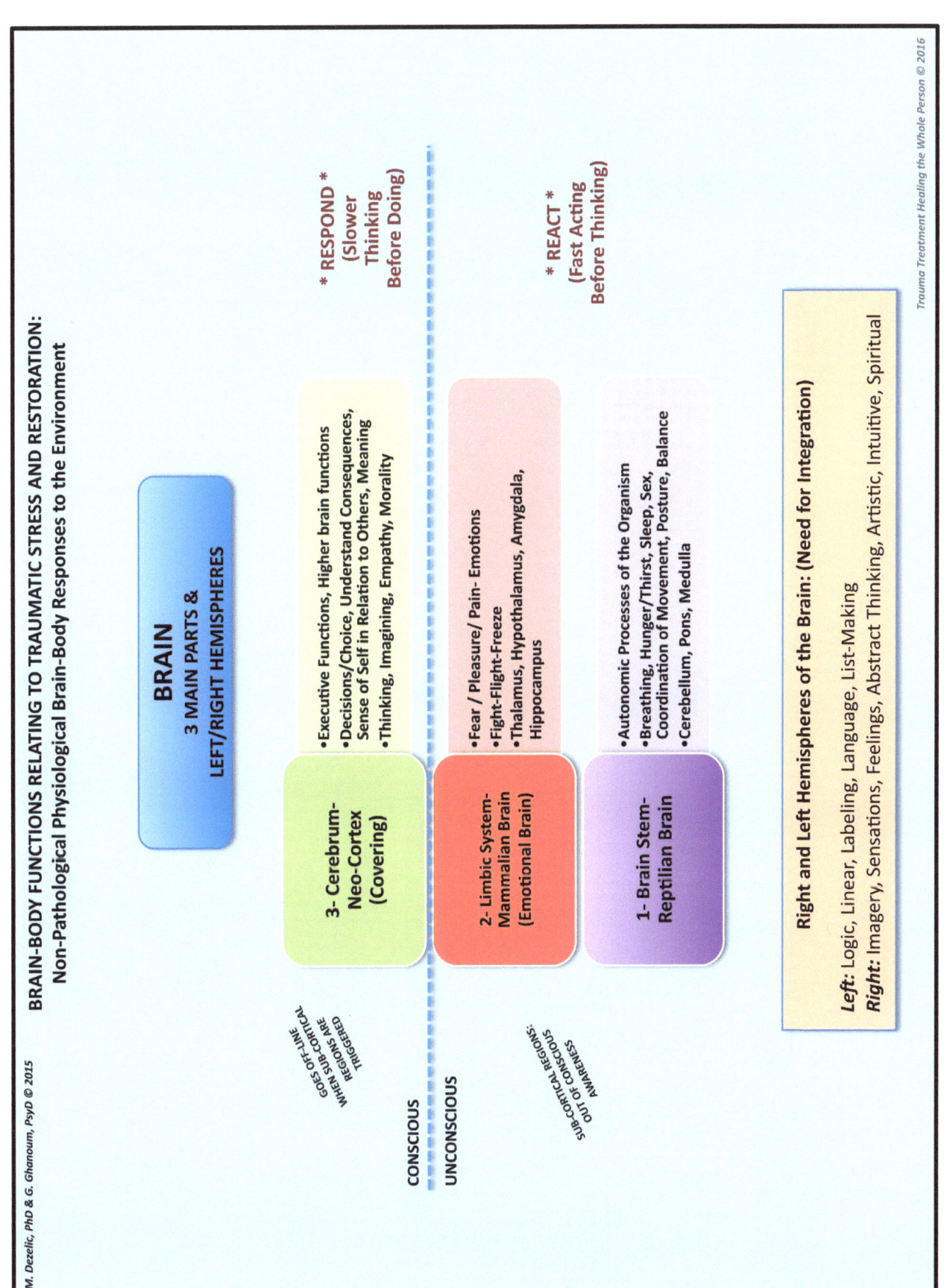

MY NOTES...

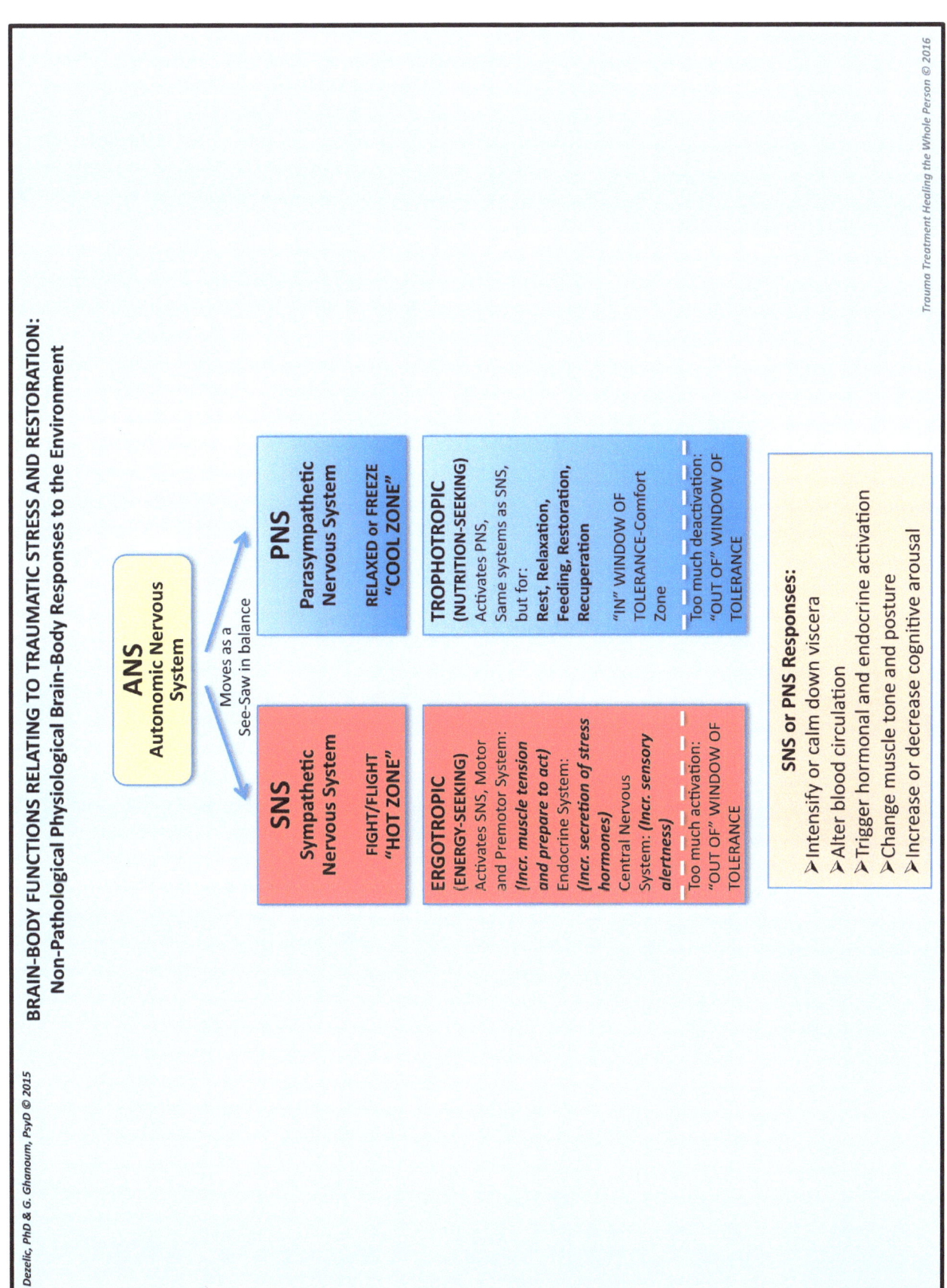

MY NOTES…

BRAIN-BODY FUNCTIONS RELATING TO TRAUMATIC STRESS AND RESTORATION:
Non-Pathological Physiological Brain-Body Responses to the Environment

ATTENDING TECHNIQUES- 4 C's (Dezelic & Ghanoum)

1- "CALM" THE BODY
Regulate the Body to the "Cool Zone," Re-Set and Stabilize to present, Demonstrate Somatic Regulation

2- "CHOICE" OF THINKING
Psychoeducation, Discussion, Neo-Cortex & Pre-Frontal Cortex gets back online when physiology is calmed down and safe

3- "CONFRONT" THE CONCERNS
Address the Trauma/Concerns, Re-process, Re-work, New Meanings

4- "CHANGE" BEHAVIORS- CHANGE THE WIRING
Changing beliefs, try new behaviors, with new results, while staying calm and regulated, creating and stabilizing new neural networks

MY NOTES...

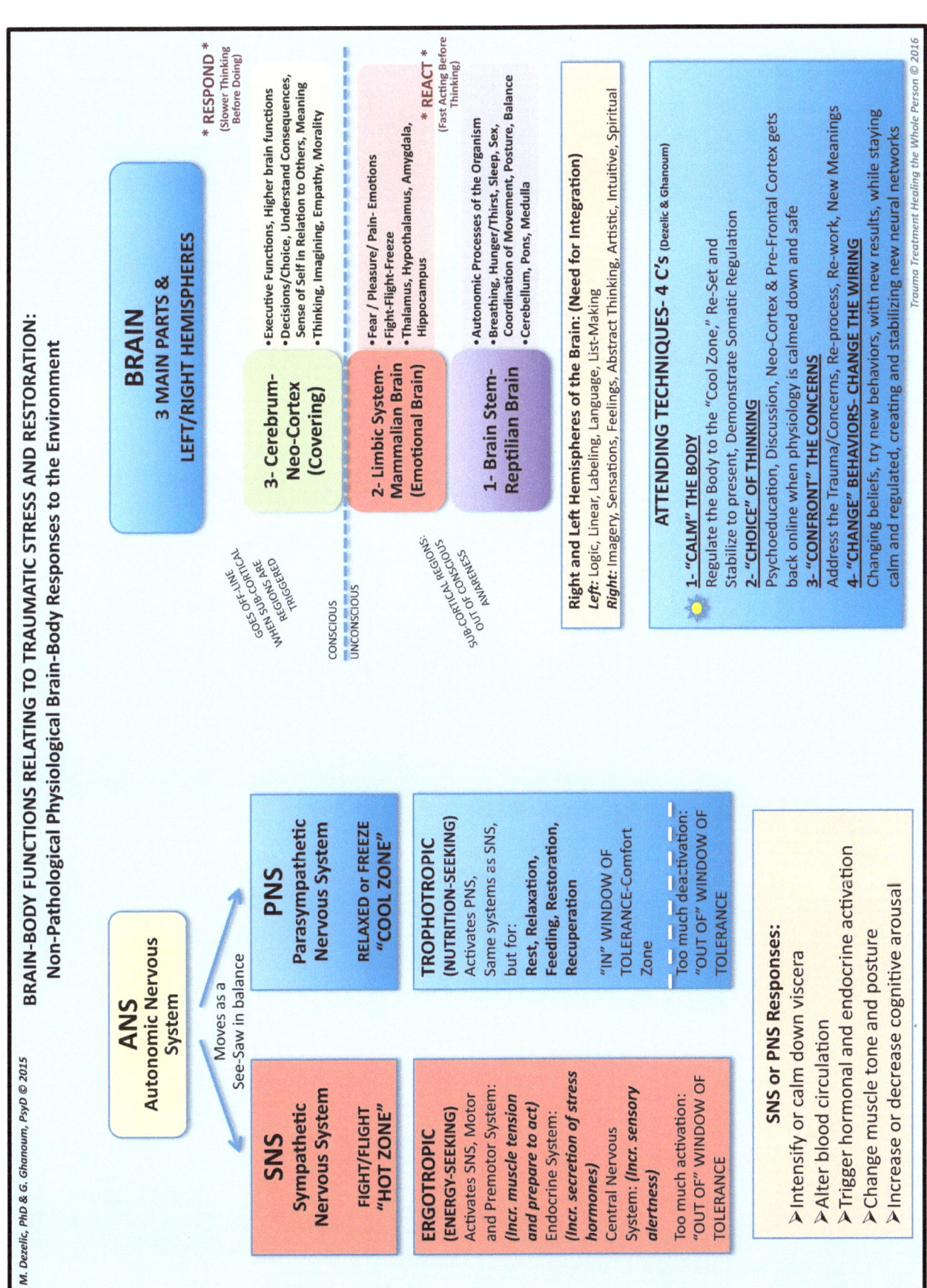

MY NOTES...

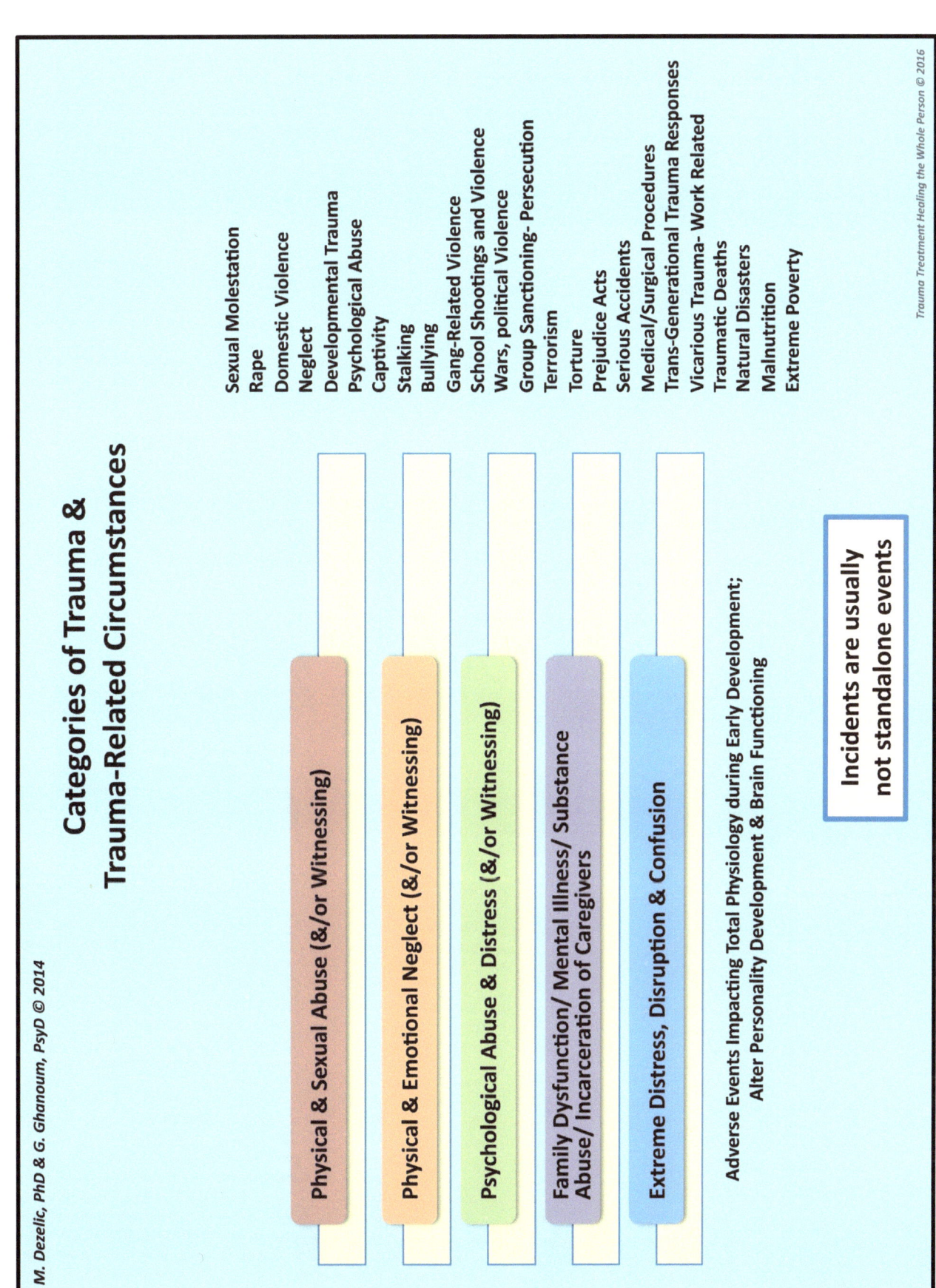

MY NOTES…

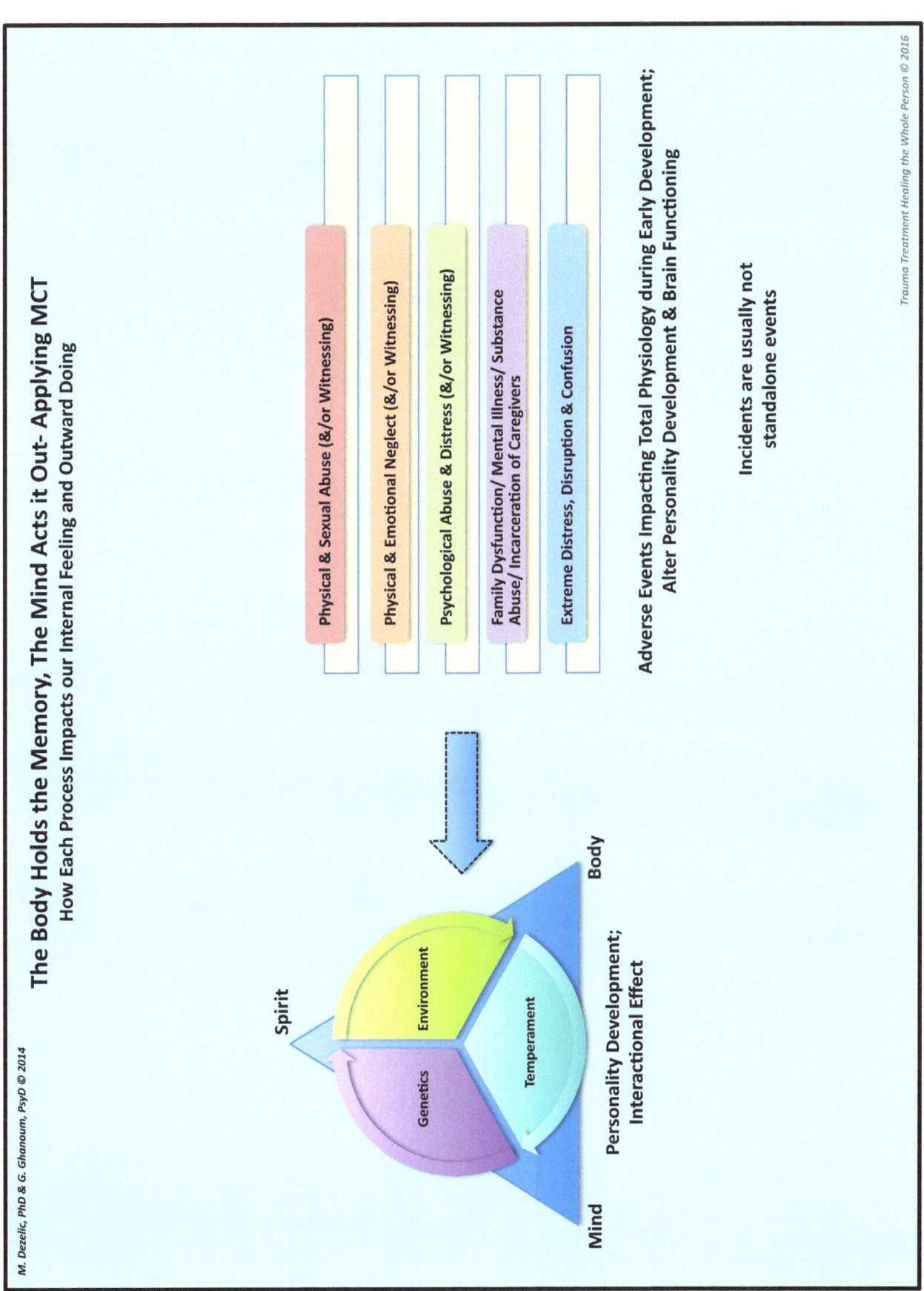

MY NOTES...

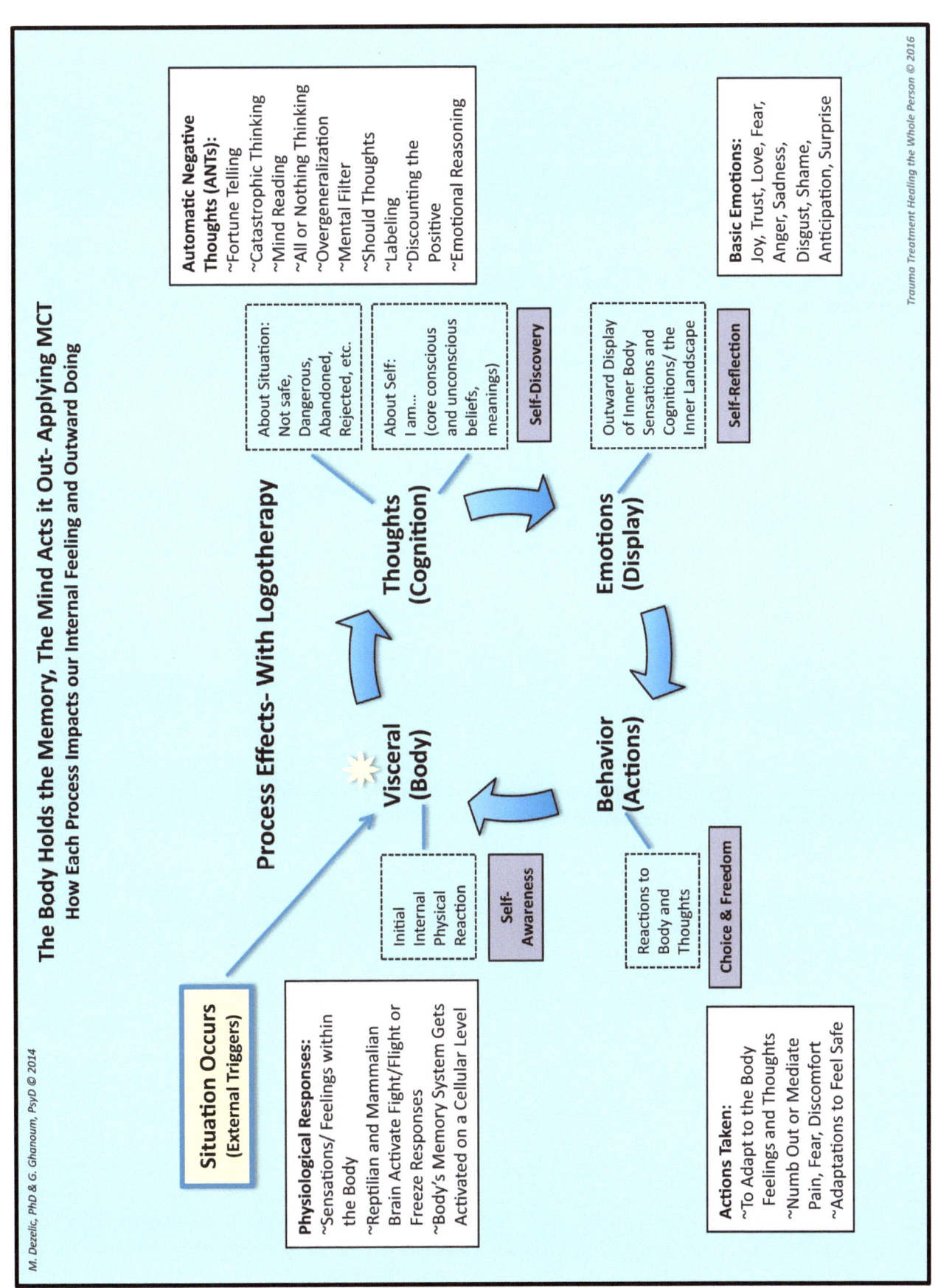

MY NOTES...

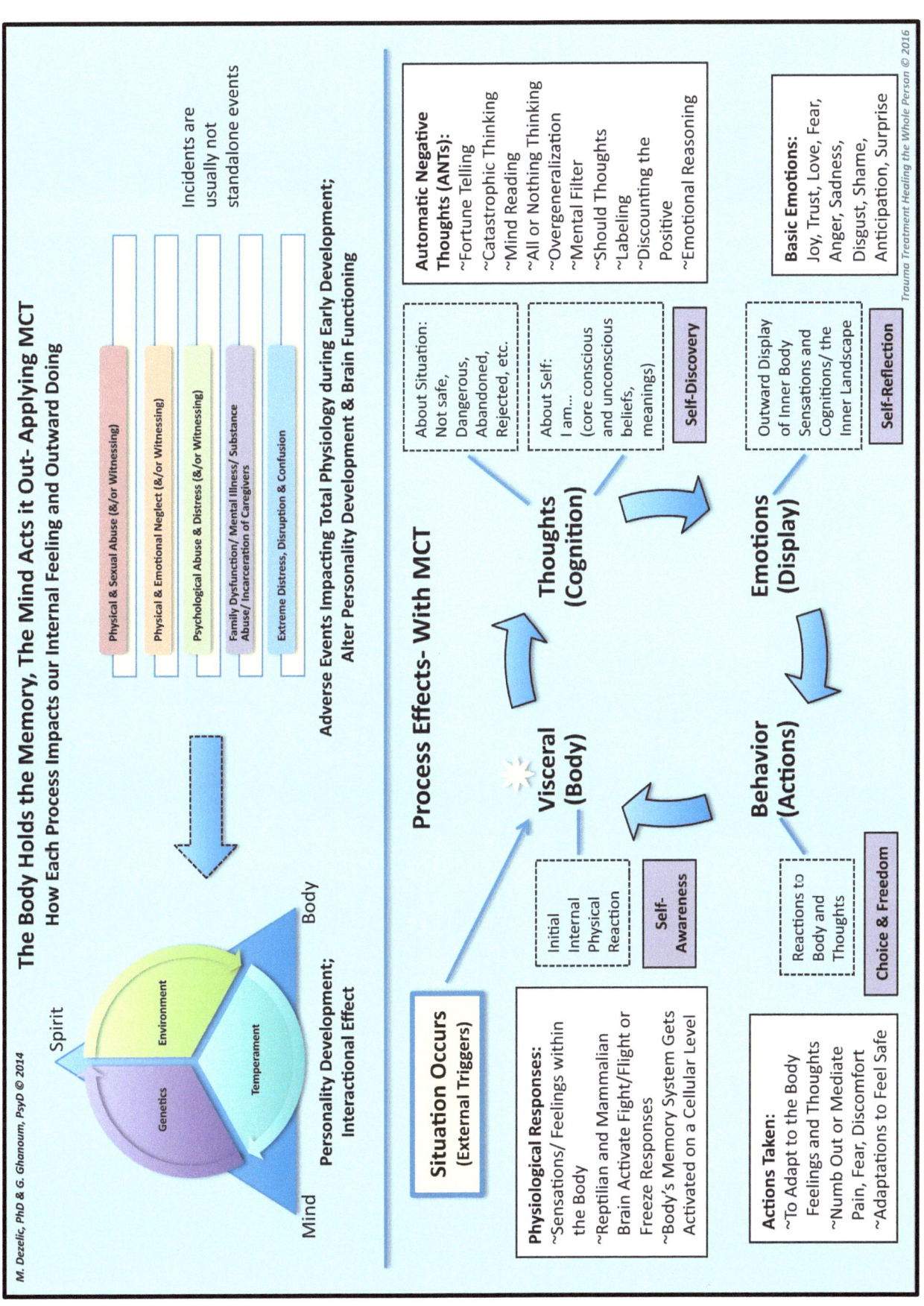

MY NOTES...

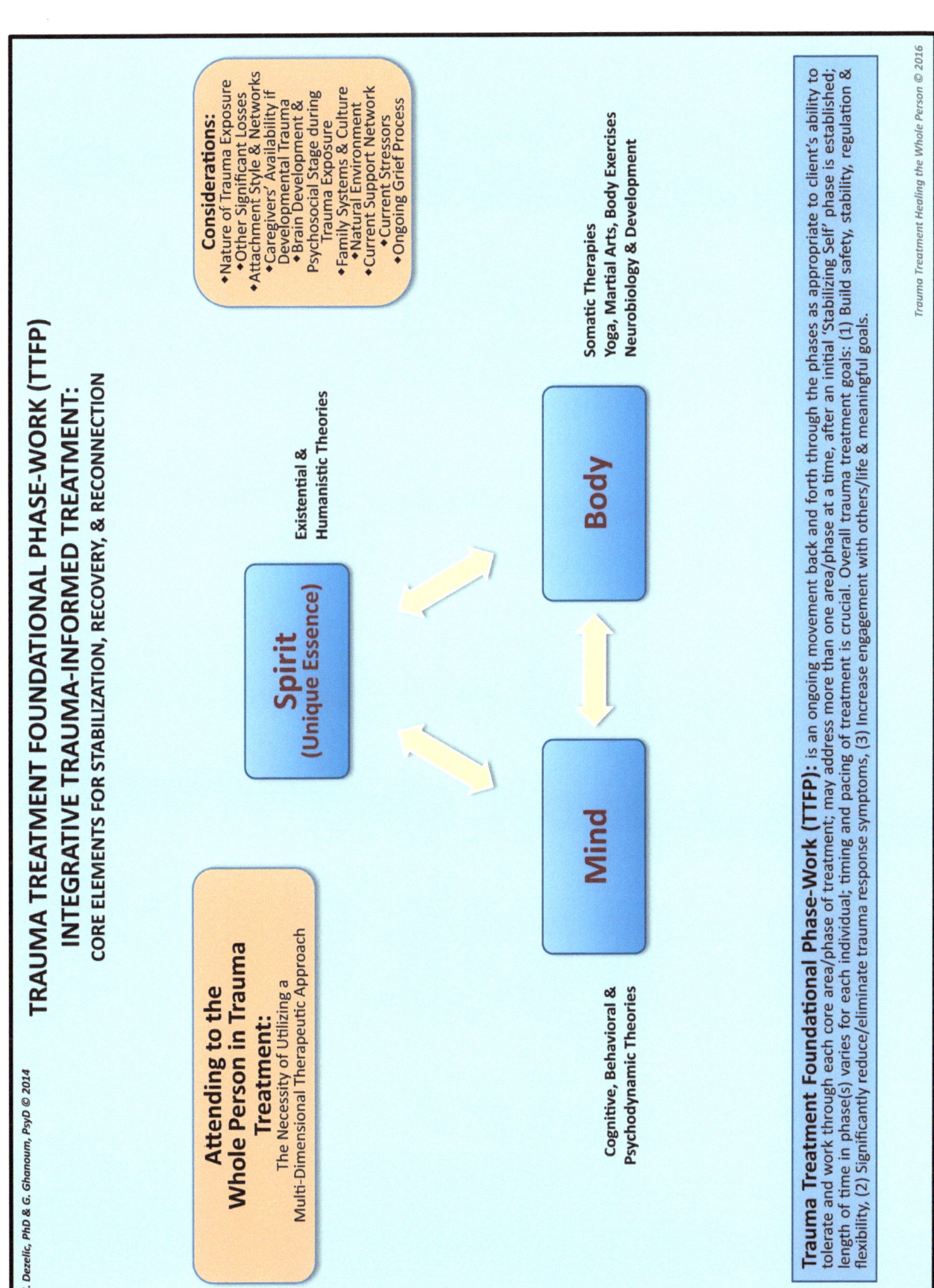

MY NOTES...

M. Dezelic, PhD & G. Ghanoum, PsyD © 2014

TRAUMA TREATMENT FOUNDATIONAL PHASE-WORK (TTFP)
INTEGRATIVE TRAUMA-INFORMED TREATMENT:
CORE ELEMENTS FOR STABILIZATION, RECOVERY, & RECONNECTION

Trauma Treatment Foundational Phase-Work (TTFP): is an ongoing movement back and forth through the phases as appropriate to client's ability to tolerate and work through each core area/phase of treatment; may address more than one area/phase at a time, after an initial 'Stabilizing Self' phase is established; length of time in phase(s) varies for each individual; timing and pacing of treatment is crucial.

Overall trauma treatment goals: (1) Build safety, stability, regulation & flexibility, (2) Significantly reduce/eliminate trauma response symptoms, (3) Increase engagement with others/life & meaningful goals.

- ❖ **Stabilizing Self** — Creating safety and stabilization in the present; trust with therapist; grounding techniques; self-regulation, affect regulation & modulation; increase window of tolerance/comfort zone, understanding responses; coping techniques; mindfulness; yoga, martial arts, dance, or body practices; learn body awareness and states; develop boundaries; safety within self, ability to tolerate being in own body; resource building; develop sense of agency and competency; increase attachment networks.

- ❖ **Traumatic Revisiting** — Revisiting traumatic memories as "touch and go's," quick trips; dual perception, past and present with therapist; continuing safety/stable platform; visualization and feeling of the trauma - 1 key scene that can represent all the scenes; start to bring words to the body feelings, sensations, body awareness; explore meanings of feelings and perceptions; EMDR; narrative; parts work.

- ❖ **Languaging & Meaning** — Reprocessing, reworking, rewording; work on wording in the present, free association to meanings; uncover the unconscious core belief systems and how these words relate to present actions and thoughts; examine meaning constructions as they correspond with the brain development at time of trauma; uncouple trauma and original meanings, shift to present development and new meanings.

- ❖ **Re-Owning** — Owning the disowned part(s), the part that experienced the trauma which have been exiled, is hated, is shameful; identify part of self (child or older) that is stuck in the trauma; examine why it is being denied or protected from the whole system; make a choice to bring this part back to the self, without the old belief system and trauma, bringing the part of self forward to present; visualization of trauma and/or beliefs, removing it, and leave it in the scene; grieving losses.

- ❖ **Integration** — Integrating separate parts of self; neural-body-behavioral; create safe place within self, as sacred center/gentle center or internal home; dialoguing with self to get core needs met; self-care, self-reflection, self-awareness, self-discovery, existential analysis.

- ❖ **Re-Connection** — Reconnection with self, feeling safe inside one's body; more secure self allows for reconnection with others; healthy boundaries with others; engage in meaningful activities; explore meaning and purpose in life; explore attitude, experiences, and creativity for creating meaning in life; competencies and resource building, new attachment networks.

Trauma Treatment Healing the Whole Person © 2016

MY NOTES...

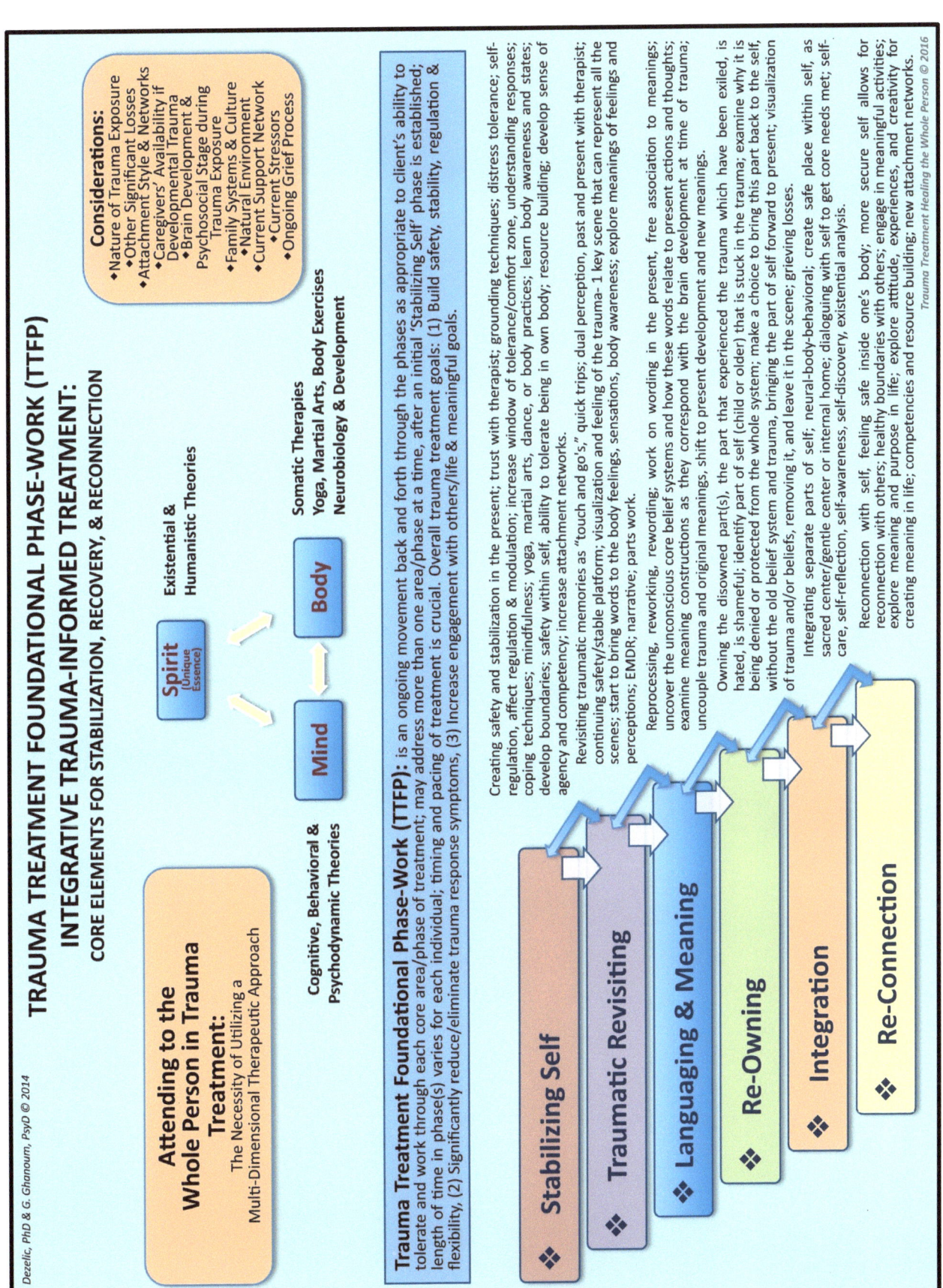

MY NOTES...

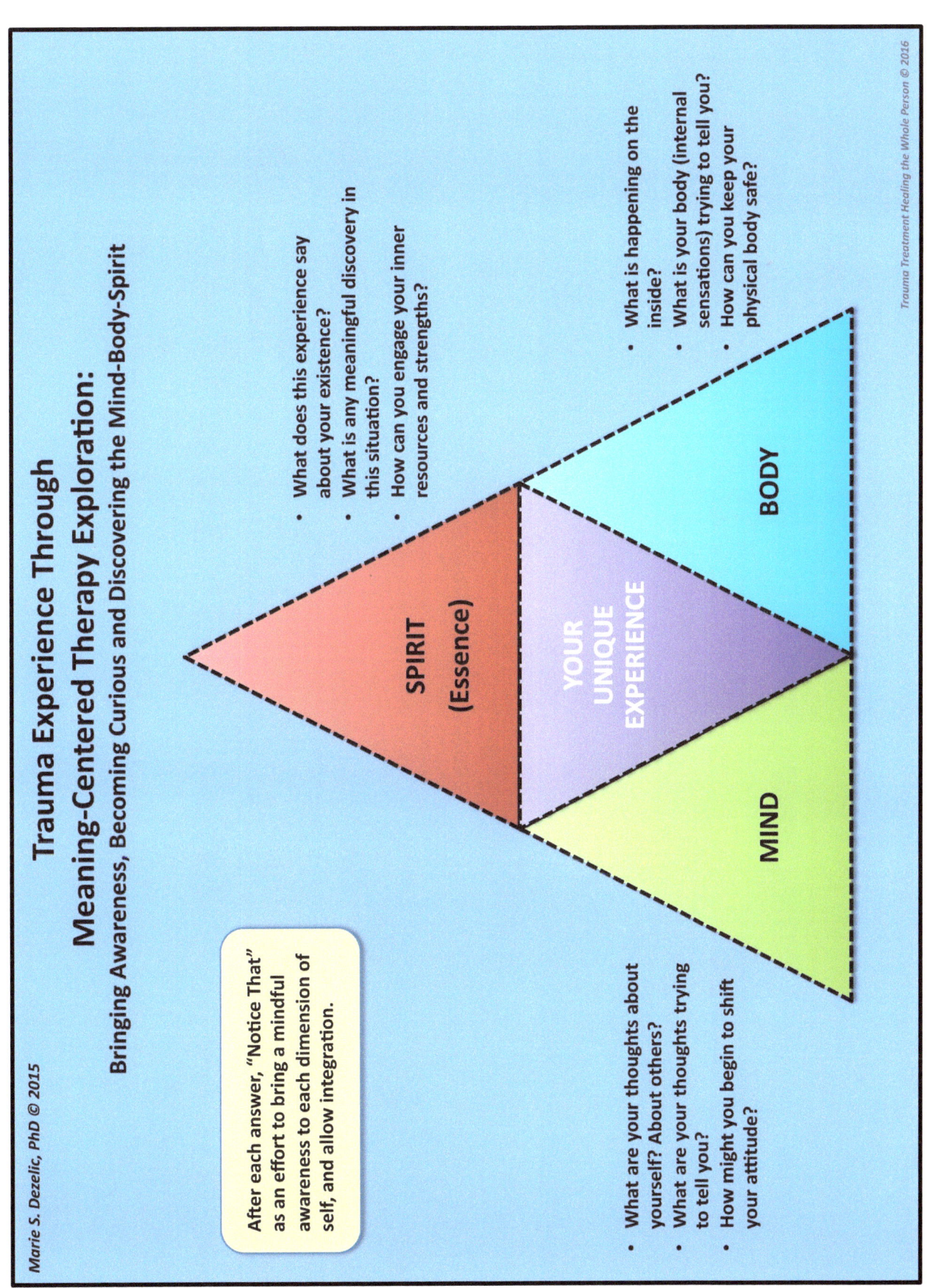

MY NOTES...

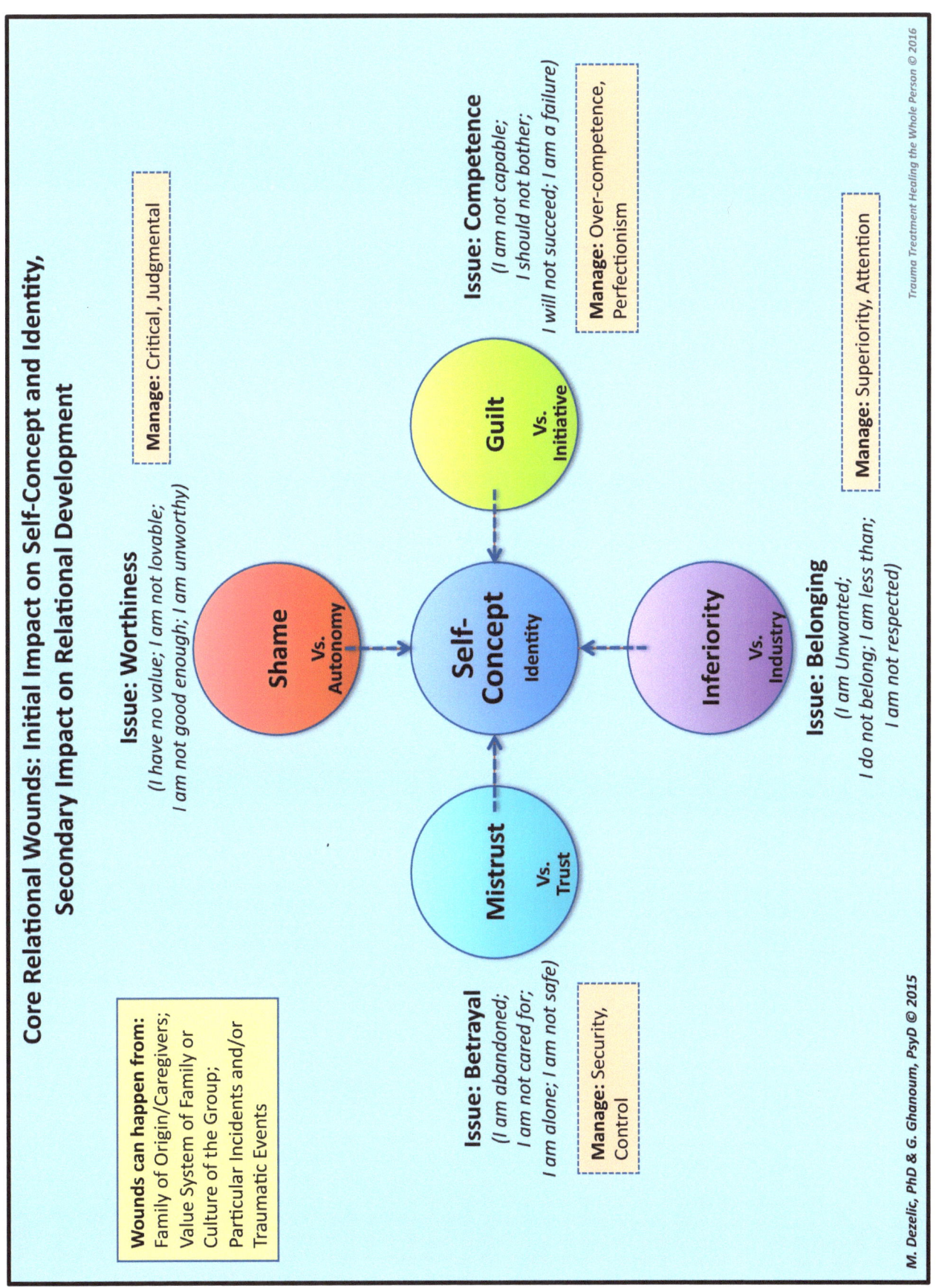

MY NOTES...

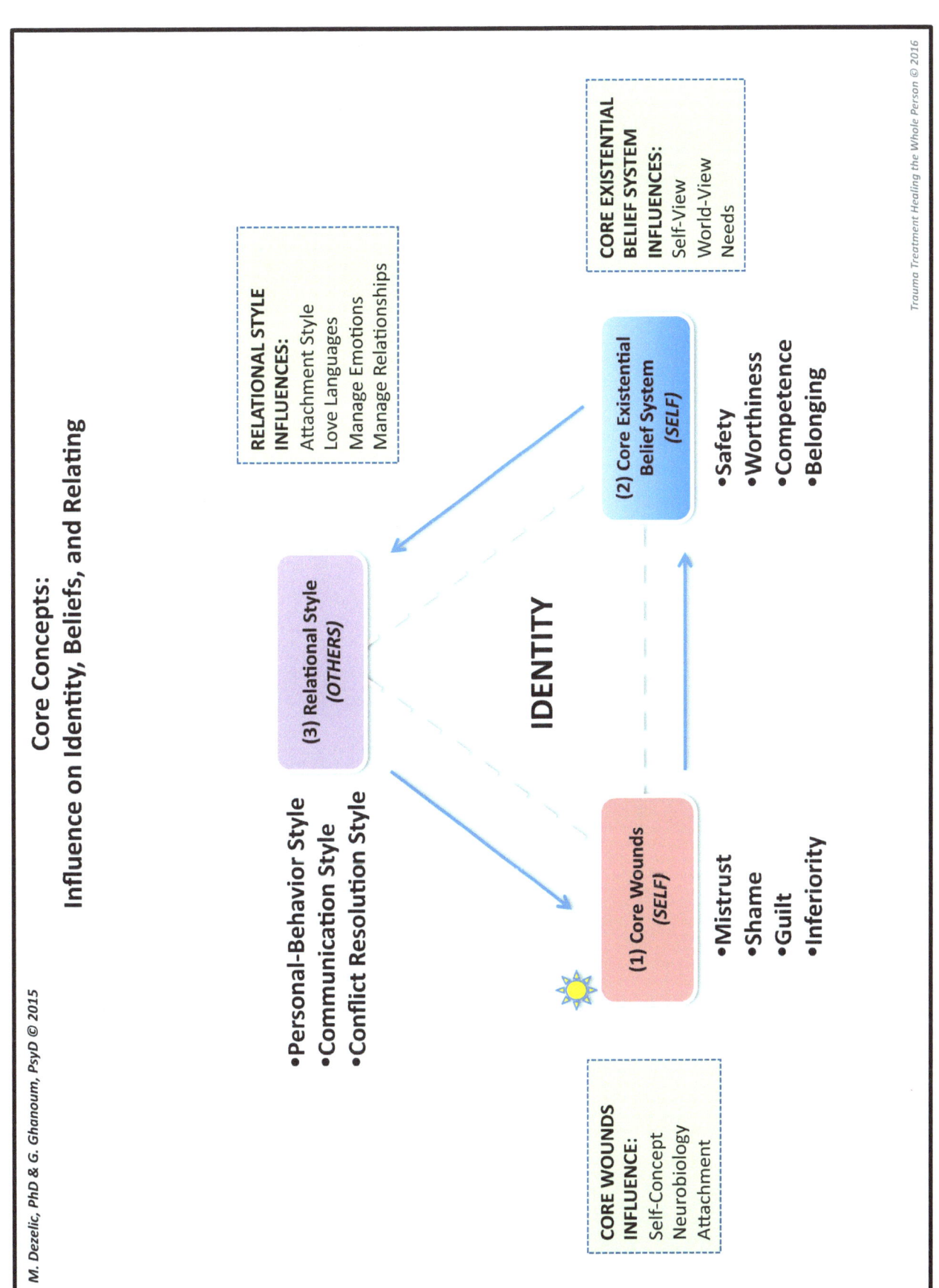

MY NOTES...

When Getting Triggered Takes Over:
Taking a "Time Out" from the Situation to Take a "Time In" for Self-Discovery

M. Dezelic, PhD & G. Ghanoum, PsyD © 2015

Examining Existence

1) **Self-Awareness**
2) **Self-Reflection**
3) **Self-Discovery**
4) **Self-Connection**
5) **Self-Acceptance**
6) **Self-Transcendence**

Creating Curiosity & Inquiring

- "I" am triggered. **Take a "Time Out" to take a "Time In."** Reframe: Is a "Part" of me is being triggered?

- What "Part" of me is being triggered? Why did this "Part" get triggered? What are the initial feelings this "Part" felt?

- What does this "Part" need, want, or is fearful of? What behavior is/was this "Part" doing to protect or try to get this need met?

- How can "I" meet the need of this "Part" of me? How can I nurture this "Part" of me? What can I do for self-care?

- How can "I" begin to create a connection between "Parts" of myself? *Creating an Interconnectedness of Self.*

- Can I recognize what might be happening in a "Part" others I engage with? How can I connect with the other and outward?

"When we create an environment of deeper self-understanding, through self-care, we can create more integration and interconnectedness within our own internal system."

MY NOTES...

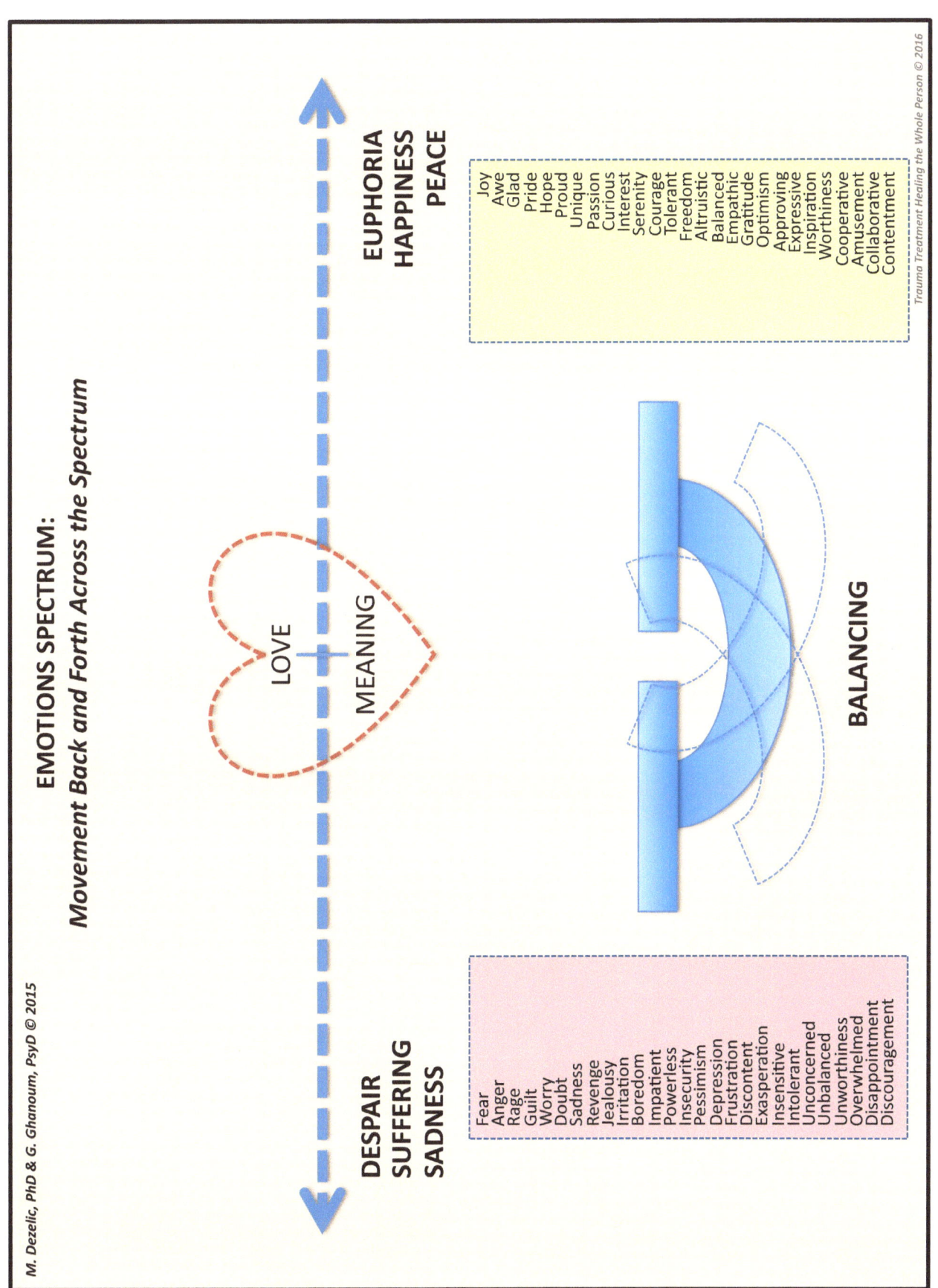

MY NOTES...

THE MEANING-ACTION TRIANGLE:
Becoming Existentially Aware

(1.) NOTICE -CONSCIOUS-

- Awareness
- Notice without judgment
- Recognize old patterns
- Become conscious of self-defeating behaviors/cycles
- Acknowledge victim role stance
- Recognize unhealthy relationship interactions
- Be fully present and conscious of self
- Acknowledge one's own existence

(2.) RESPONSIBILITY -TO SELF-

- Awareness, Self-Transcendence
- Responsible to self, to one's meaning in life, to the ultimate meaning of life
- Own one's feelings, actions and behaviors
- Acknowledge wanting to choose to change past self-limiting patterns
- Recognize one's healthy core—Spiritual Nöetic Dimension

(3.) TAKE ACTION -CHOICE-

- Awareness
- Freedom to act
- Choose to be conscious of self-improving behaviors
- Choose not to be a victim
- Decision to have healthy relationship interactions
- Be fully present to and conscious of one's actions
- Acknowledge one's own existence in the present
- Meaning in the moment
- Ultimate meaning

Meaning-Action Triangle

1. NOTICE
2. RESPONSIBILITY
3. ACTION

ATTITUDE
CREATIVITY
EXPERIENCES

Taking Flight from your PAST, While Being Pulled to your FUTURE

Marie S. Dezelic, PhD ©2013

Trauma Treatment Healing the Whole Person © 2016

MY NOTES...

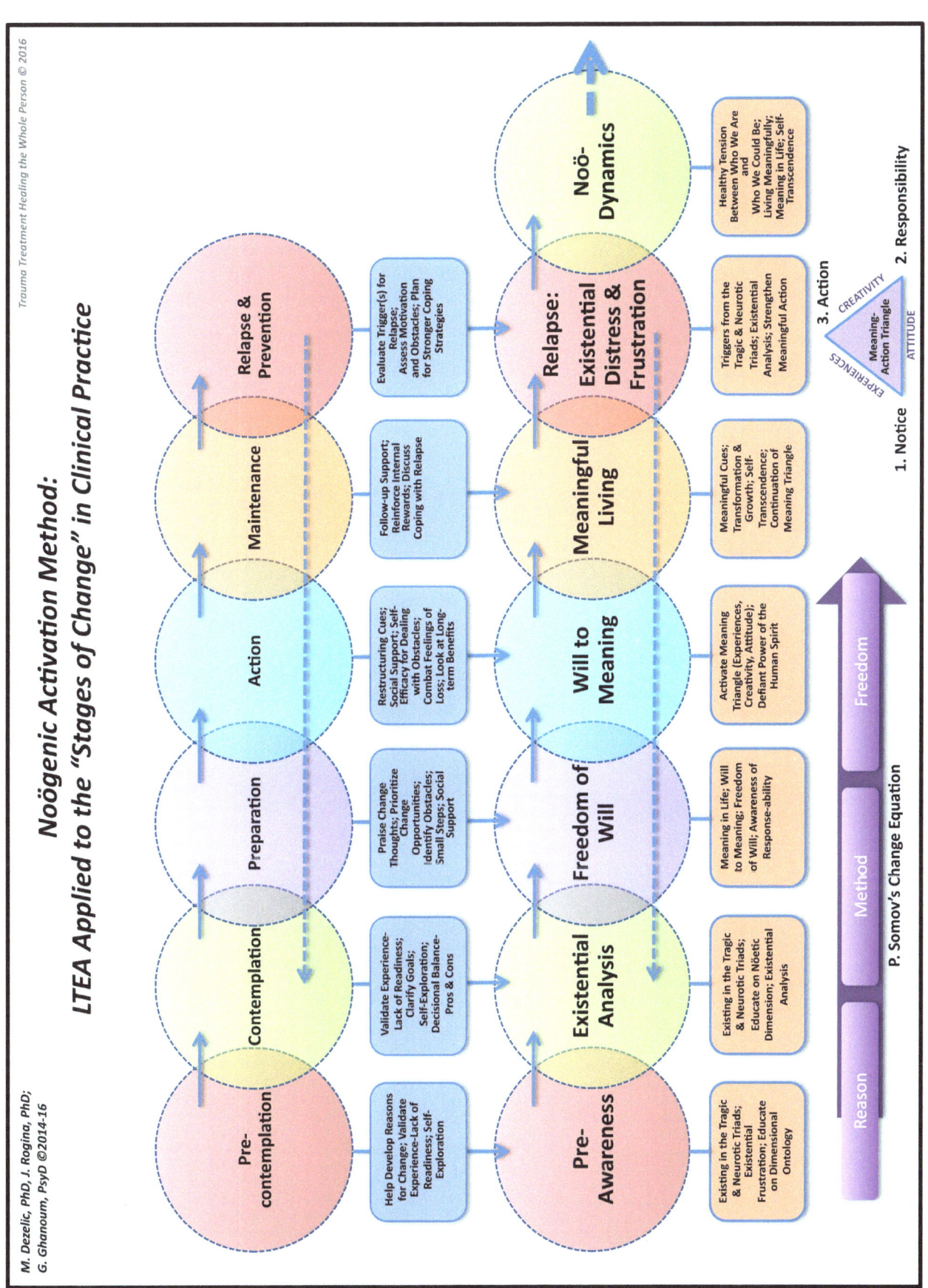

MY NOTES...

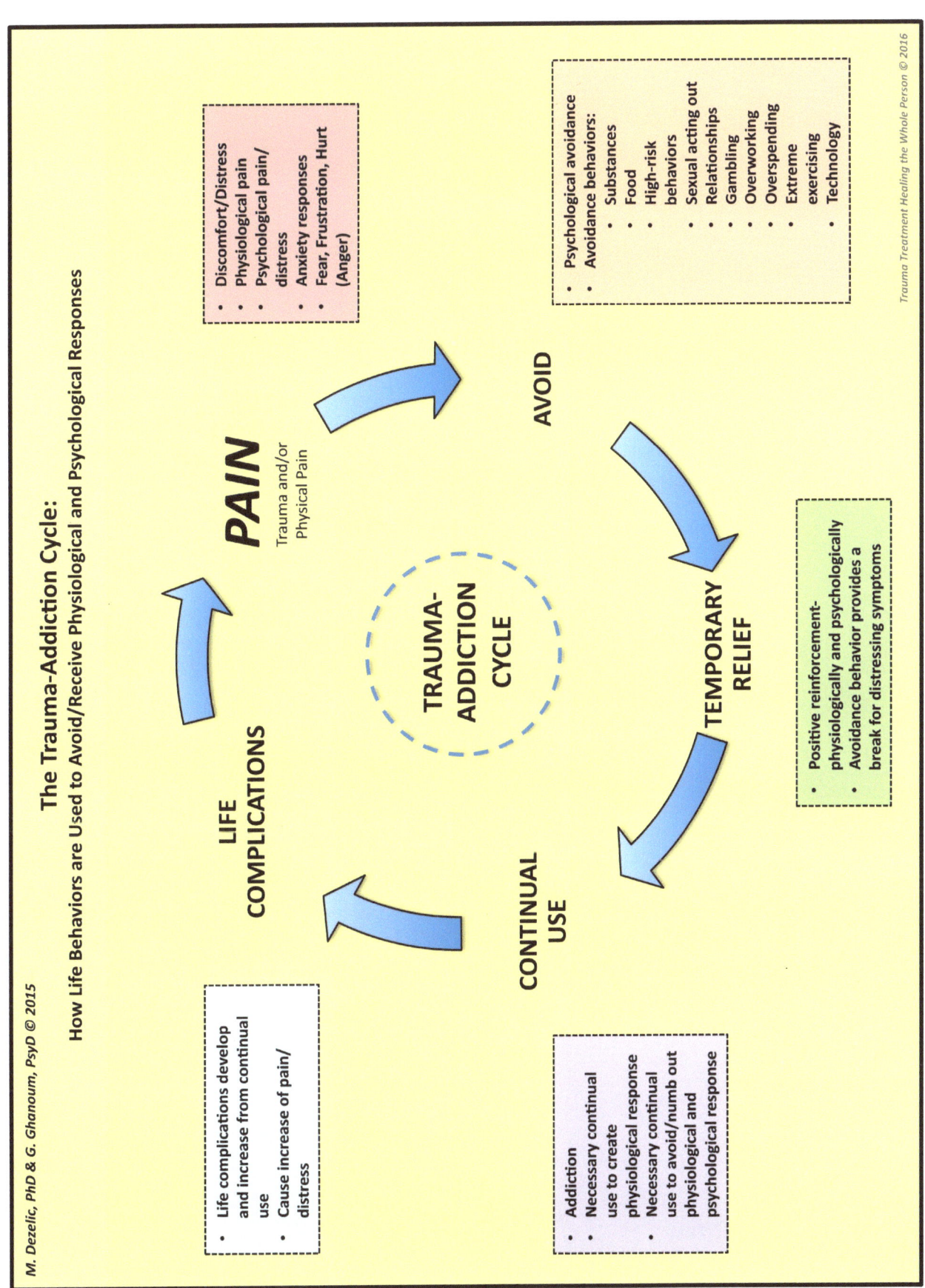

MY NOTES...

TRAUMA TREATMENT - HEALING THE WHOLE PERSON

PROCESSING THROUGH LOSS, GRIEF, TRANSITIONS AND TRANSFORMATION:
A Meaning-Centered Existential Approach

M. Dezelic & G. Ghanoum © 2013

STAGES OF DEATH, GRIEF, & TRANSITION:
- DENIAL
- ANGER
- BARGAINING
- DEPRESSION
- ACCEPTANCE

- E. Kübler-Ross & D. Kessler

MEANING-CENTERED GRIEF MODEL:
- ❖ **Processing Through Grief: (Not Linear)**
  - Spiraling and processing through all of the Stages, Feeling & Emotions, while experiencing; Somatic Pain (Body), Psychic Distress (Mind), and Spiritual Uncertainty (Spirit).
  - Validating and being present with one's inner and outer experience, multi-dimensional levels of pain
- ❖ **Continual Phase:**
  - Recovering Meaning (Meaning in Life)
  - Accessing Resources of the Spirit
  - Healing through: **Meaning, Memory, Restoration** and **Re-Activation**

- M. Dezelic & G. Ghanoum

6 "R" PROCESSES OF MOURNING:
- ❖ AVOIDANCE PHASE
  1. Recognize the loss
- ❖ CONFRONTATION PHASE
  2. React to the separation
  3. Recollect and reexperience
  4. Relinquish the old attachments and assumptive world
- ❖ ACCOMODATION PHASE
  5. Readjust to move adaptively
  6. Reinvest

- T. Rando

THE CONTINUAL PHASE: RECOVERING MEANING
Lifetime Journey of Recovery

- Ongoing Process Surviving Through the Loss
- Acceptance that Loved One is No Longer Physically Present, Yet Can Continue to Have a Presence in Life
- Growth & Thriving
- Resilience
- Transcendence

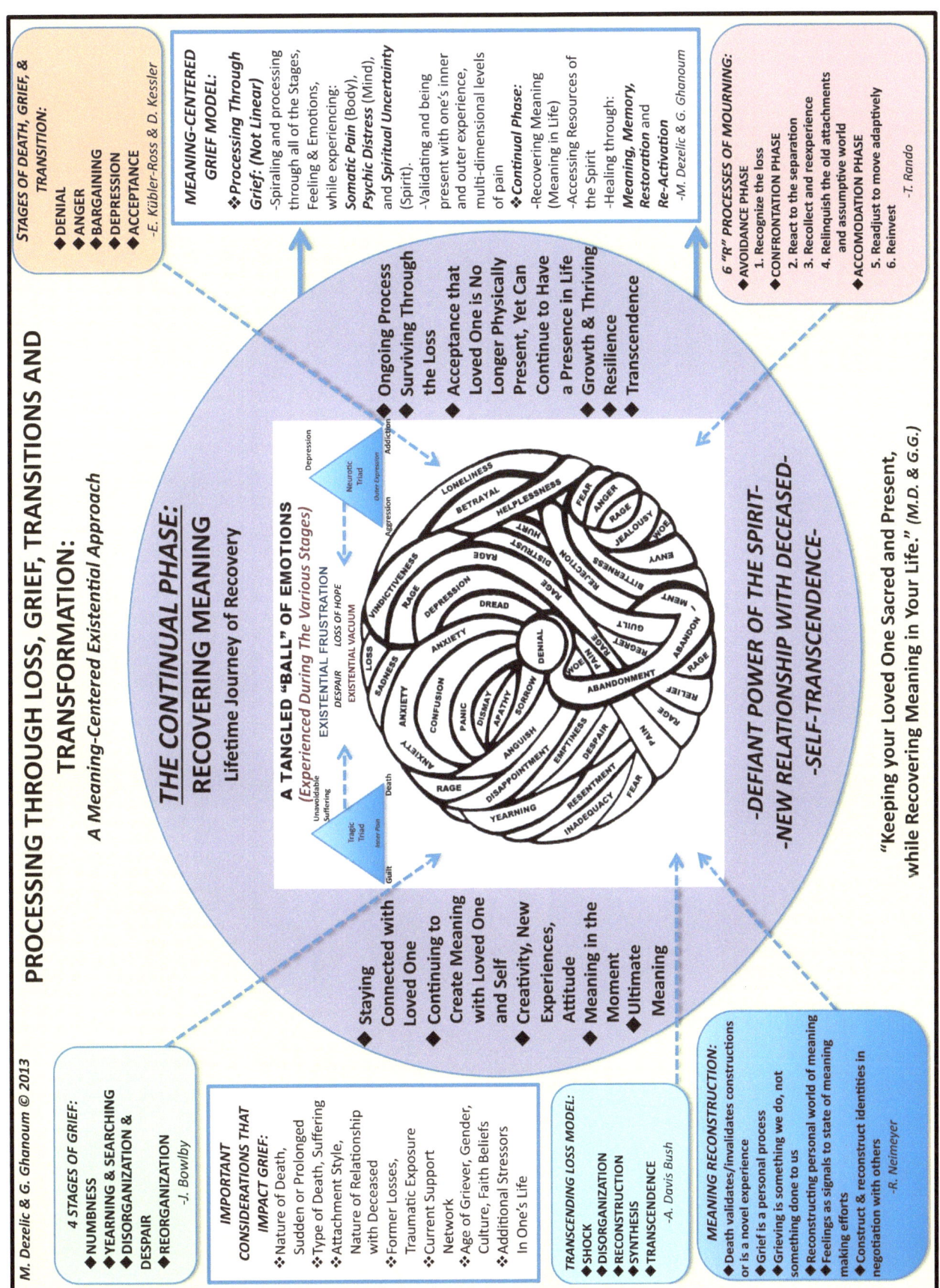

- Staying Connected with Loved One
- Continuing to Create Meaning with Loved One and Self
- Creativity, New Experiences, Attitude
- Meaning in the Moment
- Ultimate Meaning

-DEFIANT POWER OF THE SPIRIT-
-NEW RELATIONSHIP WITH DECEASED-
-SELF-TRANSCENDENCE-

"Keeping your Loved One Sacred and Present, while Recovering Meaning in Your Life." (M.D. & G.G.)

4 STAGES OF GRIEF:
- NUMBNESS
- YEARNING & SEARCHING
- DISORGANIZATION & DESPAIR
- REORGANIZATION

- J. Bowlby

IMPORTANT CONSIDERATIONS THAT IMPACT GRIEF:
- ❖ Nature of Death, Sudden or Prolonged
- ❖ Type of Death, Suffering
- ❖ Attachment Style, Nature of Relationship with Deceased
- ❖ Former Losses, Traumatic Exposure
- ❖ Current Support Network
- ❖ Age of Griever, Gender, Culture, Faith Beliefs
- ❖ Additional Stressors In One's Life

TRANSCENDING LOSS MODEL:
- SHOCK
- DISORGANIZATION
- RECONSTRUCTION
- SYNTHESIS
- TRANSCENDENCE

- A. Davis Bush

MEANING RECONSTRUCTION:
- ◆ Death validates/invalidates constructions or is a novel experience
- ◆ Grief is a personal process
- ◆ Grieving is something we do, not something done to us
- ◆ Reconstructing personal world of meaning
- ◆ Feelings as signals to state of meaning making efforts
- ◆ Construct & reconstruct identities in negotiation with others

- R. Neimeyer

MY NOTES...

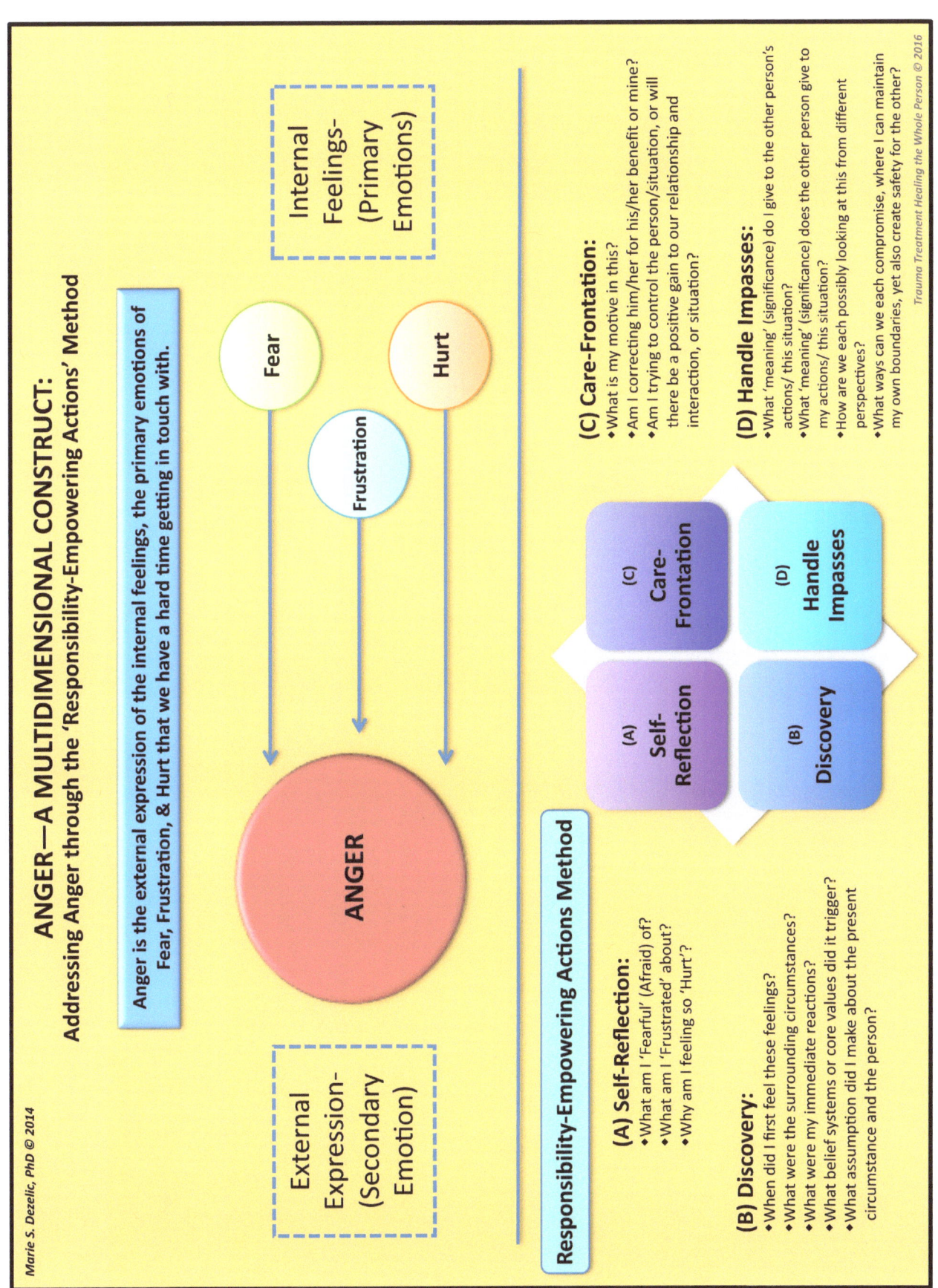

MY NOTES...

TRAUMA TREATMENT - HEALING THE WHOLE PERSON

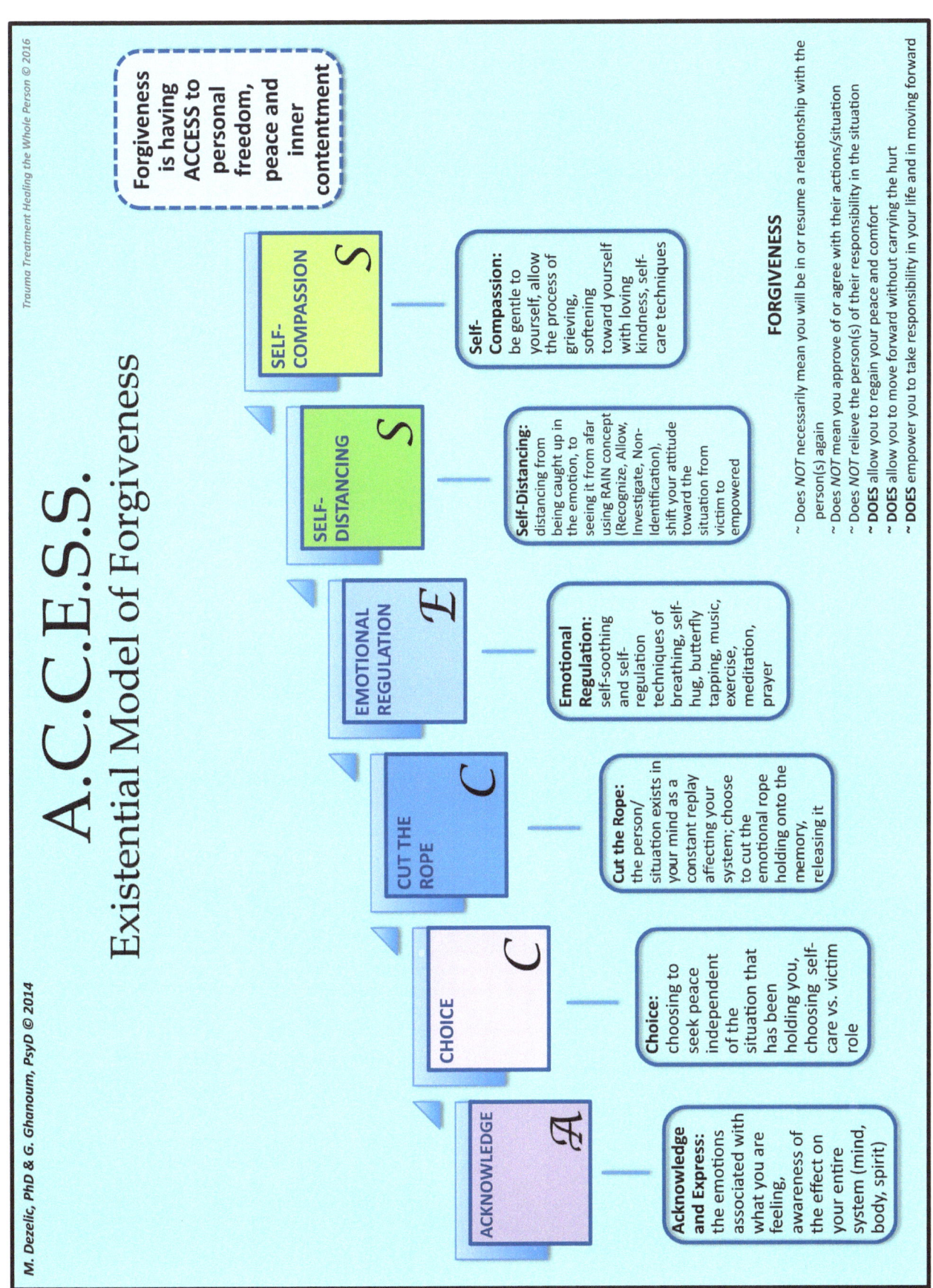

203

MY NOTES...

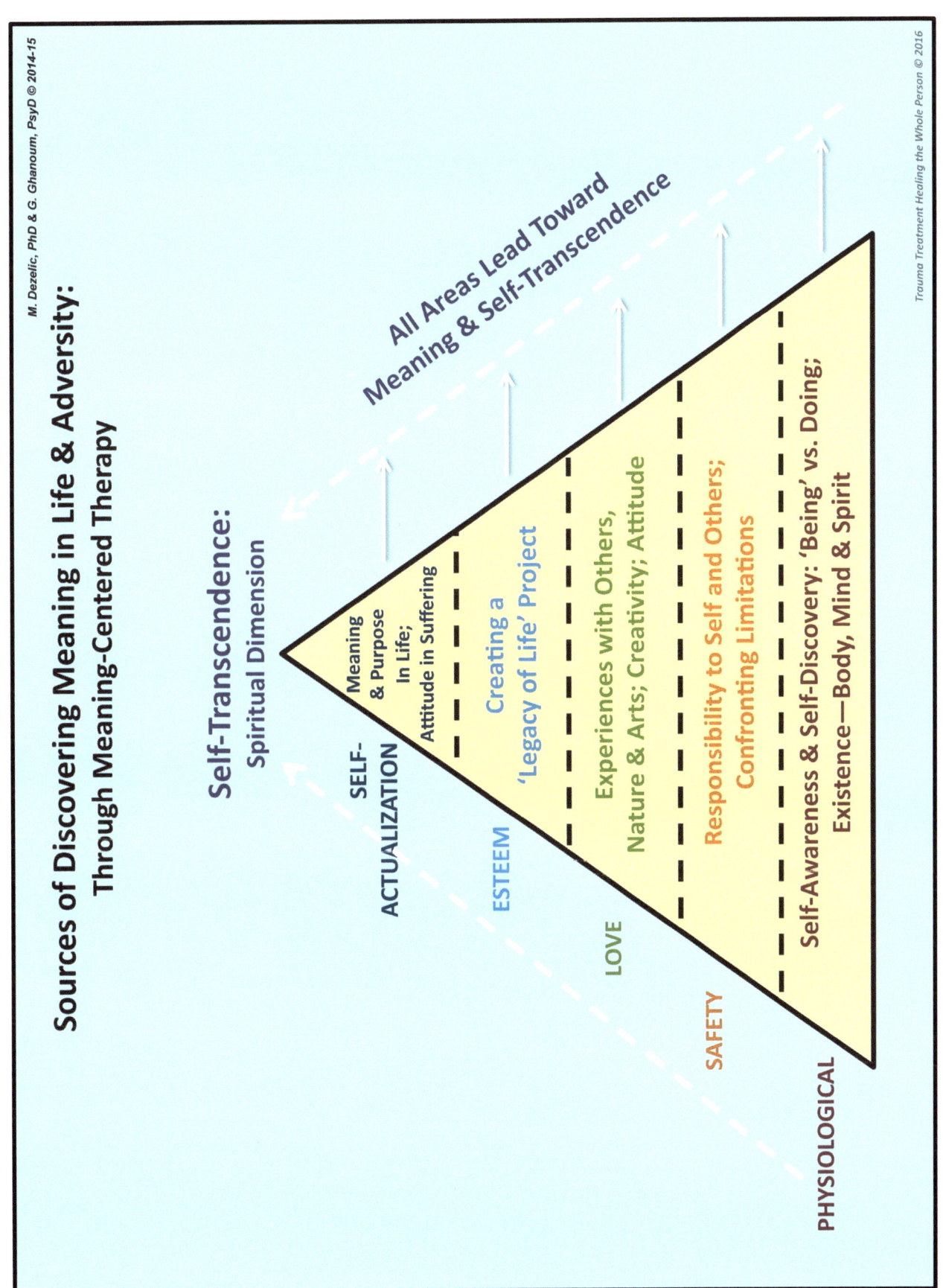

MY NOTES...

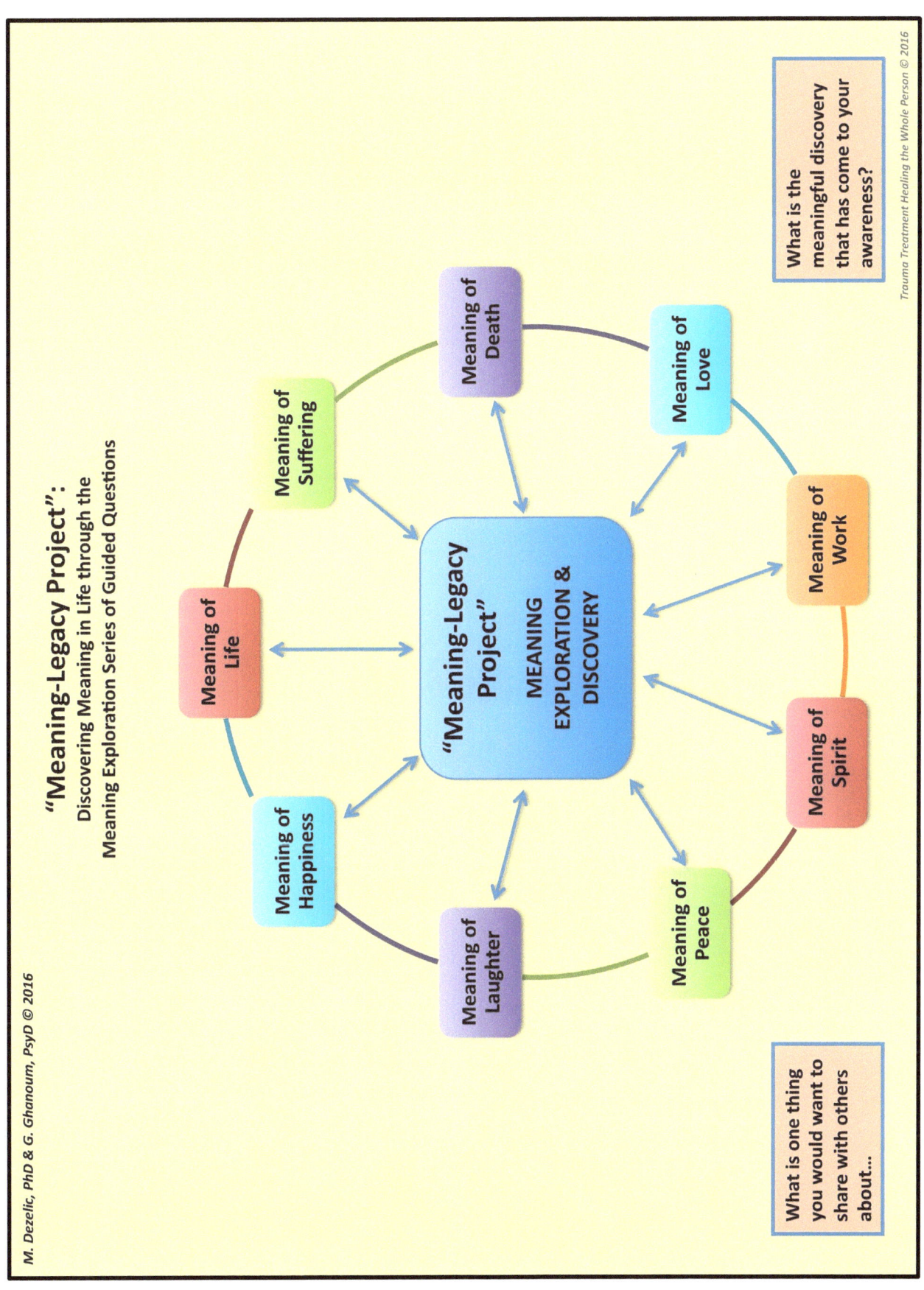

MY NOTES...

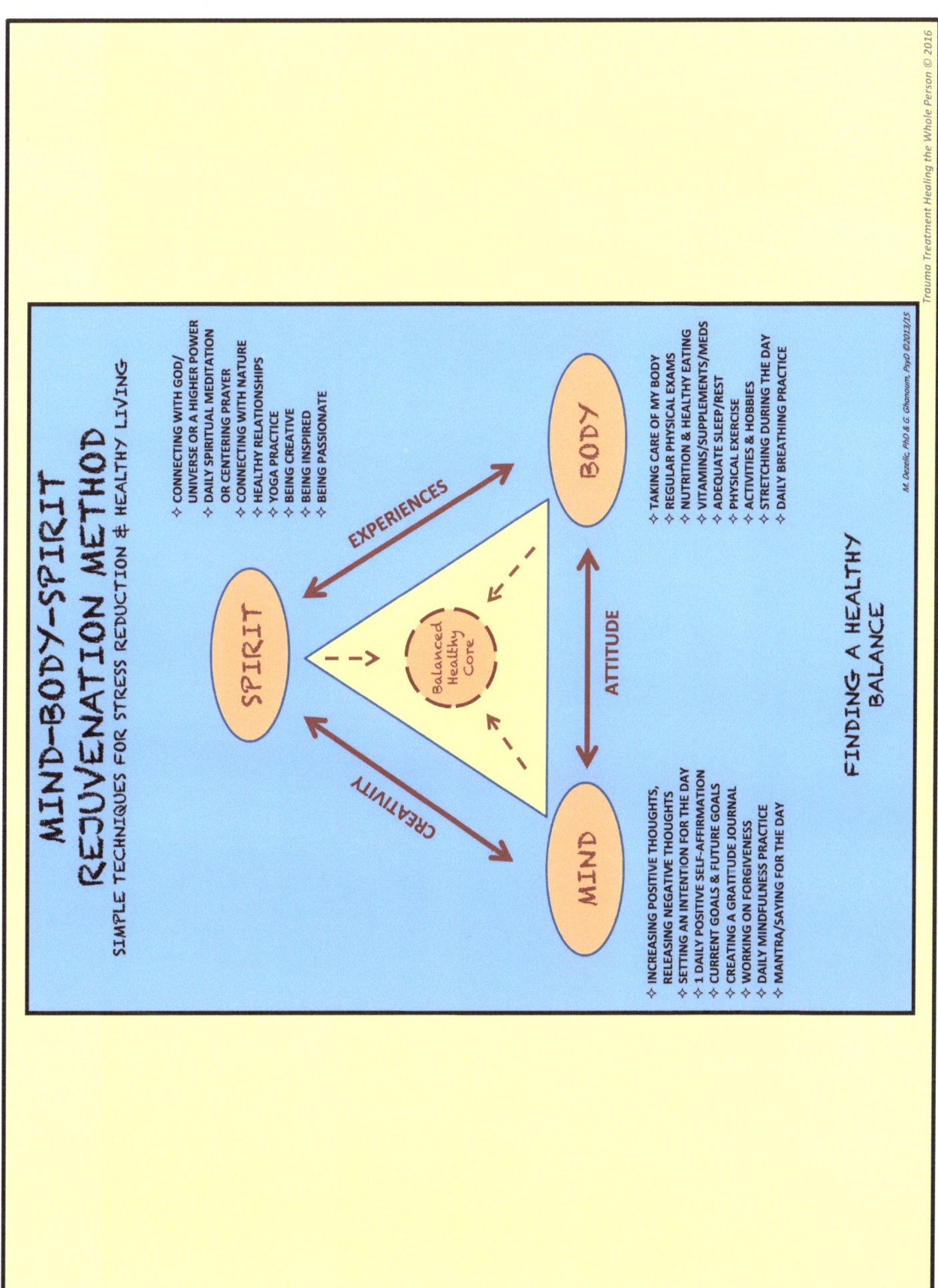

MY NOTES...

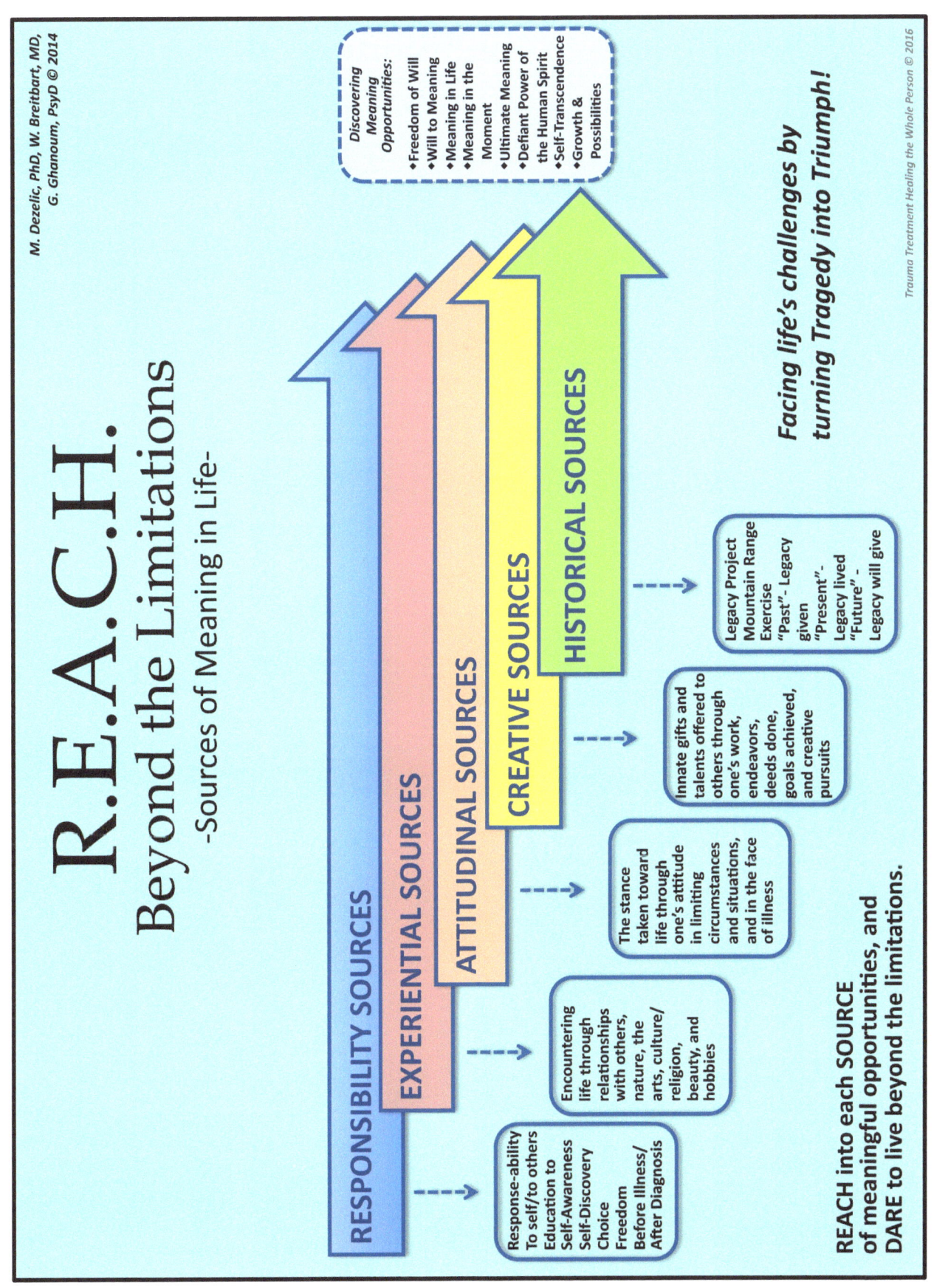

MY NOTES...

CONNECT—CREATE—CONVEY
Living Life with Meaning and Purpose

Create:
- Access your inner strengths and resources, discovering your natural talents and gifts, and possibilities to bring your uniqueness to the world.
- Be in your life creatively; discover how you bring your unique creativity to tasks, to projects, to your work, to your hobbies, to all of your relationships.

Connect:
- With others who inspire you, motivate you, lift you up, support you, whom you can help, and give of yourself to.
- You can connect with great thinkers, writers, actors, people you look up to, role models (from the past or present).
- You can connect with nature, the arts, culture.

Convey:
- Teach it, give it, bring it, write it, play it, paint it, say it, sing it, dance it; offer your unique creativity in your work, hobbies, causes you serve, and in all of your relationships.
- Convey to the world who you are and live your greater purpose with passion and meaning.

"By connecting we create, by creating we convey, by conveying we connect and create...
By connecting, creating, and conveying we can experience purpose and meaning in life..."

M. Dezelic, PhD & G. Ghanoum, PsyD © 2014

Trauma Treatment Healing the Whole Person © 2016

MY NOTES...

III.
"CLINICIAN & CLIENT HANDOUTS"

BLACK-AND-WHITE VERSION
FOR PHOTOCOPYING

TRAUMA TREATMENT - HEALING THE WHOLE PERSON

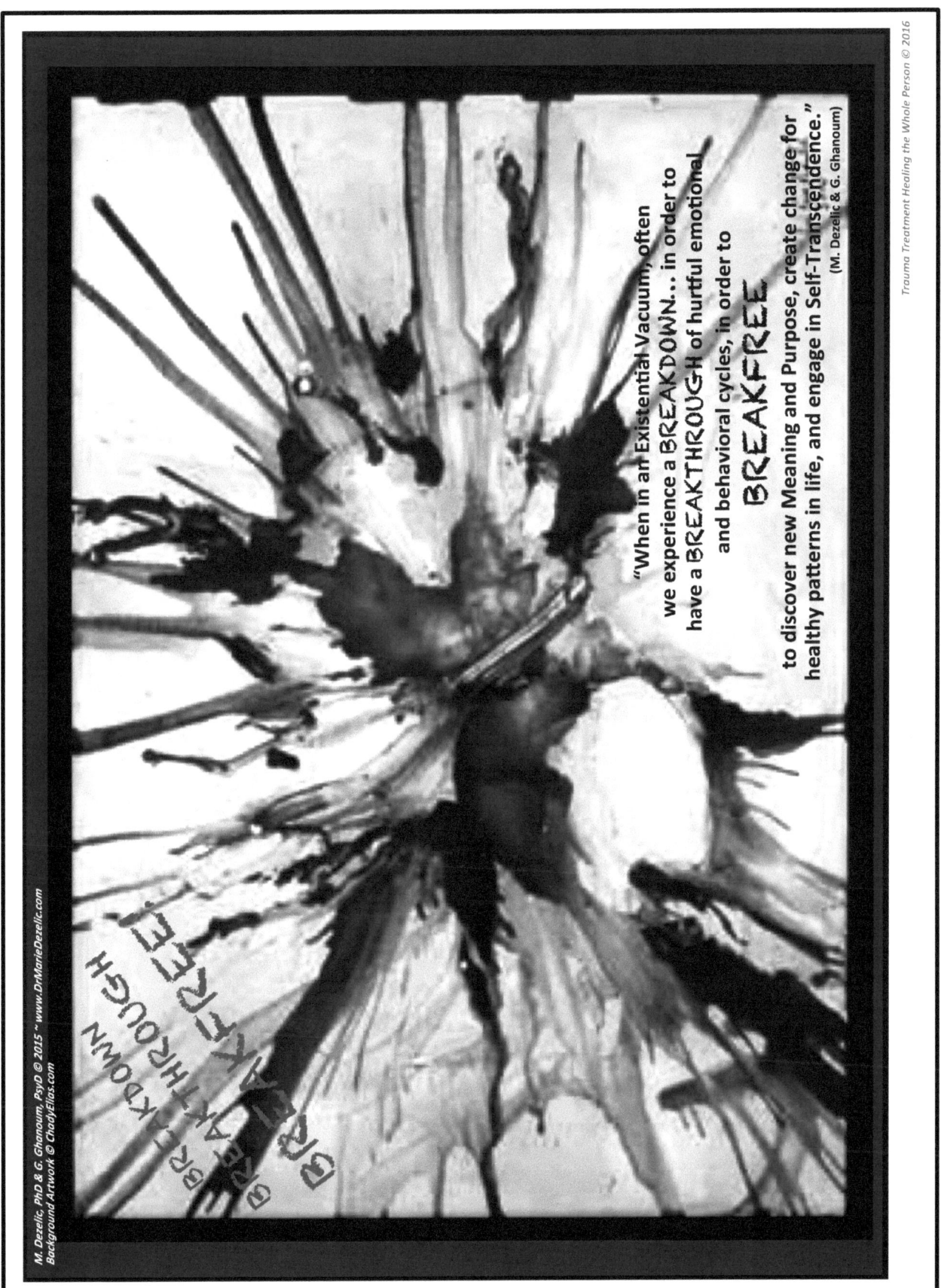

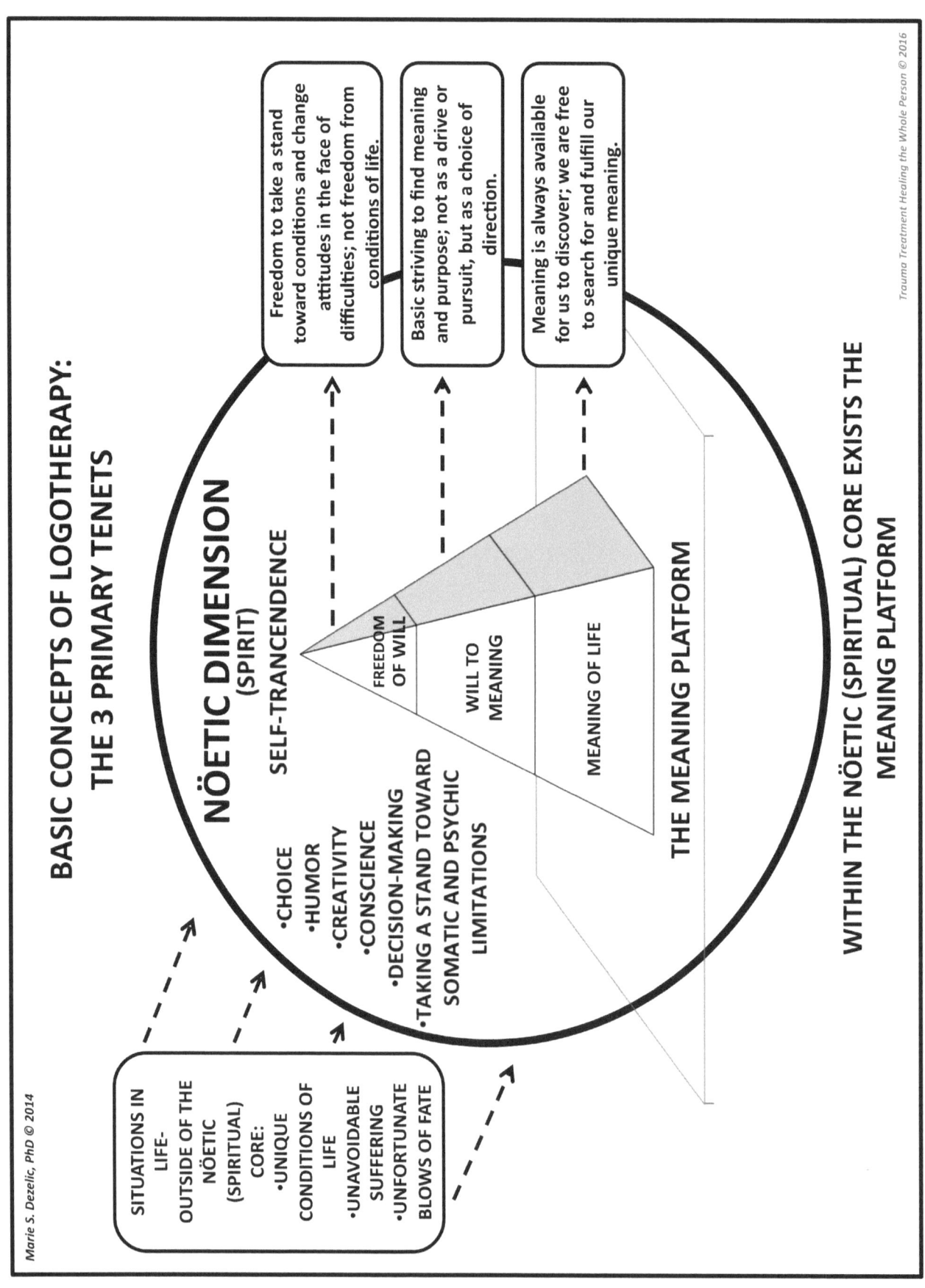

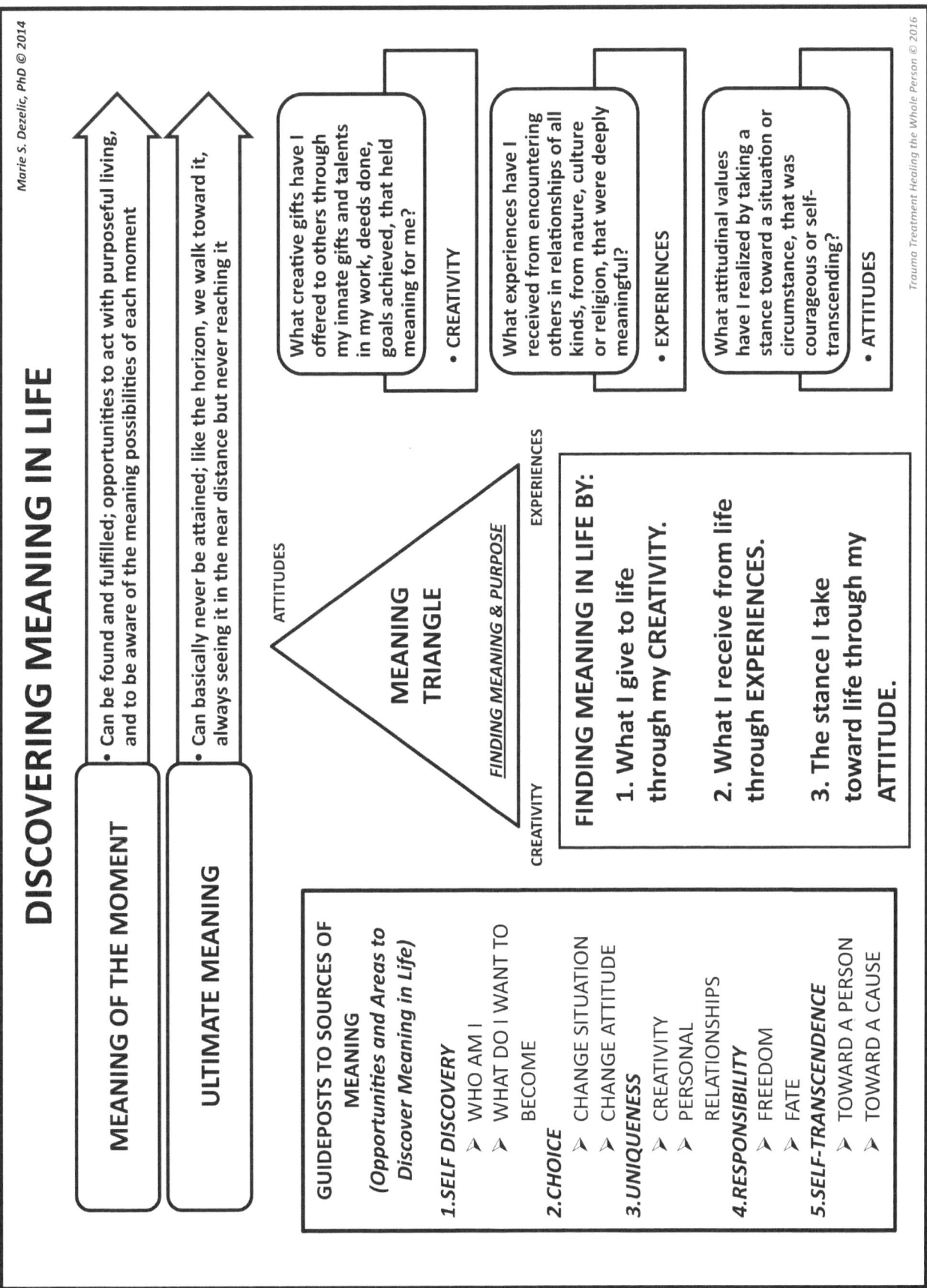

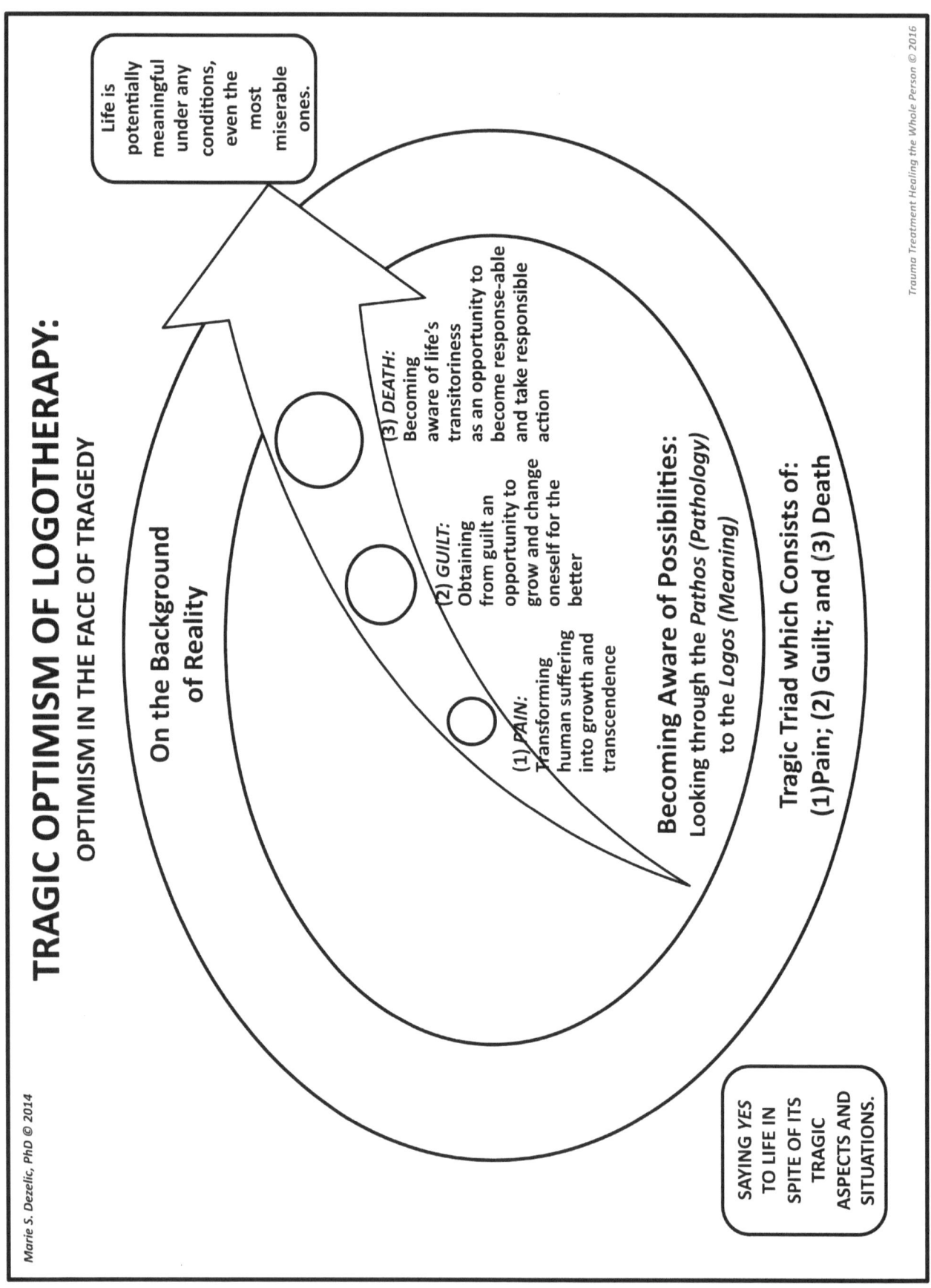

TRAUMA TREATMENT - HEALING THE WHOLE PERSON

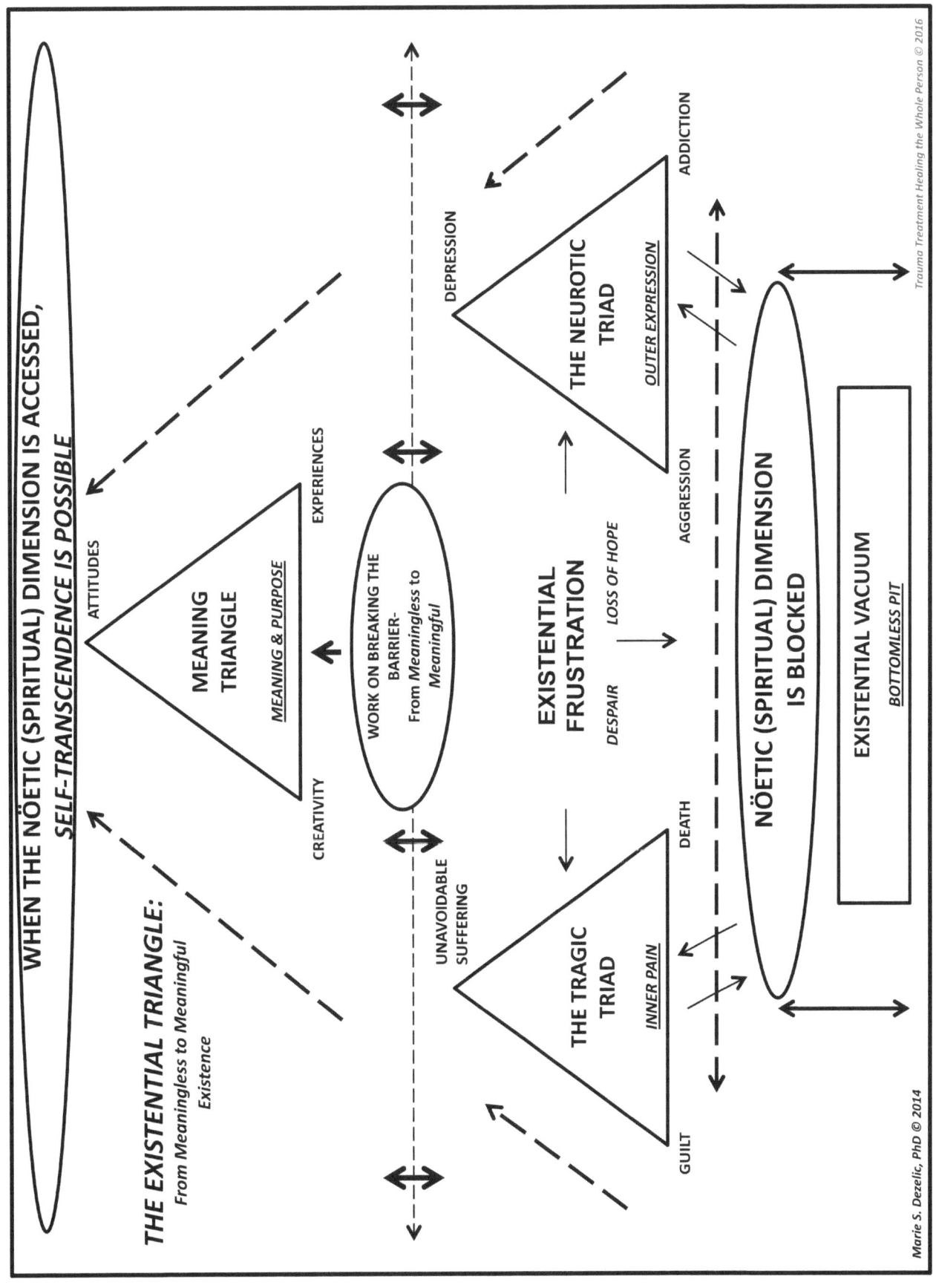

METHODOLOGY OF LOGOTHERAPY:
ELICITING WISDOM AND MEANING INHERENTLY HIDDEN WITHIN THE SPIRIT OF EACH SEEKER

Marie S. Dezelic, PhD © 2014

SOCRATIC (MAIEUTIC) DIALOGUE
A conversation that enables the birth of a latent idea, where the therapist acts as a midwife to help the patient give birth to new ideas; maieutic questioning awakens an innate knowledge into new attitudes, choices, and actions during the meaningful encounter.
• **Encounter, Meaning, Creativity, Self-Transcendence**

PARADOXICAL INTENTION
Having the patient try to do, or wish to have happen, precisely that which he/she fears; the effect is to disarm the anticipatory anxiety which accounts for much of the feedback mechanism that initiate and perpetuate the neurotic condition.
• **Self-Distancing, Humor, Self-Transcendence**

DEREFLECTION
Used when a problem is caused for the patient by too much reflection (hyperreflection), or by too much attention to solving the problem (hyperintention); consists of putting a stop on pathological hyperreflection and turning the mind to other thoughts or actions.
• **Self-Distancing, Self-Transcendence**

MEDICINE CHEST
Therapist makes the patient aware of the tremendous and often untapped resources of health within their healthy core- the spiritual dimension; activates will to find meaning, orientation toward goals, freedom to make decisions, creativity, imagination, love beyond physical.
• **Defiant Power of the Human Spirit**

Methodology & Outcome:

MODIFICATION OF ATTITUDES
Therapist facilitates and awakens attitudinal changes when the patient is in despair or finds him/herself in a situation that cannot be changed, i.e. unfortunate blows of fate, tragedies; each moment presents a unique opportunity in which we can respond to and discover meaning.
• **Attitudinal Change, Meaning, Self-Transcendence**

COMPLEMENTATRY METHODS:
- ACT AS IF
- ALTERNATIVE LISTS
- APPEALING TECHNIQUE
- ART THERAPY
- DREAMS
- GUIDED FANTASIES/ IMAGERY
- IDENTIFICATION WITH OBJECTS
- IMPROVISATIONS
- JOURNAL WRITING
- LIFE MAPS
- LIST MAKING- (Good/Bad Consequences)
- LOGOANALYSIS- 7-STEP/ 10-STEP
- LOGOANCHOR TECHNIQUE
- LOGODRAMA
- LOGOHOOK
- METAPHORS
- MOUNTAIN RANGE
- MOVIE EXPERIENCE
- NOÖGENIC ACTIVATION
- POSITIVE SELF-TALK
- SCULPTING
- STORIES/PARABLES

Trauma Treatment Healing the Whole Person © 2016

Meaning-Centered Therapy

Integrative Meaning-Centered, Existential and Humanistic Treatment Concepts

Meaning – *Meaning in life, Meaning in the Moment, Will to Meaning,* and *Meaning Triangle—Creativity, Experiences, and Attitude* create *Hope* and foster *Resilience.*

Personal-Existential Responsibility – Freedom to take ownership to one's own life through *Becoming Conscious (Aware), Becoming Responsible (Response-Able),* and *Taking New Actions (Choice);* building *Resource* capacity.

Education – Learning about each aspect of *Mind-Body-Spirit, Responsibility, Neurobiology, Trauma Triggers* and *Responses, Tools, Freedom, Choice, Meaning/Engagement* in life.

Self Awareness – Through personal responsibility and education, *Making Choices* that support safety, well-being, boundaries, and trauma recovery; uncovering and discovering *Inner Strengths* and *Resources.*

Support – *Safe Environment, Safety* with others, *Connection* with others, *Reciprocity, Self-Transcendence-* going beyond oneself through giving, collaboration, community, and serving.

Treatment – *Collaborative* and *Guiding* approach, address experiences of *Human Existence* and the *Human Condition,* unconditional *Acceptance,* specialized *Trained* clinician, ongoing *Support.*

M. Dezelic, PhD & G. Ghanoum, PsyD © 2015

DARE
Existential Therapy
-Live Life in Each Moment & 'REACH' Beyond Limitations-

M. Dezelic, PhD, W. Breitbart, MD, & G. Ghanoum, PsyD © 2014

D: Dialectics
- Holding opposing dialectical and paradoxical internal states, feelings, emotions, circumstances, recognition of before and after diagnosis.
- Focus on becoming comfortable with interoceptive and emotional states.
- Notice, recognize belief systems, understand meaning held within each state.

A: Attitude
- Acknowledging and validating the dialectical positions; accepting to hold the dialectical positions without self-judgment.
- Education to awareness of the freedom of choice in choosing one's attitude in suffering and life-limiting circumstances.

R: Resources
- Discover and focus on inner human strengths as resources to health, and the balance between difficult or limiting experiences and meaning.
- Response-ability: respond (pre-frontal cortex activation) versus react (limbic system activation) to experiences and emotions, allows for self-distancing.

E: Encounter
- Encounter, Engage, Experience: the situation, the person, or the emotion, from an emotionally balanced place, allowing it without being consumed by it.
- Evaluate options, make choices from a stance of freedom in one's attitude.
- Engage in new experiences, activating meaning and self-transcendence.

DARE Existential Therapy Focuses on:
- Developing a sense of mindful awareness, and a compassionate stance toward oneself without judgment, through self-distancing and self-transcendence, with a focus on becoming existentially aware while holding dialectical positions in the face of difficult or life-limiting conditions.
- Particular emphasis on the 'Meaning-Action Triangle' 1) Noticing; 2) Responsibility; 3) Action

Trauma Treatment Healing the Whole Person © 2016

Existential Therapeutic Process
Logotherapy & Existential Analysis

➢ Recognize strengths and weaknesses, and utilize both for growth

➢ Facilitate a greater understanding of the human condition and the experiences within it from the personal context

➢ Uncover and discover inner strengths and resources to live passionate, fulfilling and meaningful lives

➢ Live authentically, heal from traumatic experiences, and have personal and relational growth

"When we are no longer able to change a situation, we are challenged to change ourselves."

(Viktor Frankl)

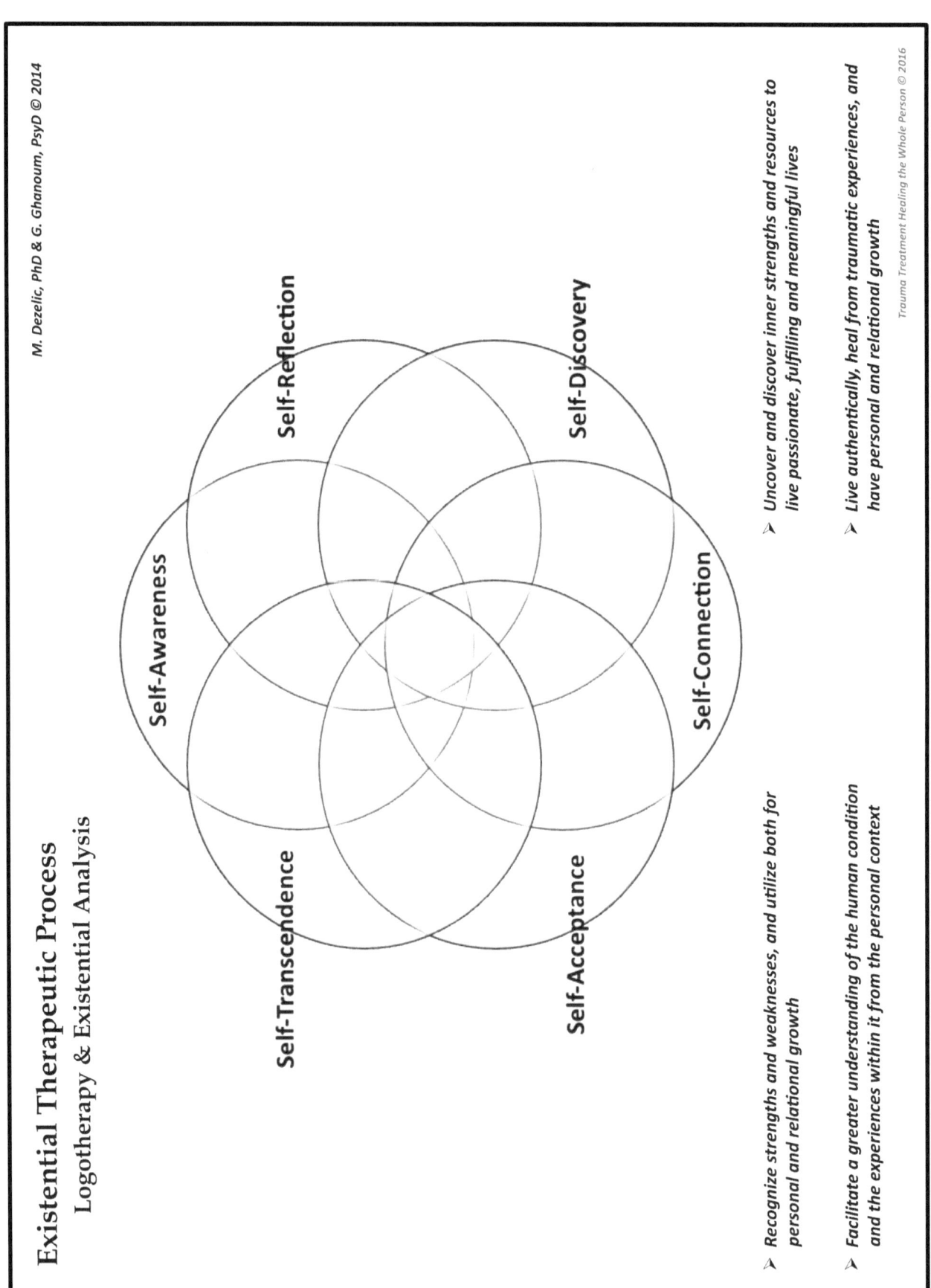

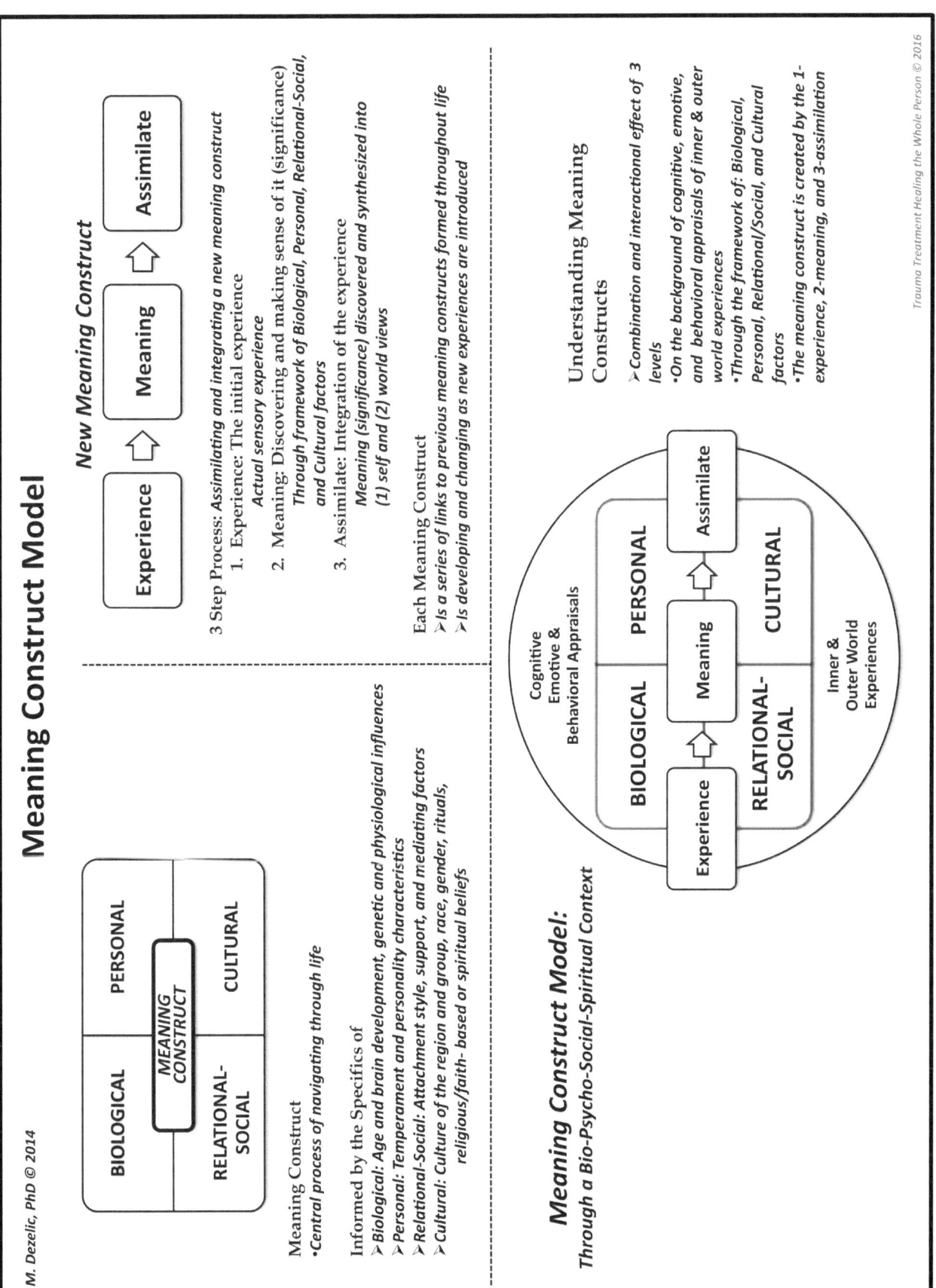

✷ HOPE ✷

= SPIRITUAL WILL
(To Meaning)

+

MEANINGFUL DISCOVERY
(Through Psychological, Physiological, and Spiritual Abilities in Creativity, Experiences, and Attitude)

M. Dezelic, PhD & G. Ghanoum, PsyD © 2015

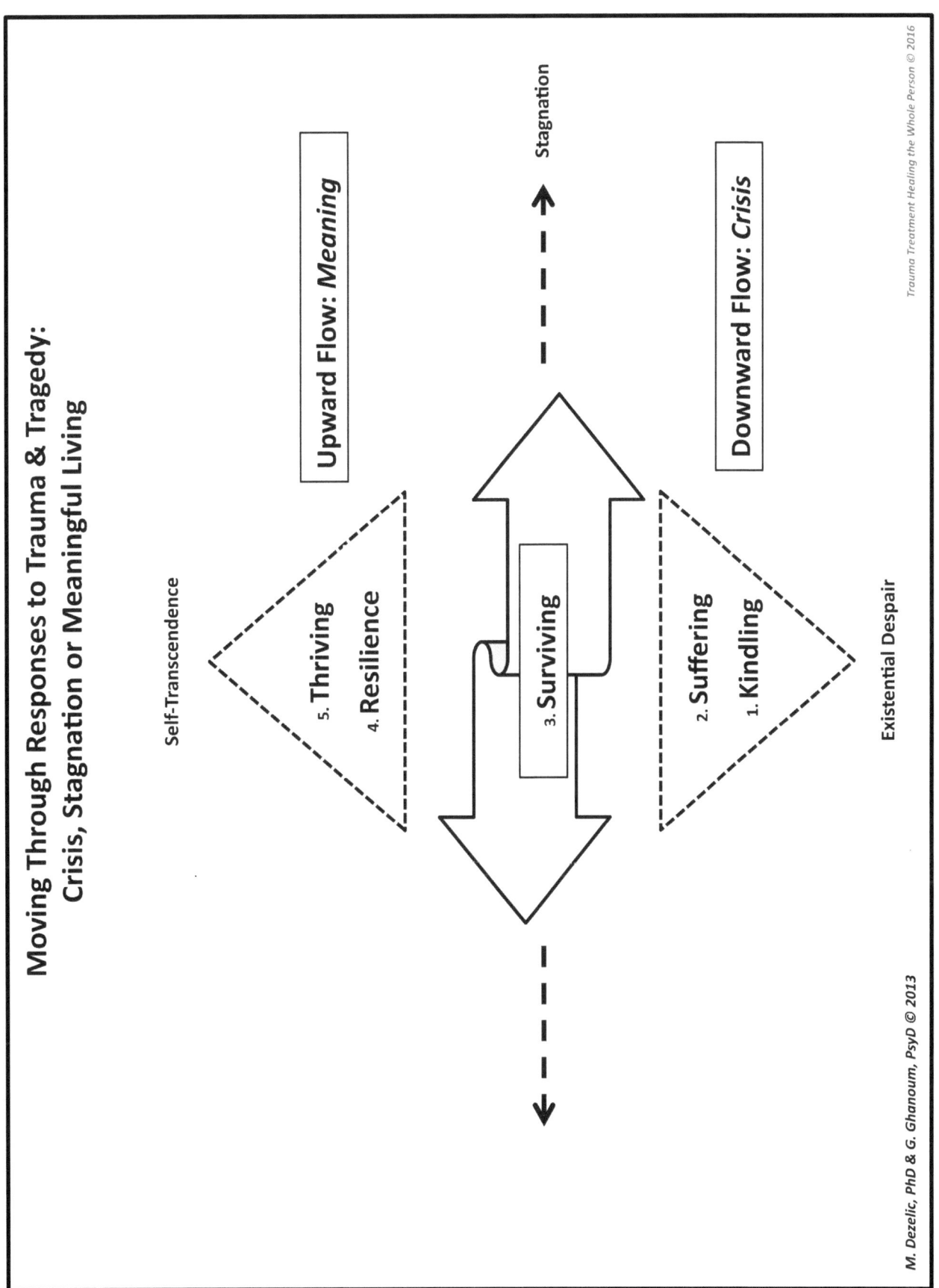

TRAUMA Elements

Overwhelming-Traumatic Event

T = TRIGGERS ARE A THREAT

R = REACTIVE RESPONSES

A = ALIENATION & ISOLATION

U = UNSAFE & UNCERTAIN

M = MEMORY DISTORTION, FRAGMENTED PIECES

A = AUTONOMIC NERVOUS SYSTEM DYSREGULATION

Marie S. Dezelic, PhD © 2015

Trauma Treatment Healing the Whole Person © 2016

M. Dezelic, PhD & G. Ghanoum, PsyD © 2015

TRAUMA Definitions

- A "wound."
- Physical or psychological injury.
- Extremely distressing or disturbing experience.
- A deeply emotional upset.
- Extremely overwhelming experience to the body, mind, and spirit.
- Altered psychological or behavioral state resulting from an overwhelming or disorganizing experience.
- Inability to integrate an emotional experience that threatened one's life, bodily integrity or psychological capacities.
- Inability to tolerate physiological and psychological symptoms.
- Unique to the person experiencing it.

TRAUMA Experience
Fragmented… in disarray

~ Past, Present, and Future become entangled

~ The symptoms tell us the "story"

~ Trauma is saved as feelings, images, emotions, sensations

~ Trauma survivors usually don't have the words (or right words) to tell the story

Trauma Treatment Healing the Whole Person © 2016

TRAUMA Elements
Trauma Affects Each Person Differently

Marie S. Dezelic, PhD © 2015

Traumatic Event(s)

Psychological Impacts

Emotional Impacts

Spiritual-Existential Impacts

Physiological Impacts

Social-Relationship Impacts

Practical Impacts

Emotional / Psychological / Spiritual-Existential:
- Sadness
- Depression
- Decreased Interest
- Irritability
- Chronic Frustration
- Intolerance
- Hopelessness
- Despair
- Anger
- Rage
- Foreshortened Future
- Altered Belief in Humanity
- Altered Belief in Spirituality
- Meaninglessness
- Shame
- Self-Loathing
- Self-Blame
- Self-Hatred
- Shattered Assumptions
- Damaged Goods
- Aggressive Communication
- Passive Communication

Physiological:
- Numbing
- Insomnia
- Hypersomnia
- Nightmares
- Amnesia
- Decreased Concentration
- Physiological Hyperarousal
- Physiological Hypoarousal
- Psychomotor Agitation
- Somatic Dysregulation
- Exaggerated Startle Response
- Hypervigilance
- Emotional Pain

- Stigmatization
- Intrusive Memories
- Flashbacks
- Fragmented Memories
- Disorganization
- Paranoia
- Explosive Outbursts
- Somatic Symptoms
- Chronic Pain
- Hyper-Sexualization
- Loss of Sexual Desire/Response
- Sexual Diseases

Social-Relationship / Practical:
- Isolation
- Alienation
- Disempowerment
- Disconnection from Community
- Chronic Relationship Attempts
- Ruptured Relationships
- Chronic Breakups
- Trust Issues
- Co-Dependency
- Overly Caretaking
- Emotional Dysregulation
- Homelessness
- Incarceration

- Lack of Life Skills
- Vocational Obstacles
- Educational Obstacles
- Learning Disabilities
- Attention Deficit Disorder
- Attention Deficit Hyperactivity
- Panic Attacks
- Phobias
- Agoraphobia
- Chronic Grief
- Substance Abuse
- Generalized Anxiety
- Eating Disorders
- Addictive Behaviors
- Dissociative Symptoms
- Alexithymia
- Self-Harming Behaviors
- Self-Destructive Behaviors
- High-Risk Behaviors
- Suicidal Ideation
- Suicidal Attempts
- Feel Like Failure

Trauma Treatment Healing the Whole Person © 2016

TRAUMA Elements
Trauma Responses – Survival Responses

SEEK CONNECTION (Cry for help)

SUBMIT

FREEZE

FLIGHT-FLEE

FIGHT

Traumatic Event(s)

- What are the symptoms you generally experience?
- How did the symptom(s) help you to survive, cope, deal with others, and deal with the environment?
- Which symptoms are about your body, about your thoughts, about your existence?
- What happens to you now when you feel these symptom(s)?
- How does feeling this way help you to survive your current environment or triggers?
- What would you like to feel about your body, about yourself and others, about your existence?

Marie S. Dezelic, PhD © 2015

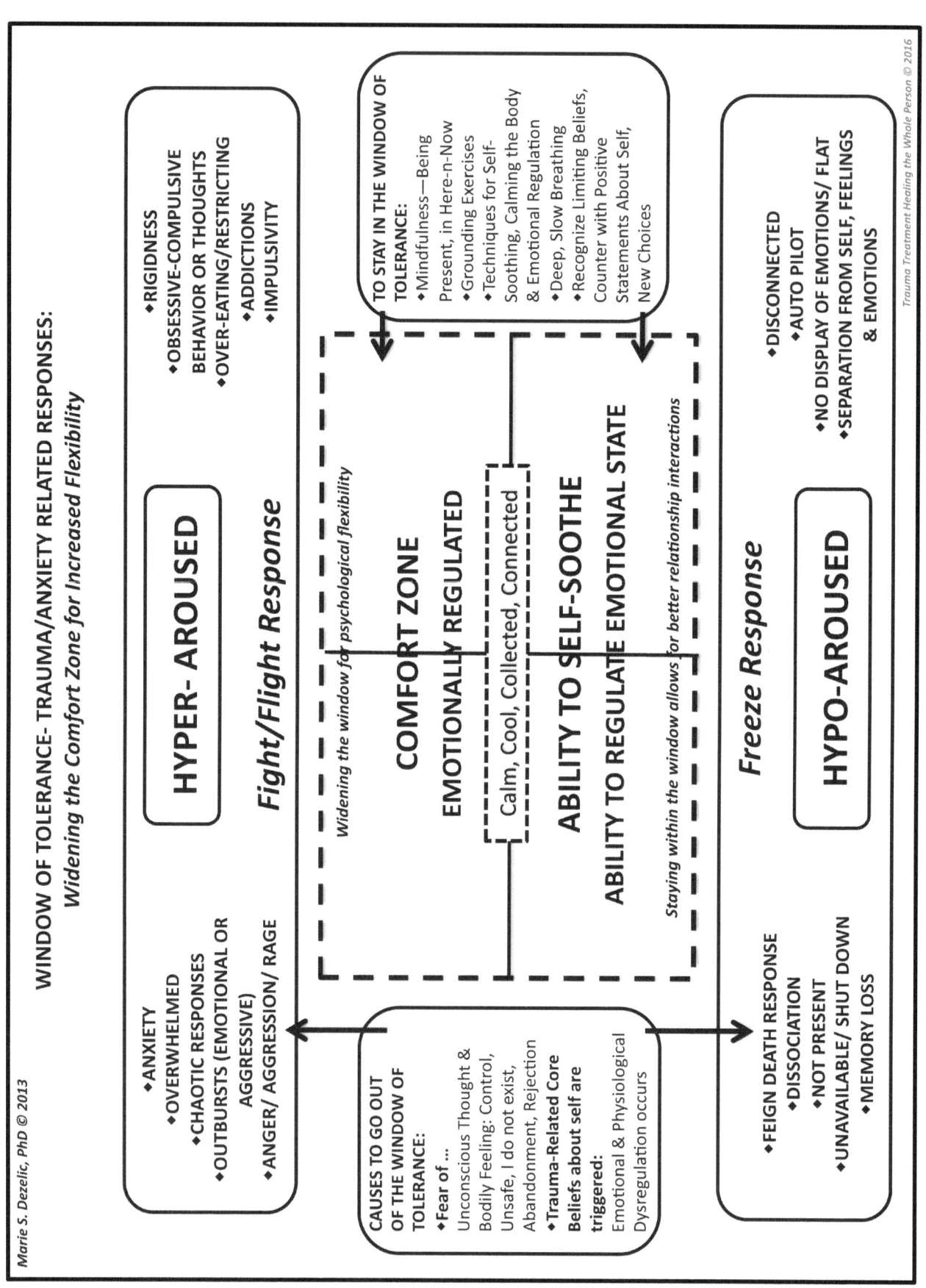

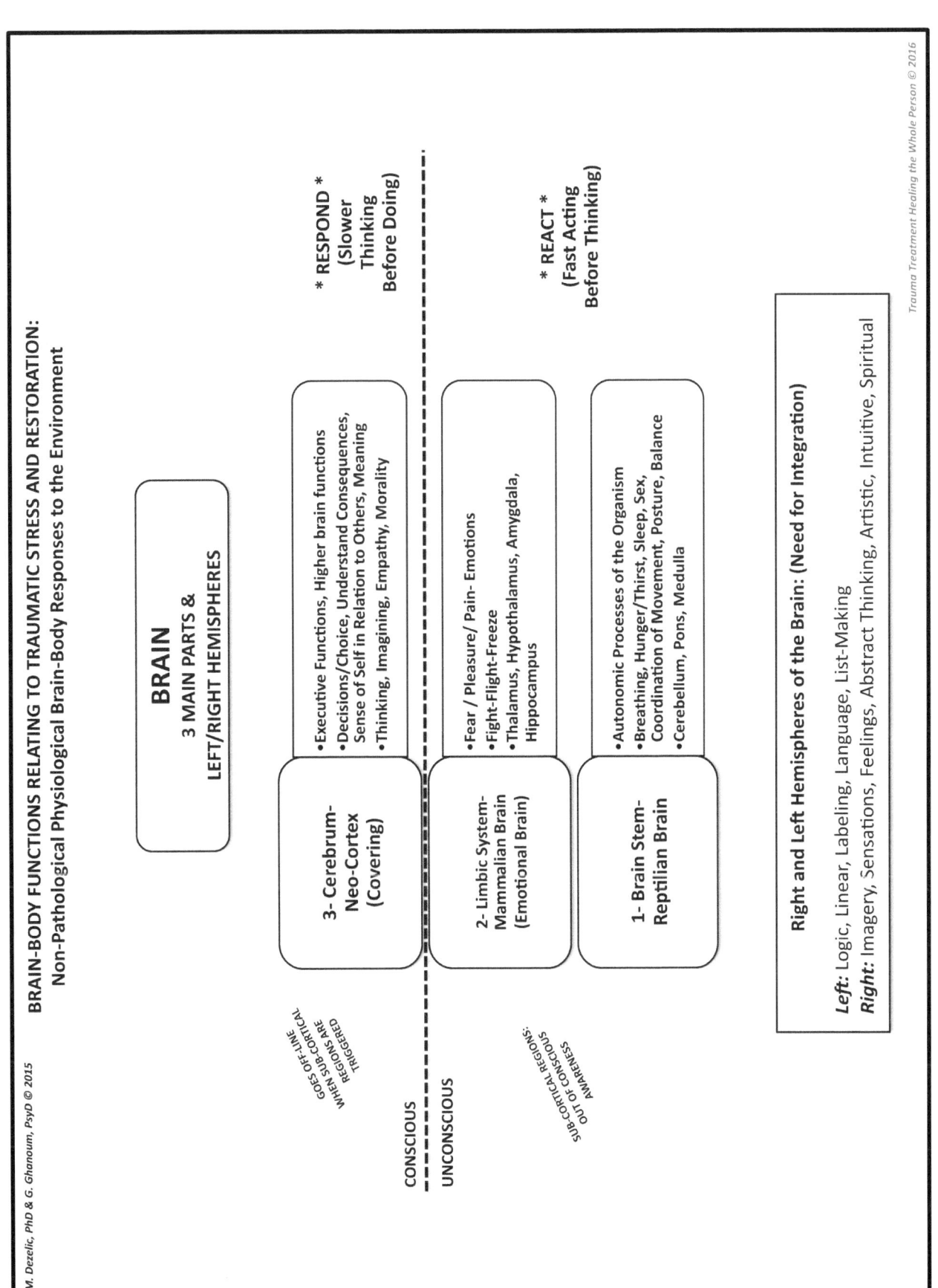

BRAIN-BODY FUNCTIONS RELATING TO TRAUMATIC STRESS AND RESTORATION:
Non-Pathological Physiological Brain-Body Responses to the Environment

ANS — Autonomic Nervous System

Moves as a See-Saw in balance

SNS — Sympathetic Nervous System
FIGHT/FLIGHT "HOT ZONE"

ERGOTROPIC (ENERGY-SEEKING)
Activates SNS, Motor and Premotor System: *(Incr. muscle tension and prepare to act)*
Endocrine System: *(Incr. secretion of stress hormones)*
Central Nervous System: *(Incr. sensory alertness)*

Too much activation: "OUT OF" WINDOW OF TOLERANCE

PNS — Parasympathetic Nervous System
RELAXED or FREEZE "COOL ZONE"

TROPHOTROPIC (NUTRITION-SEEKING)
Activates PNS, Same systems as SNS, but for:
Rest, Relaxation, Feeding, Restoration, Recuperation

"IN" WINDOW OF TOLERANCE-Comfort Zone

Too much deactivation: "OUT OF" WINDOW OF TOLERANCE

SNS or PNS Responses:
- Intensify or calm down viscera
- Alter blood circulation
- Trigger hormonal and endocrine activation
- Change muscle tone and posture
- Increase or decrease cognitive arousal

M. Dezelic, PhD & G. Ghanoum, PsyD © 2015

BRAIN-BODY FUNCTIONS RELATING TO TRAUMATIC STRESS AND RESTORATION:
Non-Pathological Physiological Brain-Body Responses to the Environment

ATTENDING TECHNIQUES - 4 C's (Dezelic & Ghanoum)

☼ **1- "CALM" THE BODY**
Regulate the Body to the "Cool Zone," Re-Set and Stabilize to present, Demonstrate Somatic Regulation

2- "CHOICE" OF THINKING
Psychoeducation, Discussion, Neo-Cortex & Pre-Frontal Cortex gets back online when physiology is calmed down and safe

3- "CONFRONT" THE CONCERNS
Address the Trauma/Concerns, Re-process, Re-work, New Meanings

4- "CHANGE" BEHAVIORS - CHANGE THE WIRING
Changing beliefs, try new behaviors, with new results, while staying calm and regulated, creating and stabilizing new neural networks

TRAUMA TREATMENT - HEALING THE WHOLE PERSON

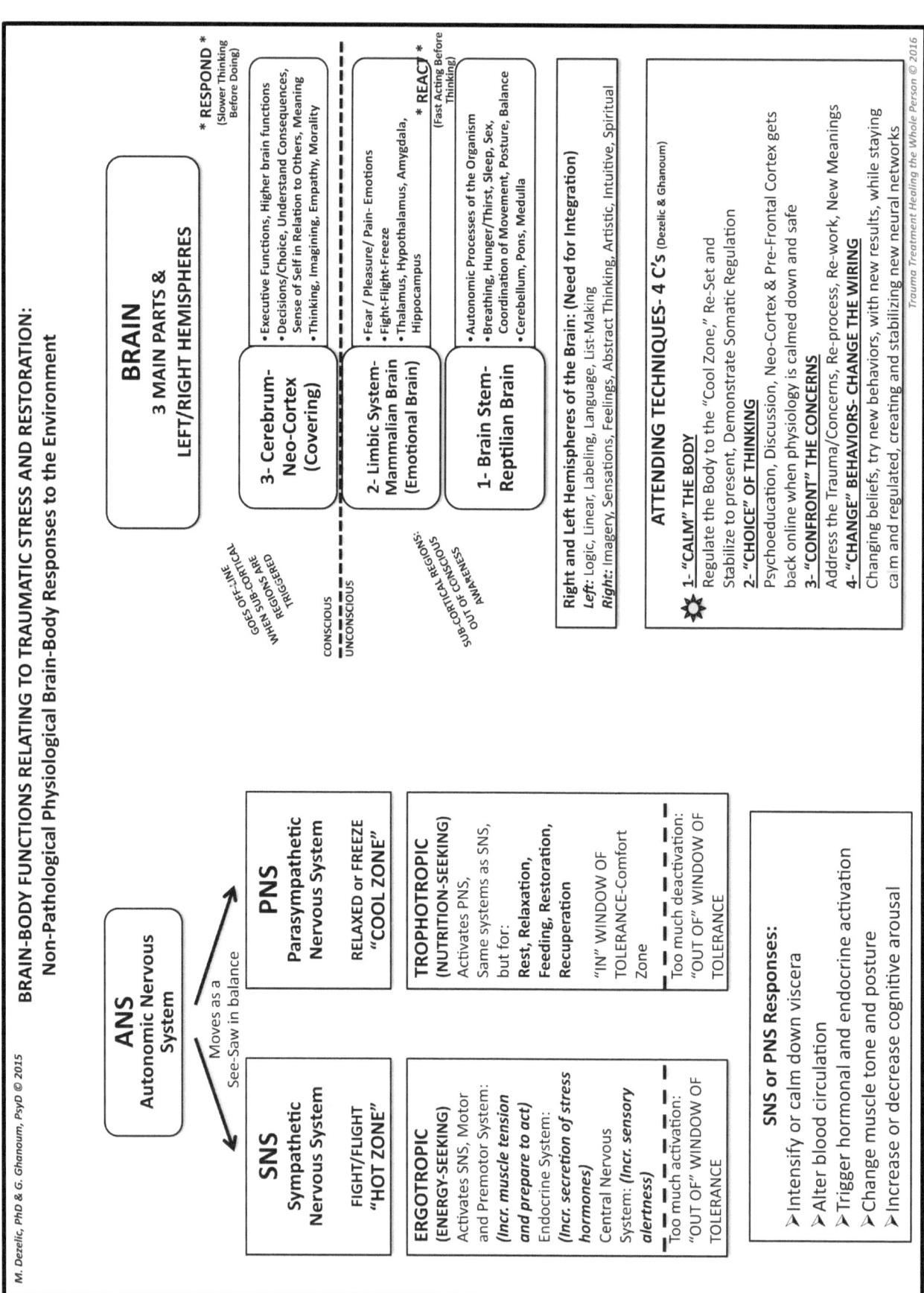

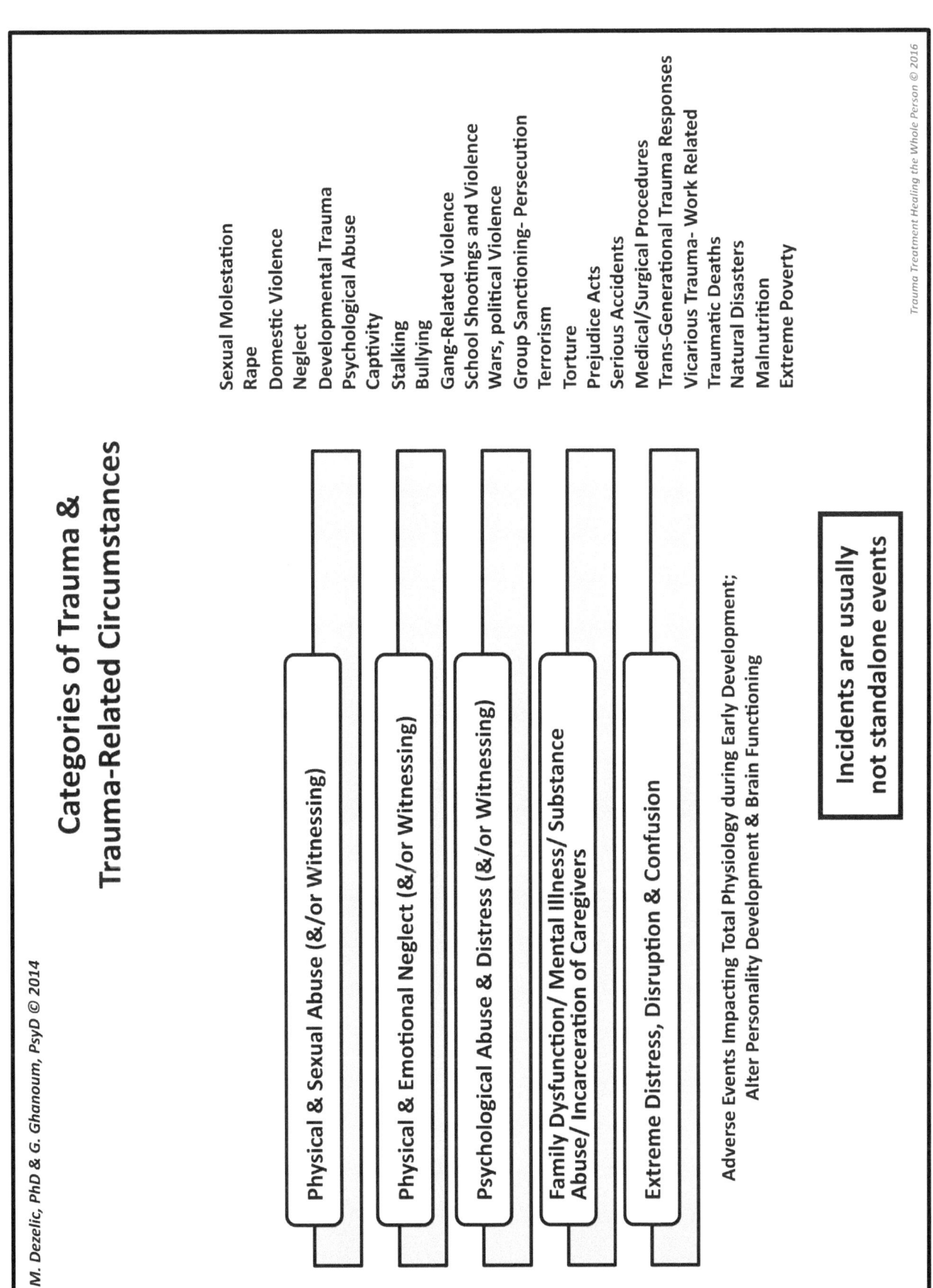

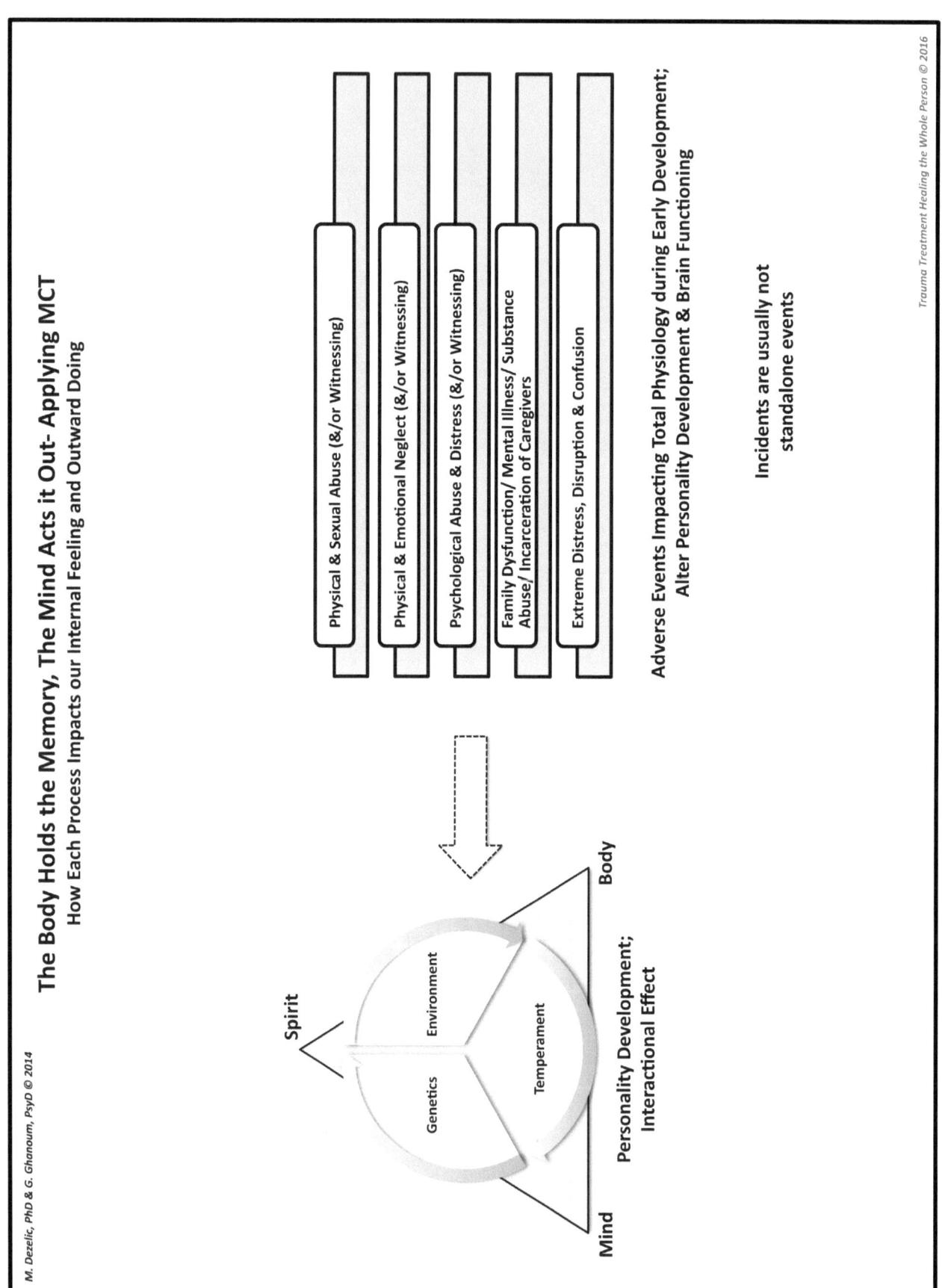

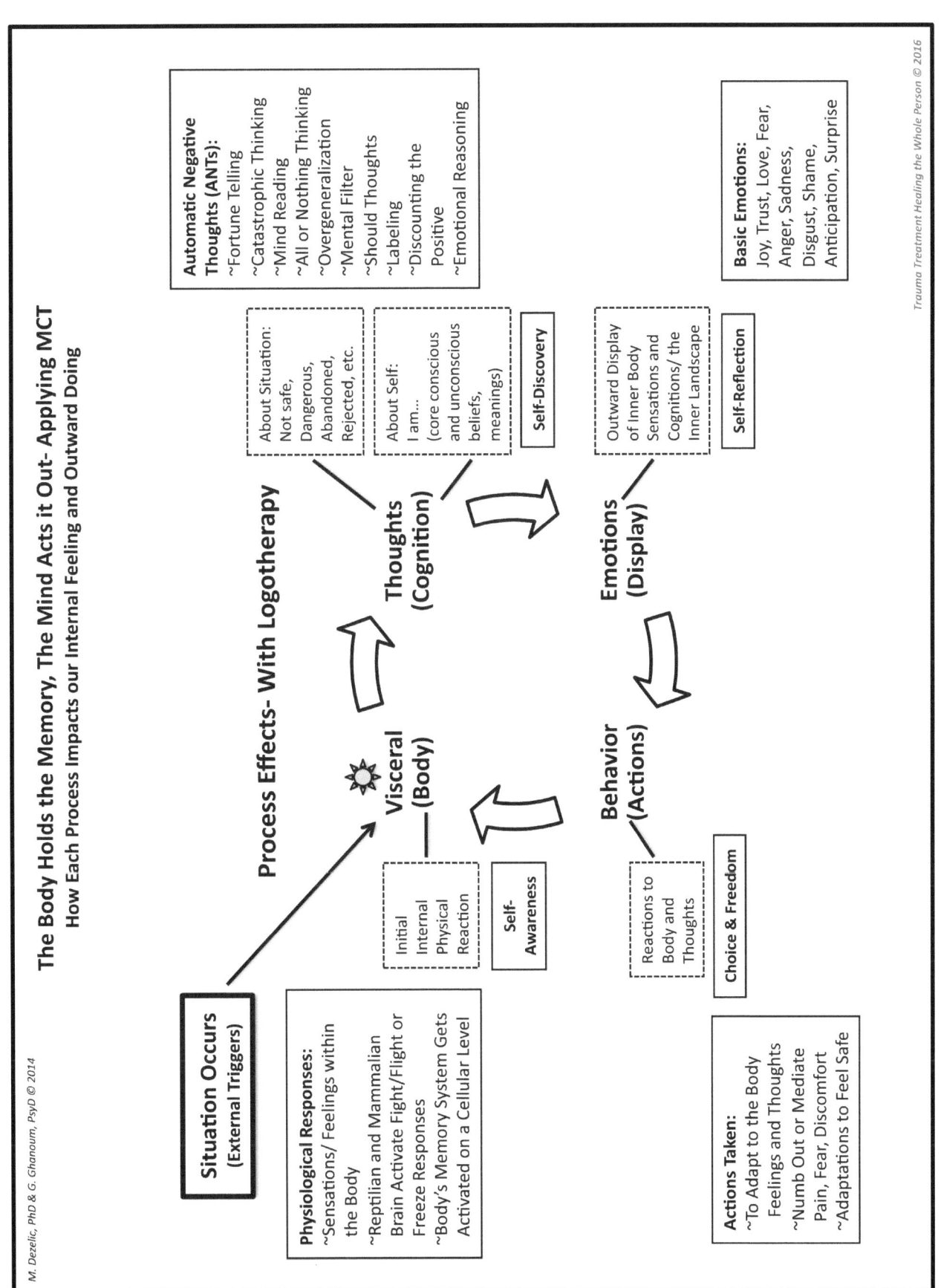

Trauma Treatment - Healing The Whole Person

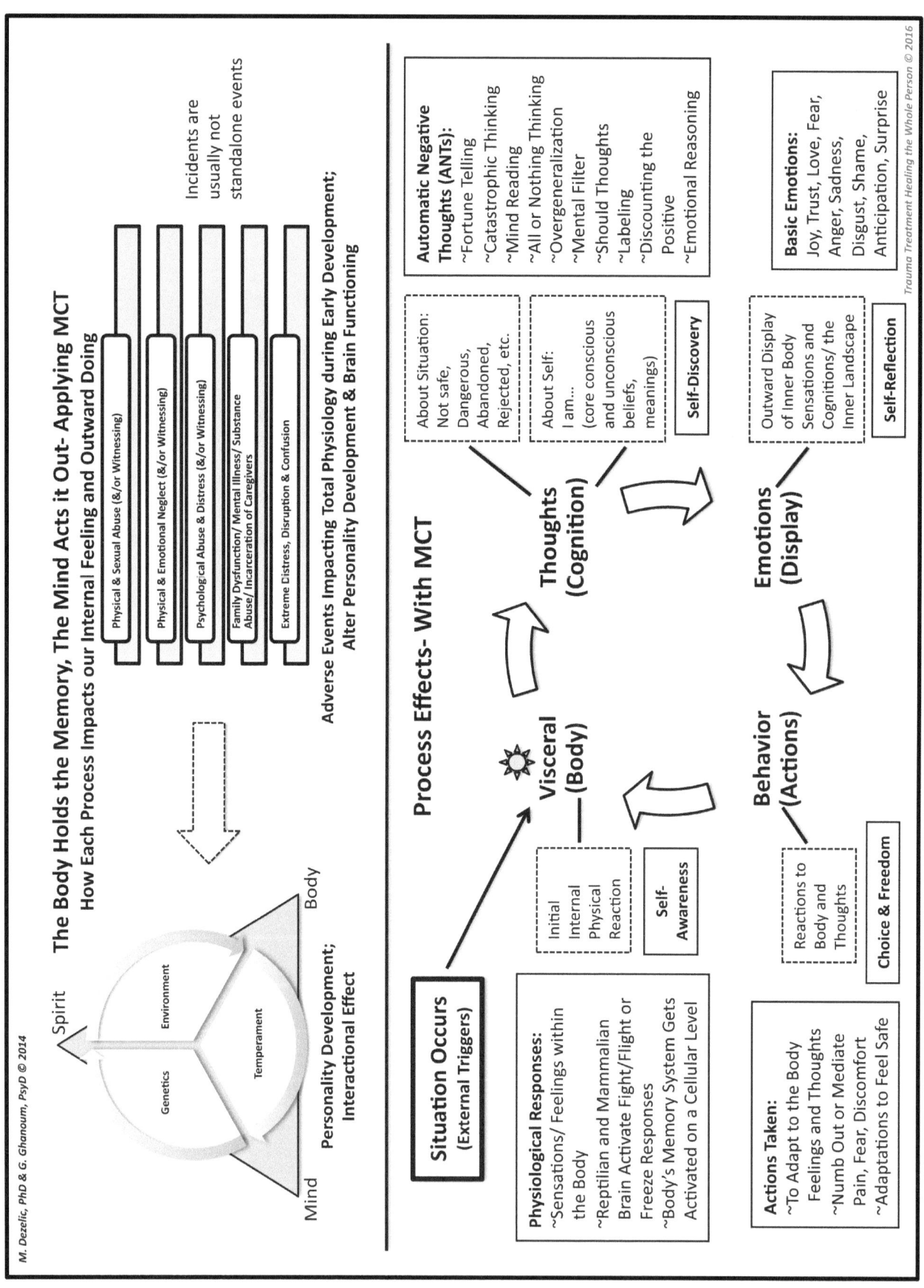

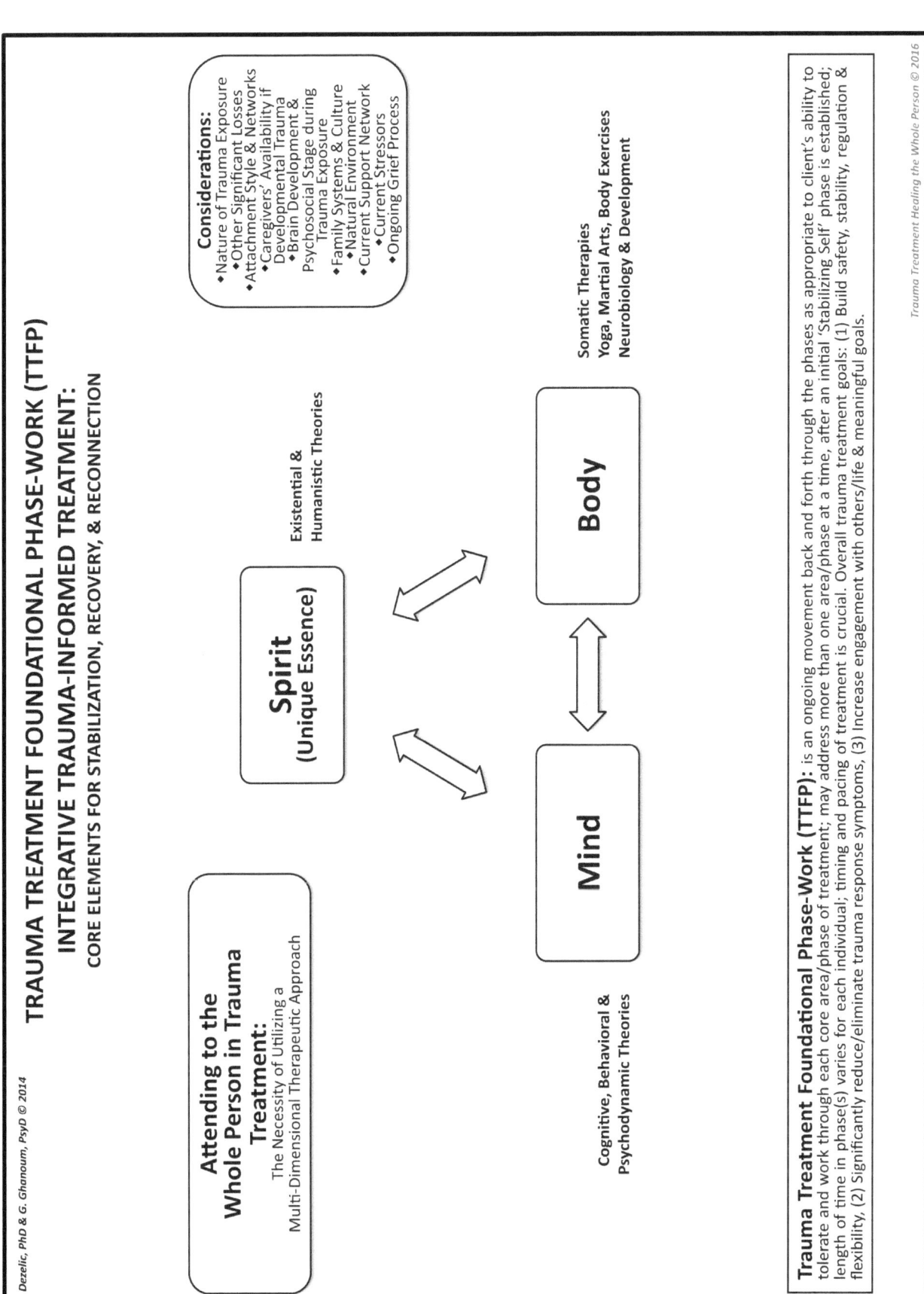

TRAUMA TREATMENT FOUNDATIONAL PHASE-WORK (TTFP)
INTEGRATIVE TRAUMA-INFORMED TREATMENT:
CORE ELEMENTS FOR STABILIZATION, RECOVERY, & RECONNECTION

Trauma Treatment Foundational Phase-Work (TTFP): is an ongoing movement back and forth through the phases as appropriate to client's ability to tolerate and work through each core area/phase of treatment; may address more than one area/phase at a time, after an initial 'Stabilizing Self' phase is established; length of time in phase(s) varies for each individual; timing and pacing of treatment is crucial.

Overall trauma treatment goals: (1) Build safety, stability, regulation & flexibility, (2) Significantly reduce/eliminate trauma response symptoms, (3) Increase engagement with others/life & meaningful goals.

- **Stabilizing Self**: Creating safety and stabilization in the present; trust with therapist; grounding techniques; distress tolerance; self-regulation, affect regulation & modulation; increase window of tolerance/comfort zone, understanding responses; coping techniques; mindfulness; yoga, martial arts, dance, or body practices; learn body awareness and states; develop boundaries; safety within self, ability to tolerate being in own body; resource building; develop sense of agency and competency; increase attachment networks.

- **Traumatic Revisiting**: Revisiting traumatic memories as "touch and go's" quick trips; dual perception, past and present with therapist; continuing safety/stable platform; visualization and feeling of the trauma-1 key scene that can represent all the scenes; start to bring words to the body feelings, sensations, body awareness; explore meanings of feelings and perceptions; EMDR; narrative; parts work.

- **Languaging & Meaning**: Reprocessing, reworking, rewording; work on wording in the present, free association to meanings; uncover the unconscious core belief systems and how these words relate to present actions and thoughts; examine meaning constructions as they correspond with the brain development at time of trauma; uncouple trauma and original meanings, shift to present development and new meanings.

- **Re-Owning**: Owning the disowned part(s), the part that experienced the trauma which have been exiled, is hated, is shameful; identify part of self (child or older) that is stuck in the trauma; examine why it is being denied or protected from the whole system; make a choice to bring this part back to the self, without the old belief system and trauma, bringing the part of self forward to present; visualization of trauma and/or beliefs, removing it, and leave it in the scene; grieving losses.

- **Integration**: Integrating separate parts of self; neural-body-behavioral; create safe place within self, as sacred center/gentle center or internal home; dialoguing with self to get core needs met; self-care, self-reflection, self-awareness, self-discovery, existential analysis.

- **Re-Connection**: Reconnection with self, feeling safe inside one's body; more secure self allows for reconnection with others; healthy boundaries with others; engage in meaningful activities; explore meaning and purpose in life; explore attitude, experiences, and creativity for creating meaning in life; competencies and resource building; new attachment networks.

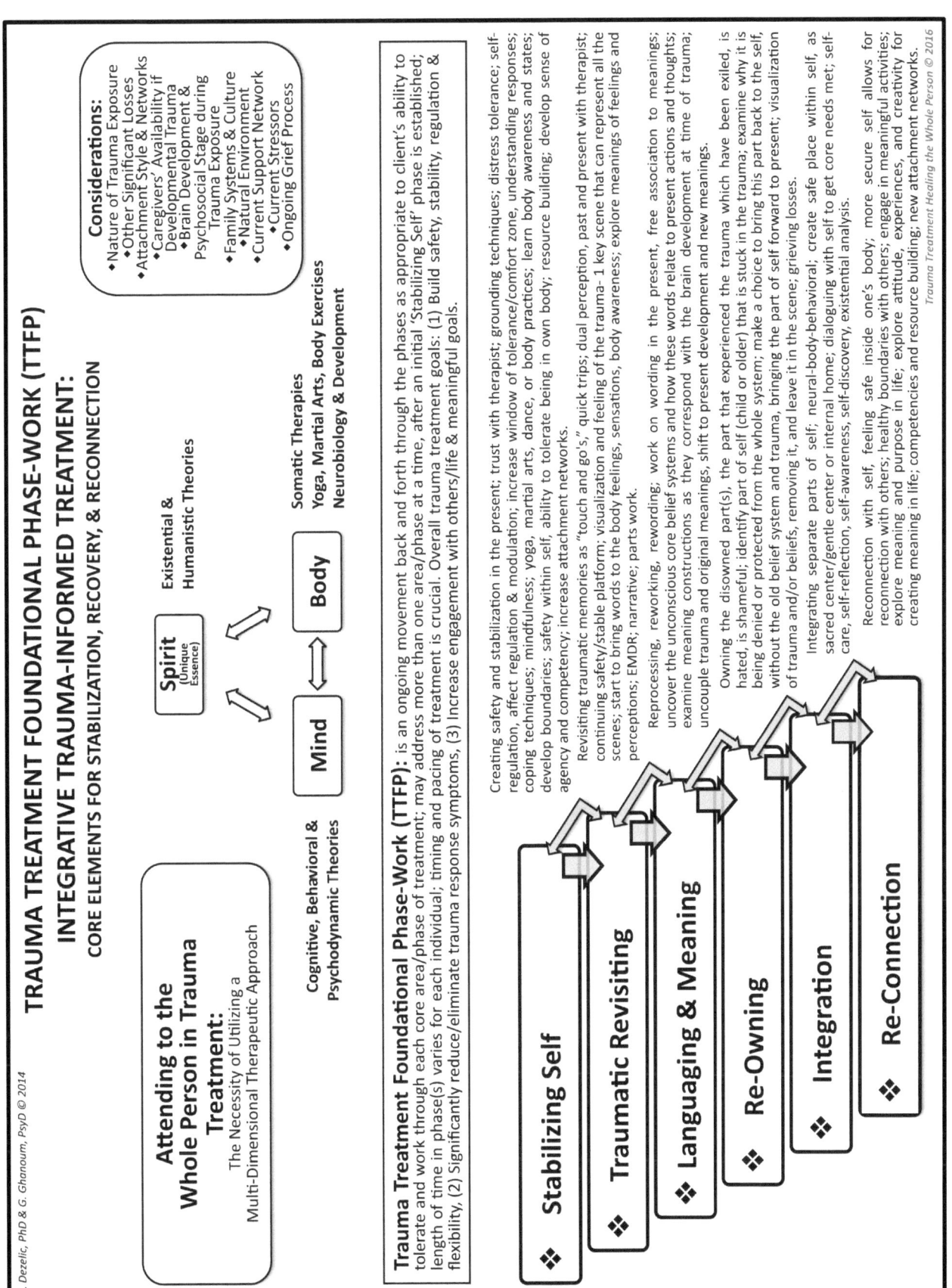

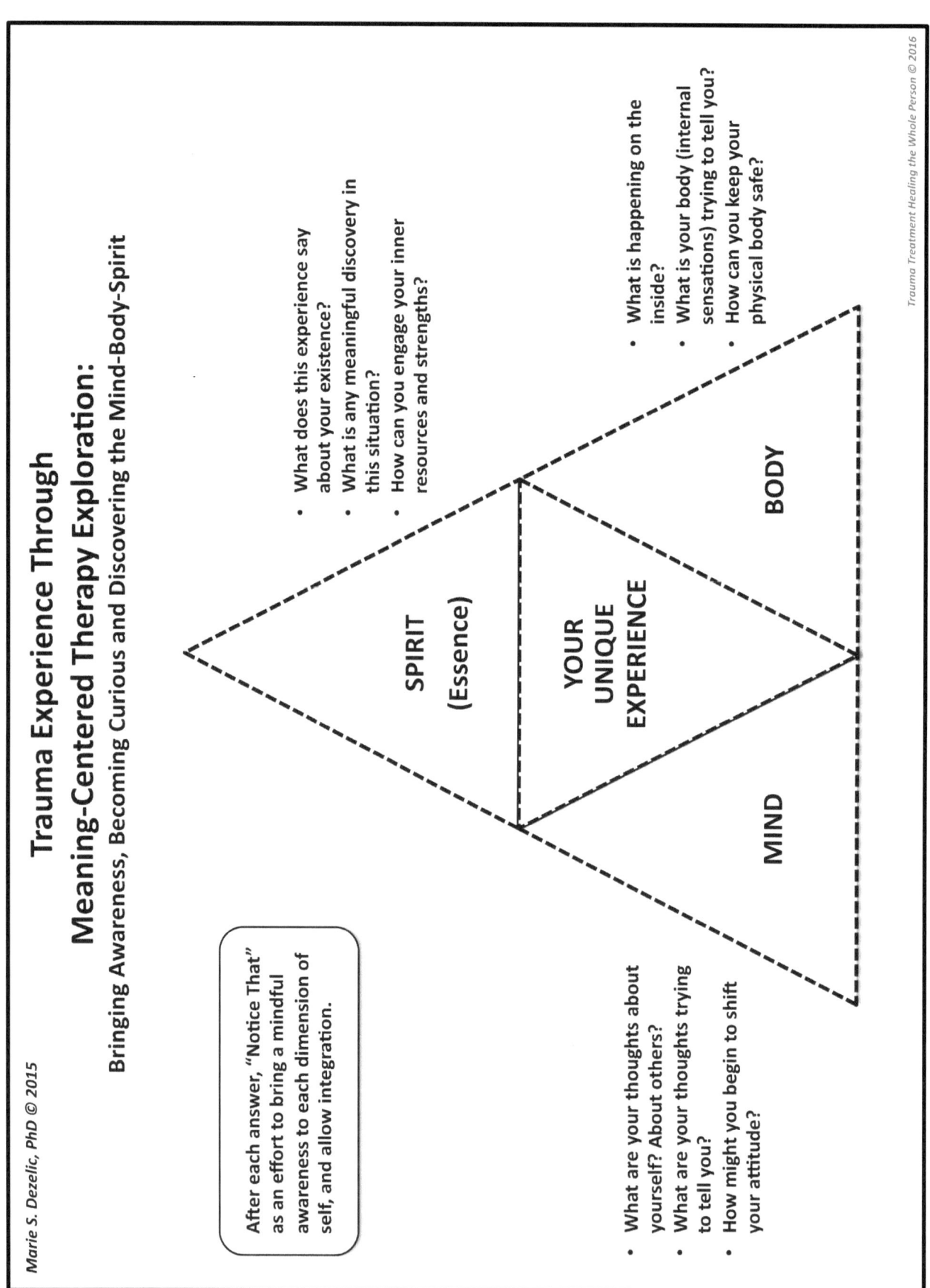

Trauma Treatment - Healing The Whole Person

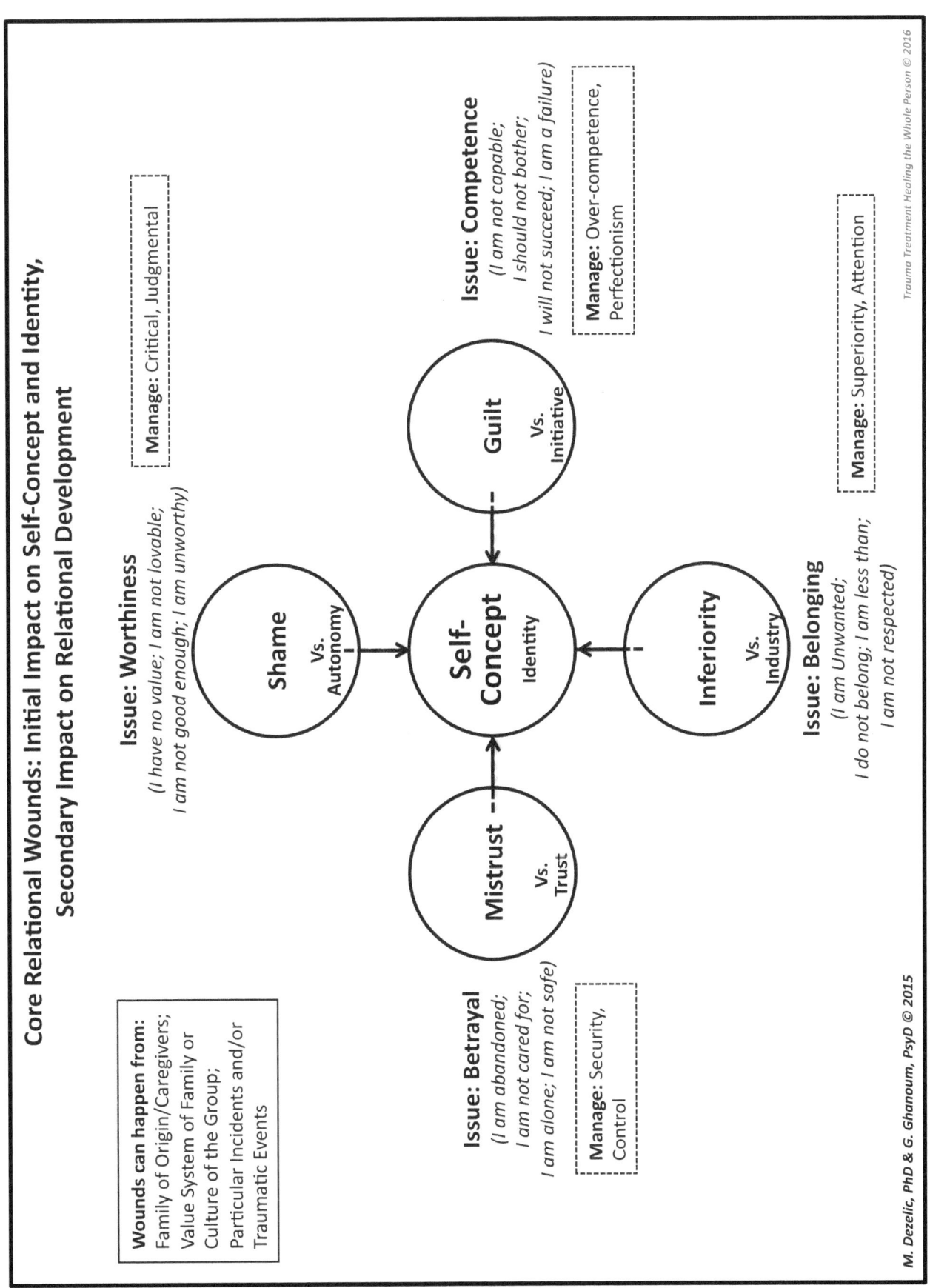

Core Relational Wounds: Initial Impact on Self-Concept and Identity, Secondary Impact on Relational Development

M. Dezelic, PhD & G. Ghanoum, PsyD © 2015

Trauma Treatment - Healing The Whole Person

Core Concepts:
Influence on Identity, Beliefs, and Relating

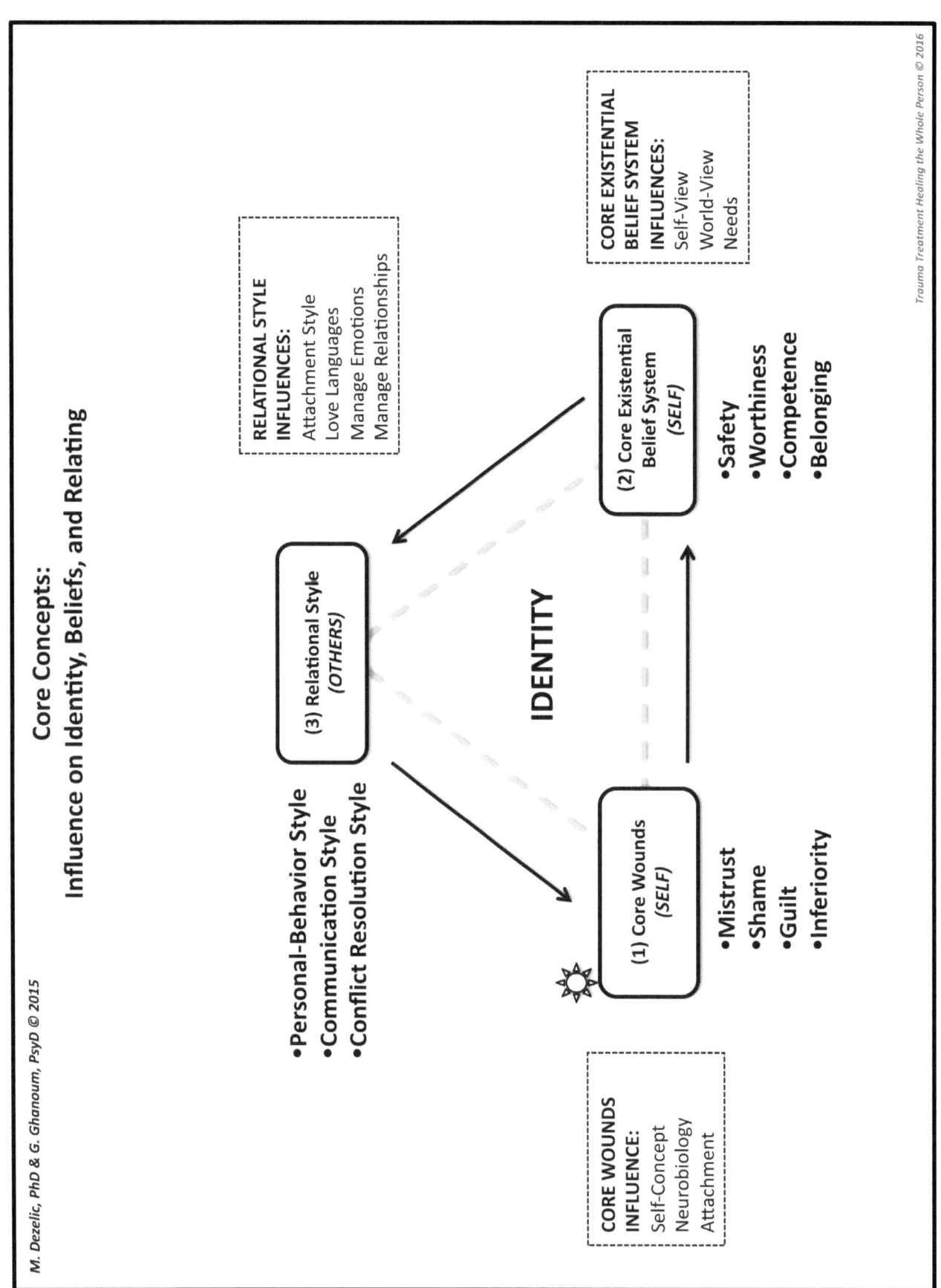

When Getting Triggered Takes Over:
Taking a "Time Out" from the Situation to Take a "Time In" for Self-Discovery

M. Dezelic, PhD & G. Ghanoum, PsyD © 2015

Examining Existence

1) **Self-Awareness**
2) **Self-Reflection**
3) **Self-Discovery**
4) **Self-Connection**
5) **Self-Acceptance**
6) **Self-Transcendence**

Creating Curiosity & Inquiring

"I" am triggered.
Take a "Time Out" to take a "Time In."
Reframe: A "Part" of me is being triggered?

What "Part" of me is being triggered?
Why did this "Part" get triggered?
What are the initial feelings this "Part" felt?

What does this "Part" need, want, or is fearful of?
What behavior is/was this "Part" doing to protect or try to get this need met?

How can "I" meet the need of this "Part"?
How can I nurture this "Part" of me?
What can I do for self-care?

How can "I" begin to create a connection between "Parts" of myself?
Creating an Interconnectedness of Self.

Can I recognize what might be happening in a "Part" of the other?
How can I connect with the other and outward?

"When we create an environment of deeper self-understanding, through self-care, we can create more integration and interconnectedness within our own internal system."

Trauma Treatment Healing the Whole Person © 2016

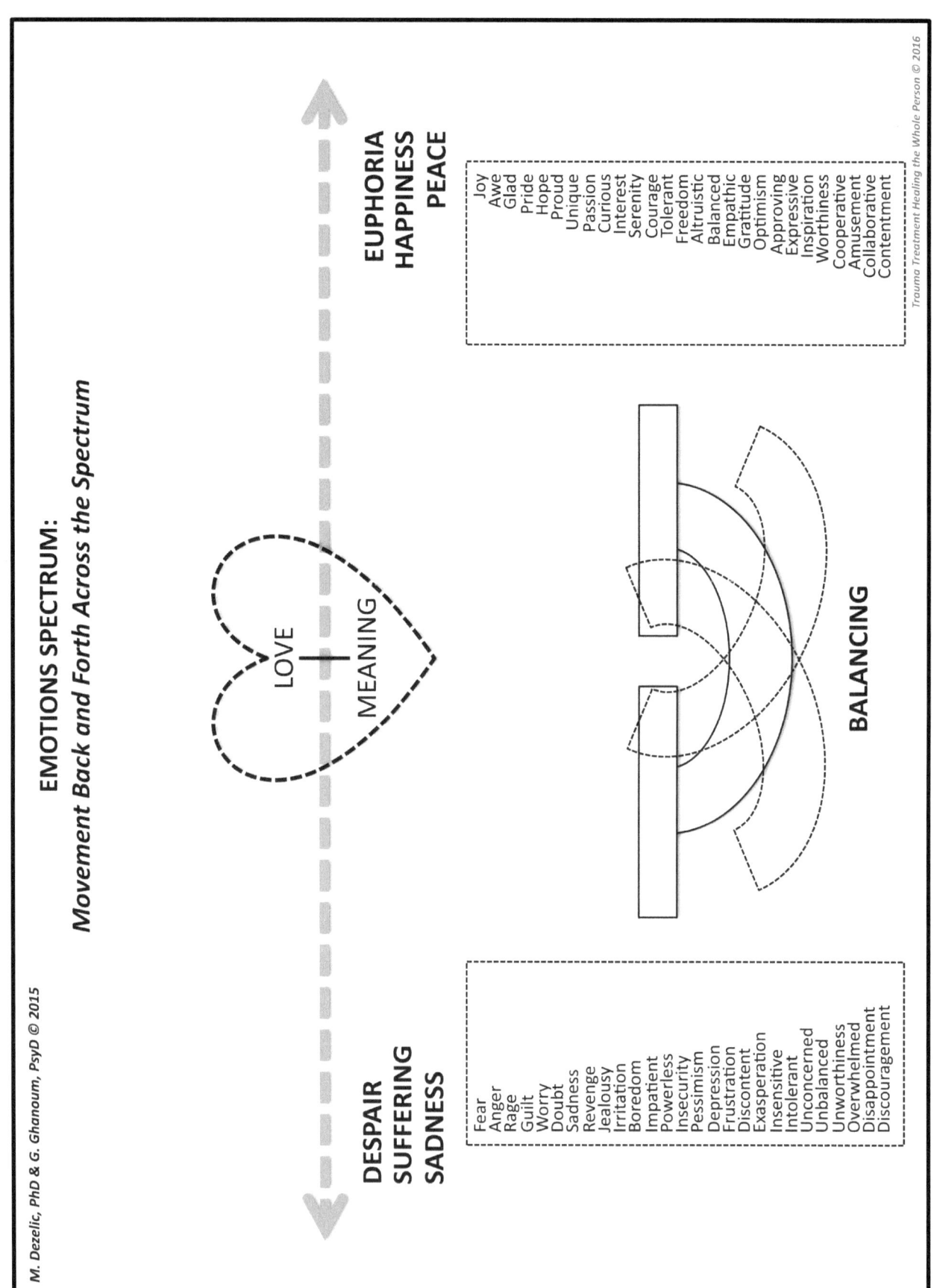

Marie S. Dezelic, PhD ©2013

THE MEANING-ACTION TRIANGLE:
Becoming Existentially Aware

(1.) NOTICE —CONSCIOUS—

- Awareness
- Notice without judgment
- Recognize old patterns
- Become conscious of self-defeating behaviors/cycles
- Acknowledge victim role stance
- Recognize unhealthy relationship interactions
- Be fully present and conscious of self
- Acknowledge one's own existence

(2.) RESPONSIBILITY —TO SELF—

- Awareness, Self-Transcendence
- Responsible to self, to one's meaning in life, to the ultimate meaning of life
- Own one's feelings, actions and behaviors
- Acknowledge wanting to choose to change past self-limiting patterns
- Recognize one's healthy core—Spiritual Nöetic Dimension

(3.) TAKE ACTION —CHOICE—

- Awareness
- Freedom to act
- Choose to be conscious of self-improving behaviors
- Choose not to be a victim
- Decision to have healthy relationship interactions
- Be fully present to and conscious of one's actions
- Acknowledge one's own existence in the present
- Meaning in the moment
- Ultimate meaning

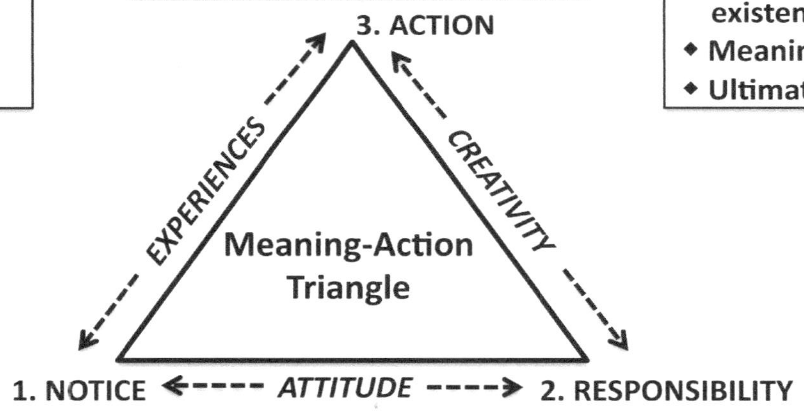

Meaning-Action Triangle

1. NOTICE ←---- ATTITUDE ----→ 2. RESPONSIBILITY
         ---- CREATIVITY ----
         ---- EXPERIENCES ----
3. ACTION

Taking Flight from your PAST, While Being Pulled to your FUTURE

Trauma Treatment Healing the Whole Person © 2016

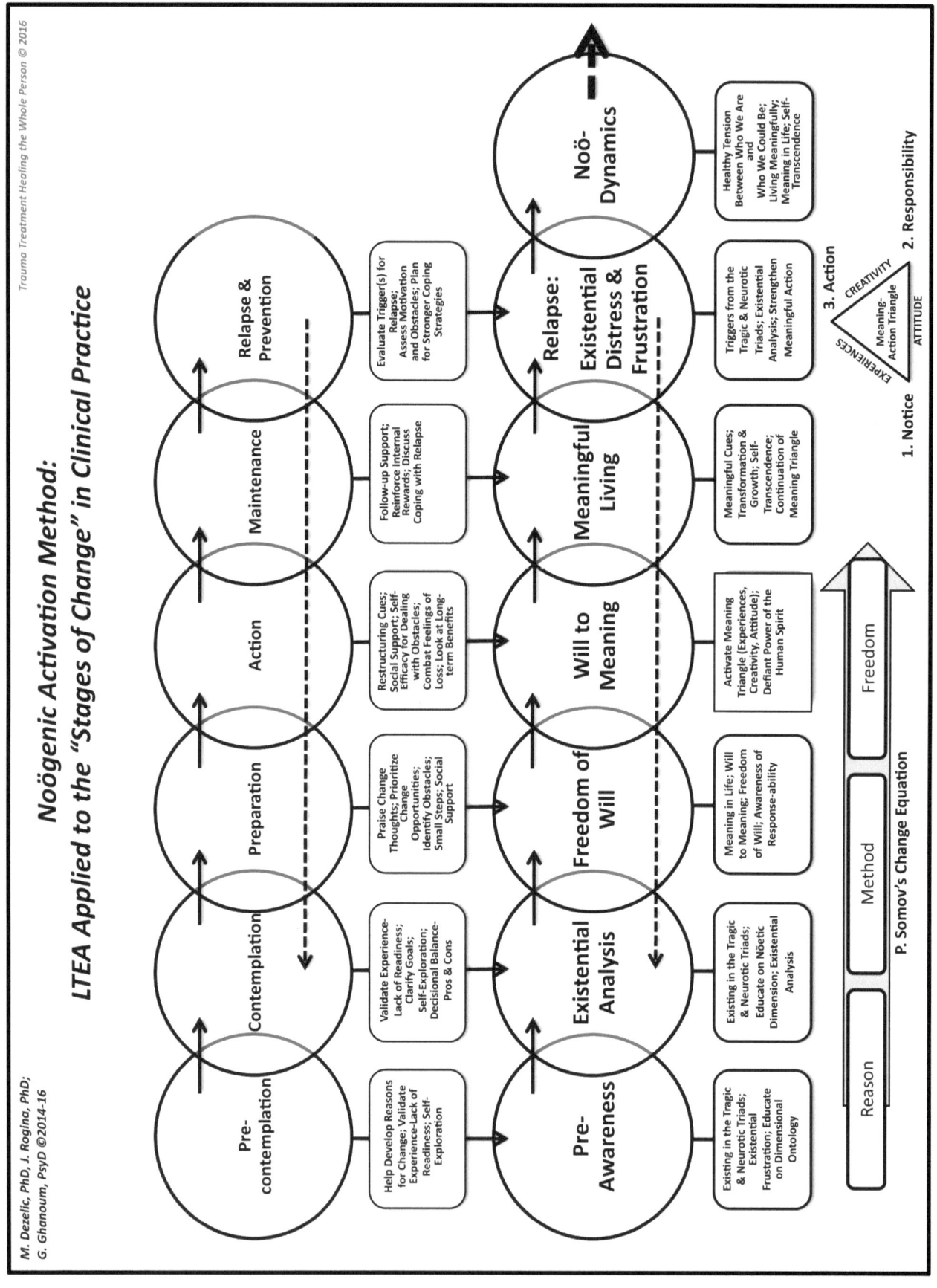

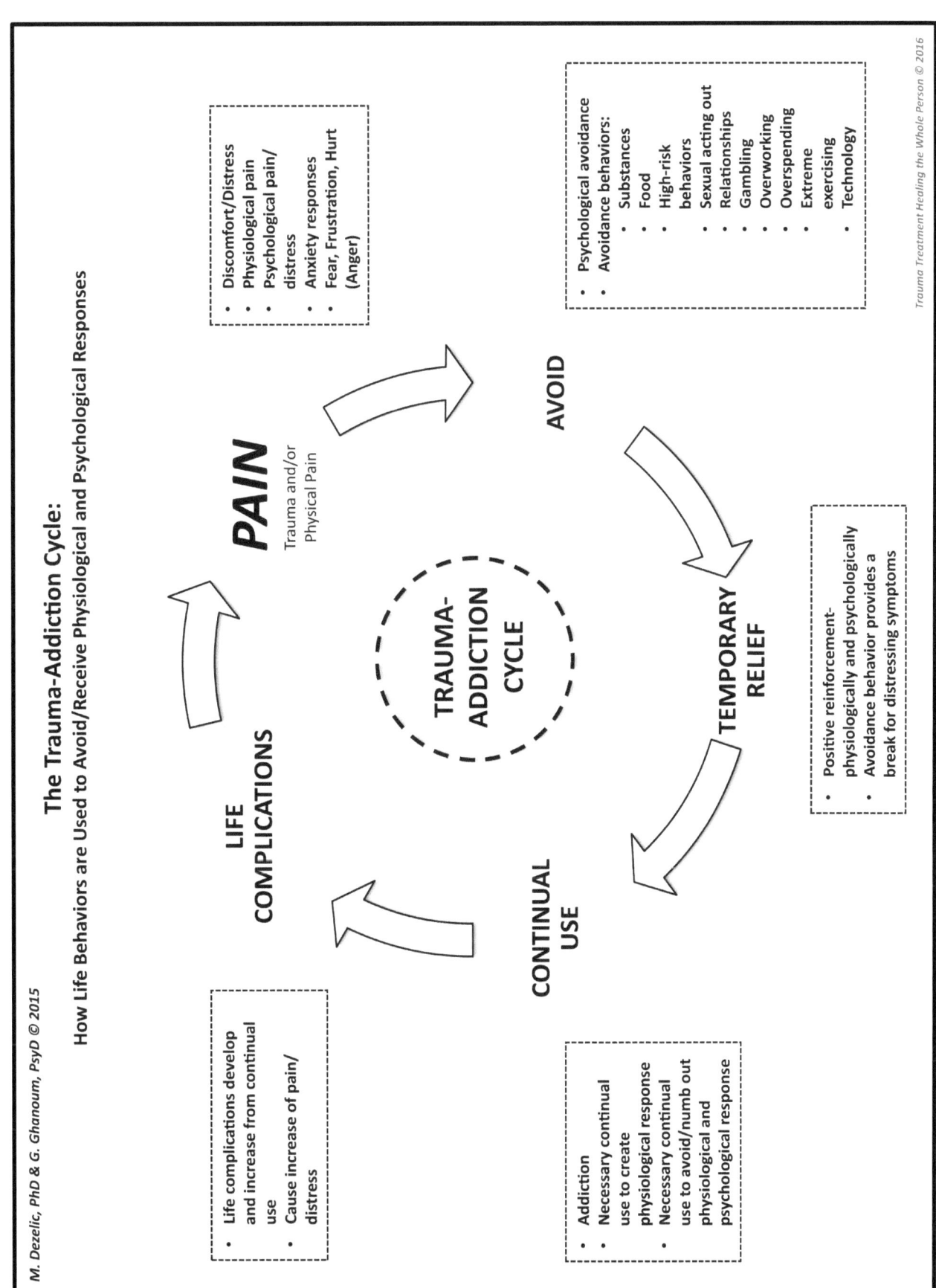

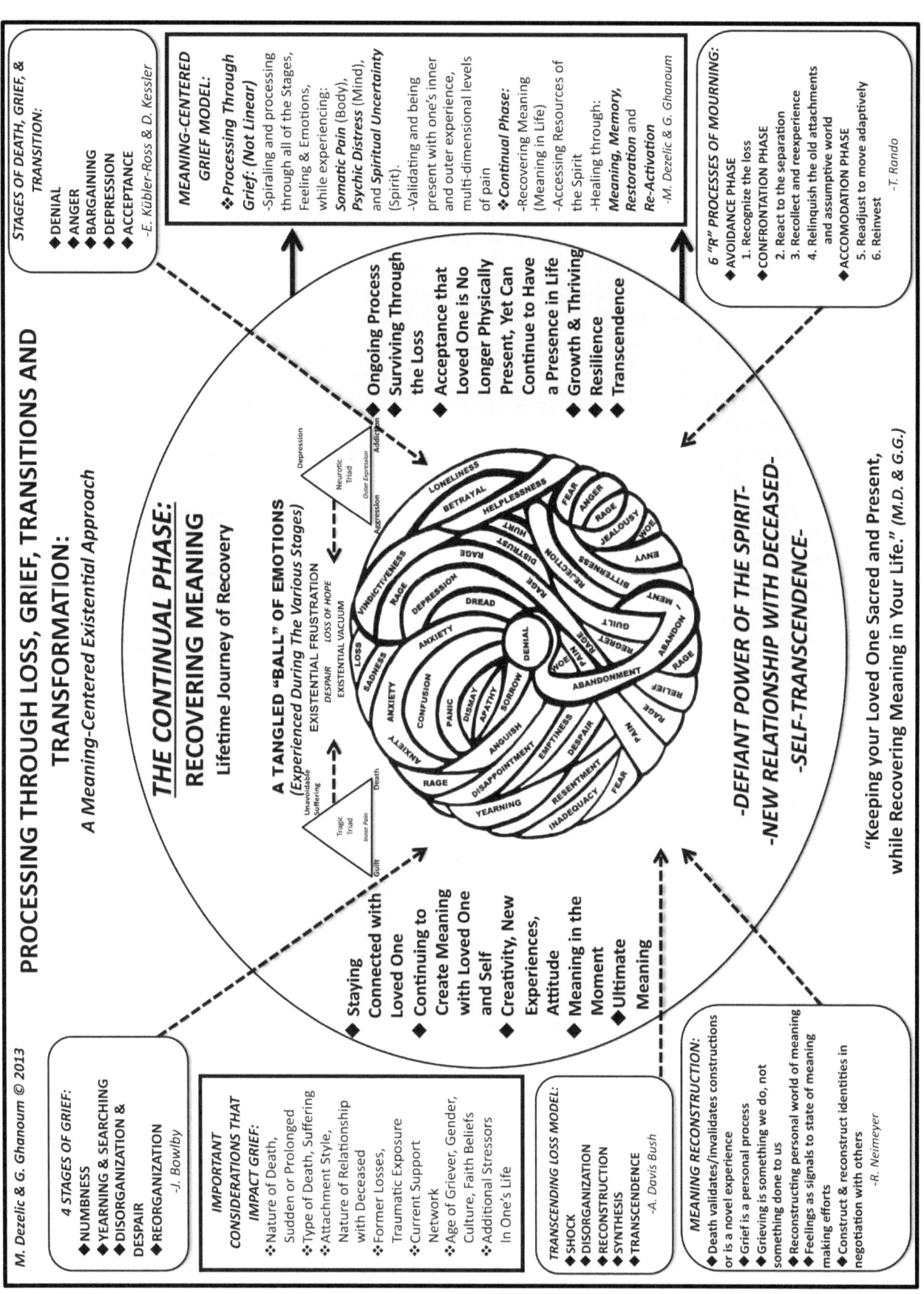

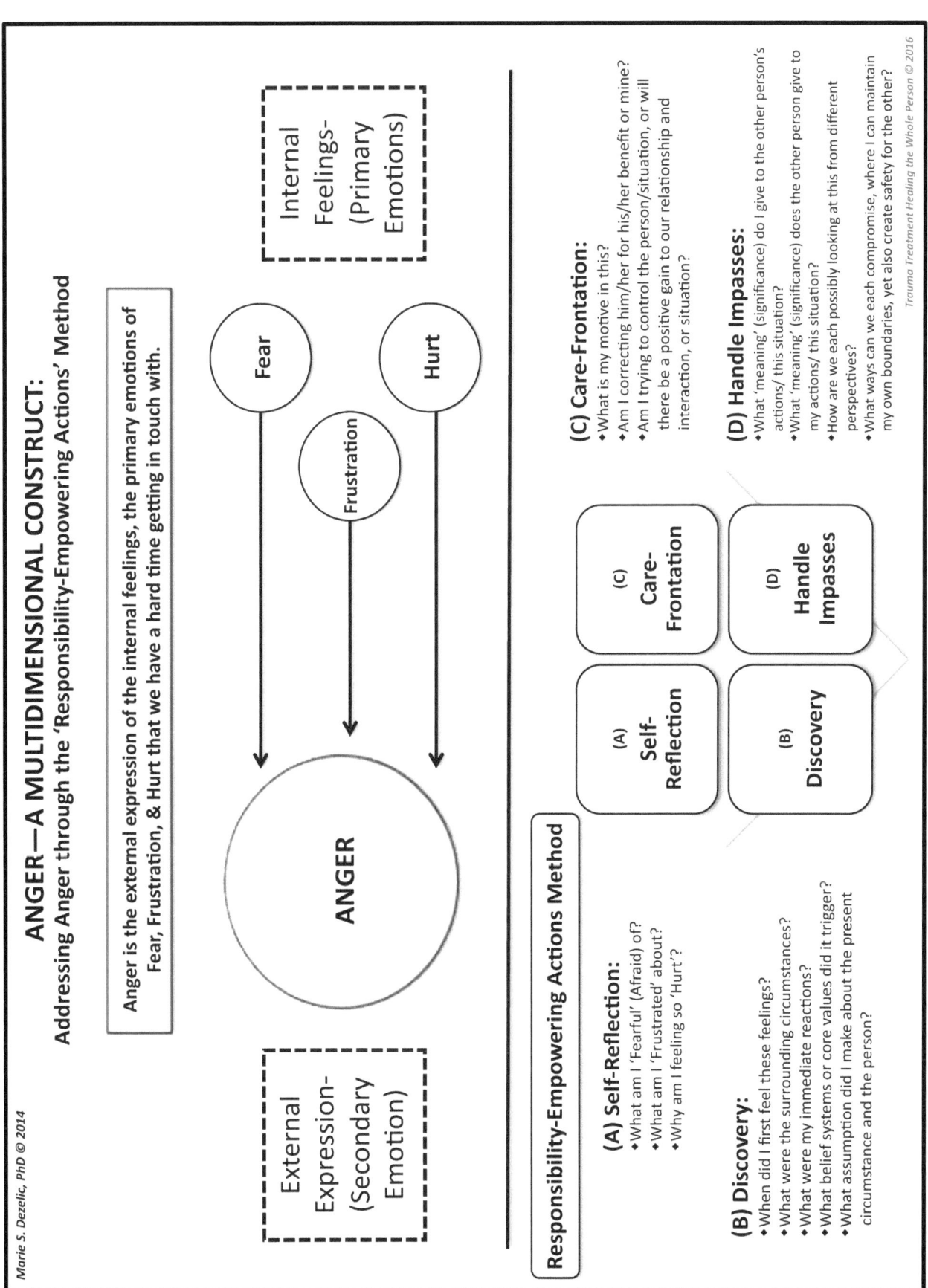

TRAUMA TREATMENT - HEALING THE WHOLE PERSON

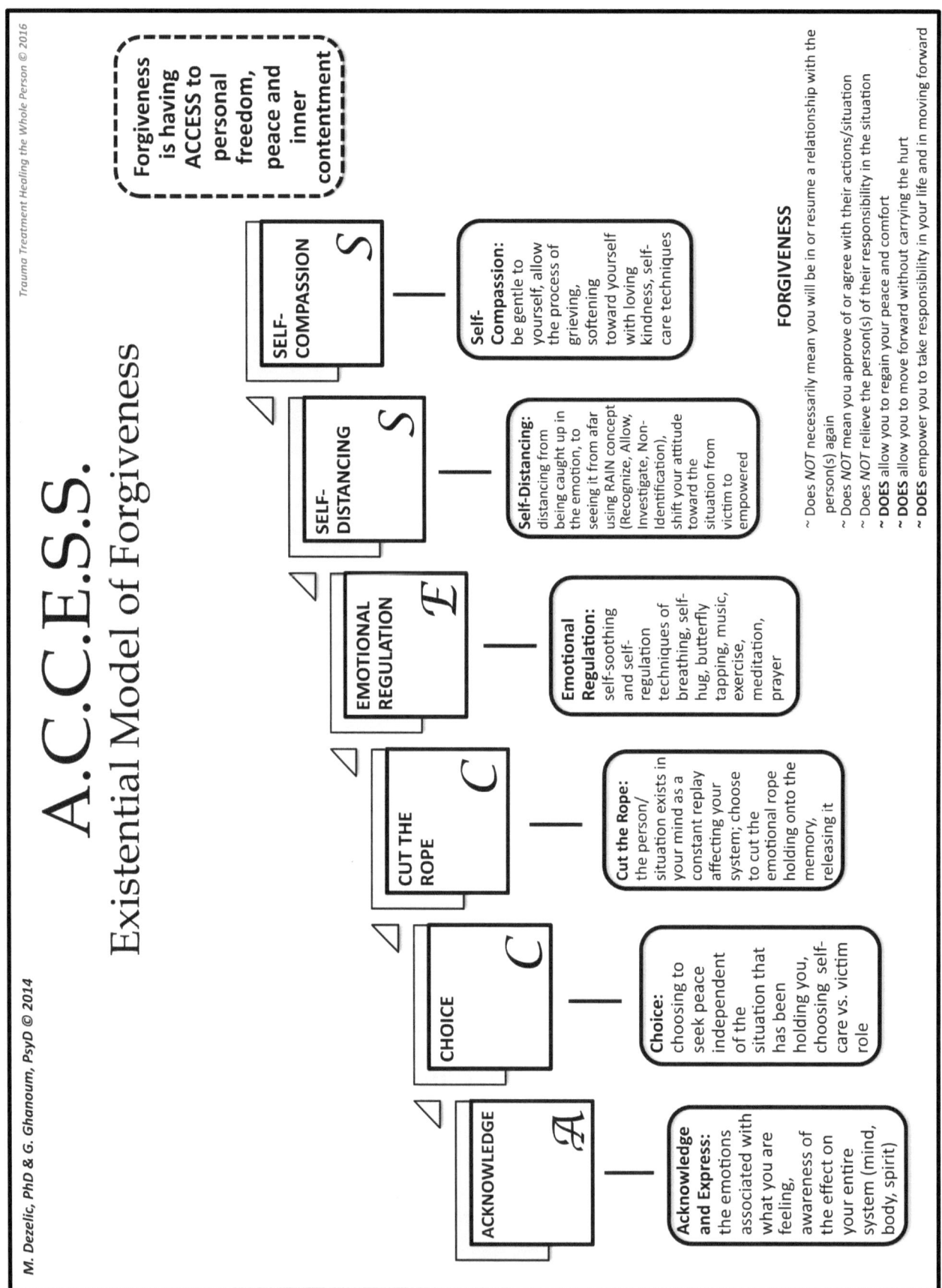

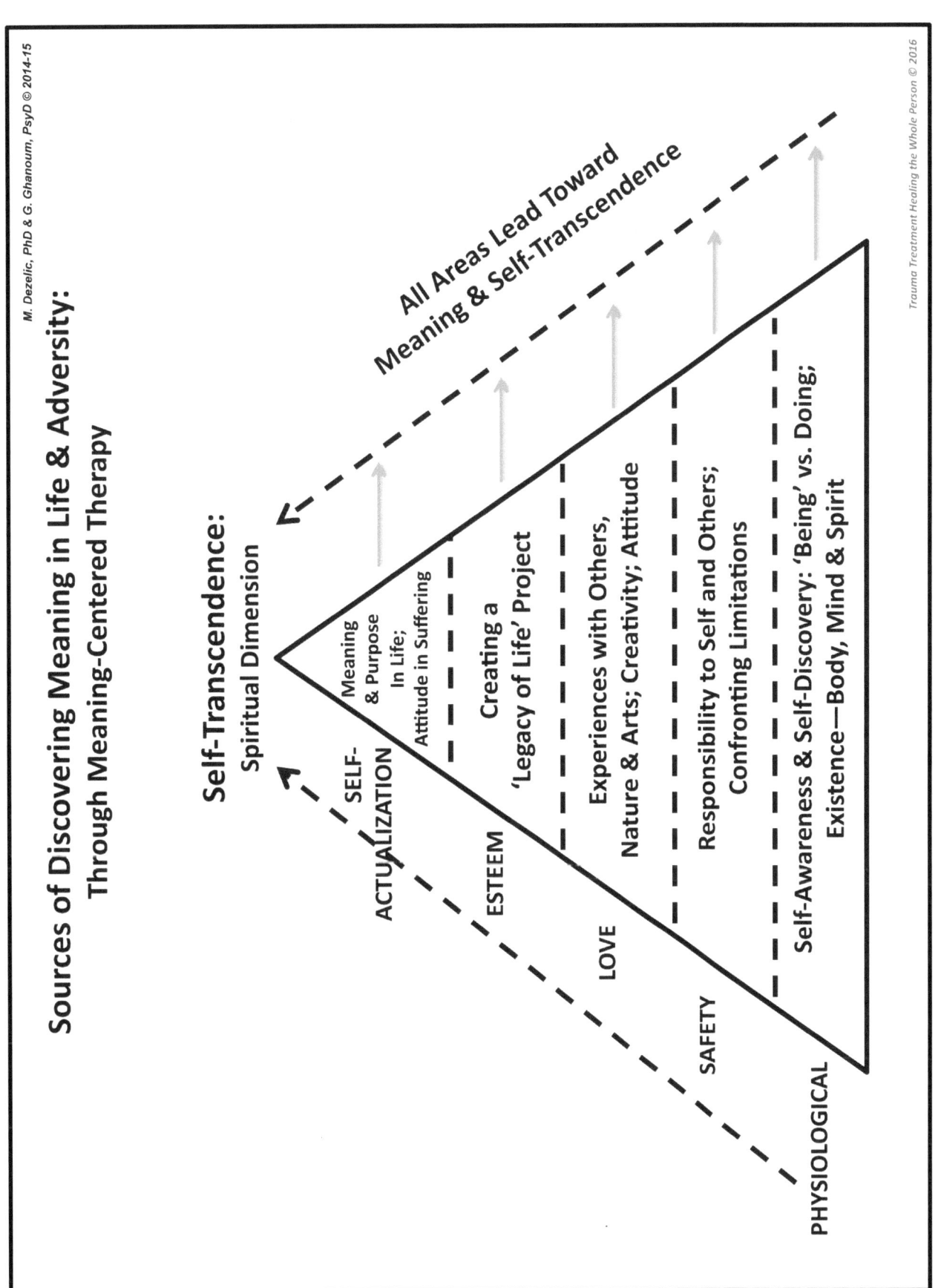

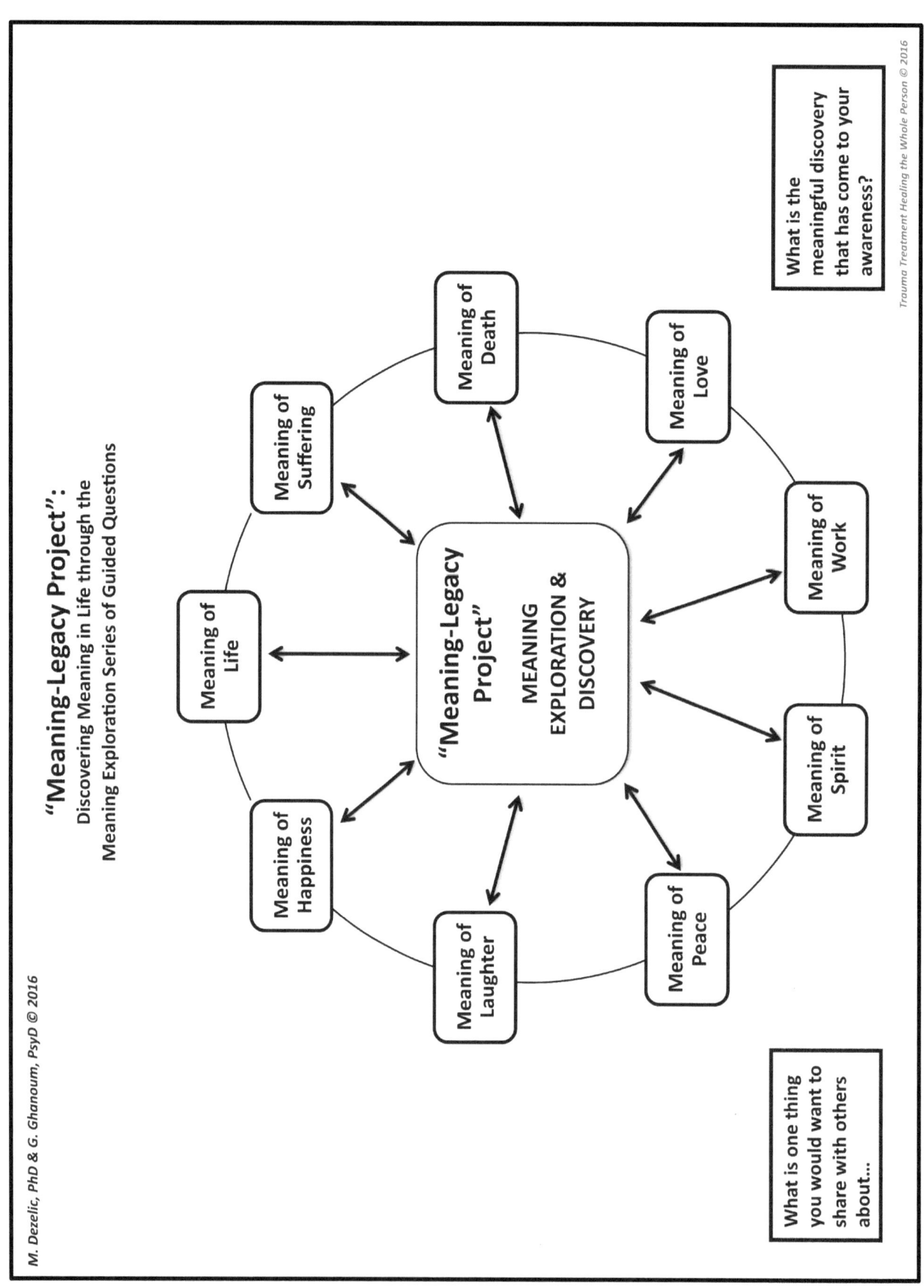

TRAUMA TREATMENT - HEALING THE WHOLE PERSON

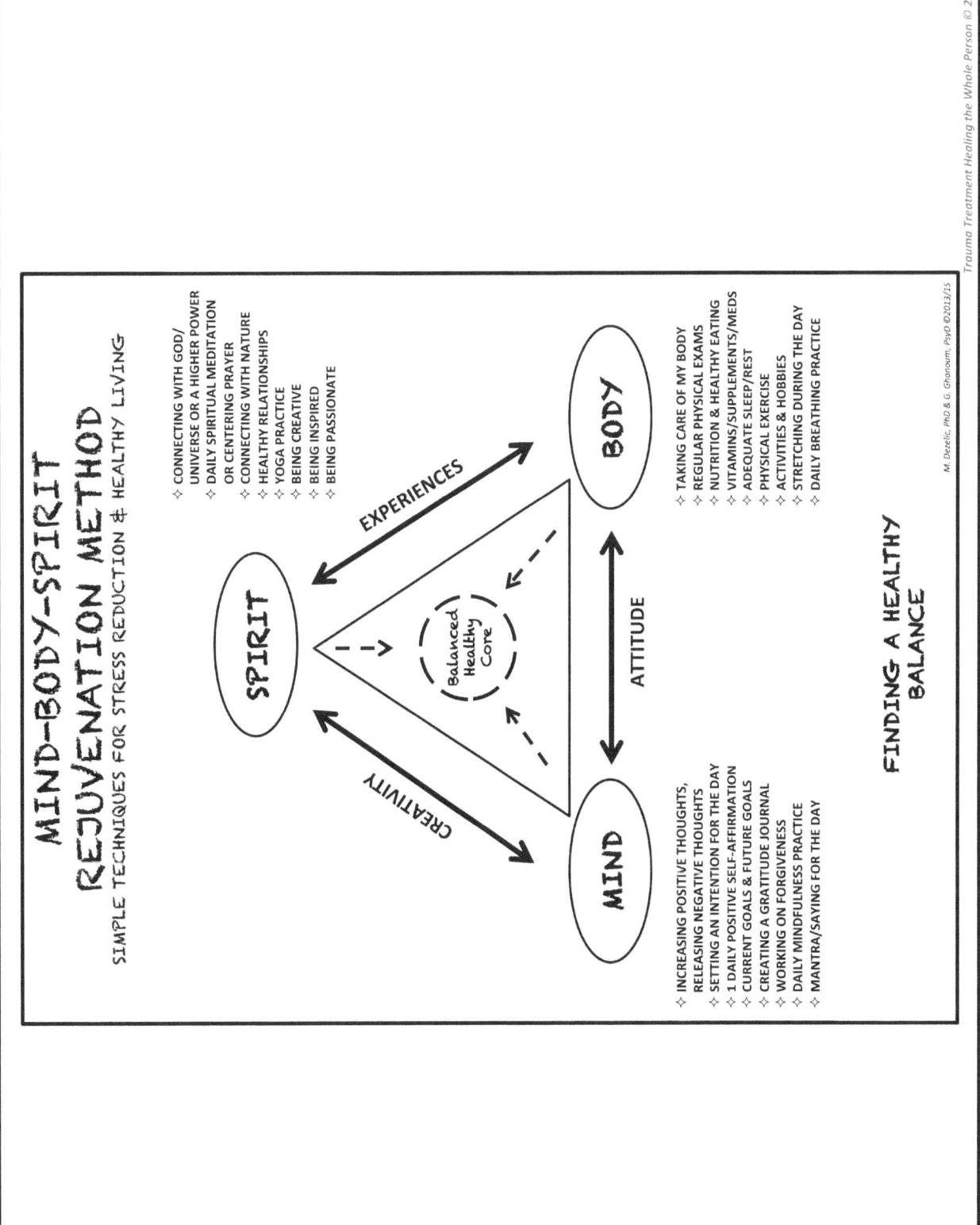

TRAUMA TREATMENT - HEALING THE WHOLE PERSON

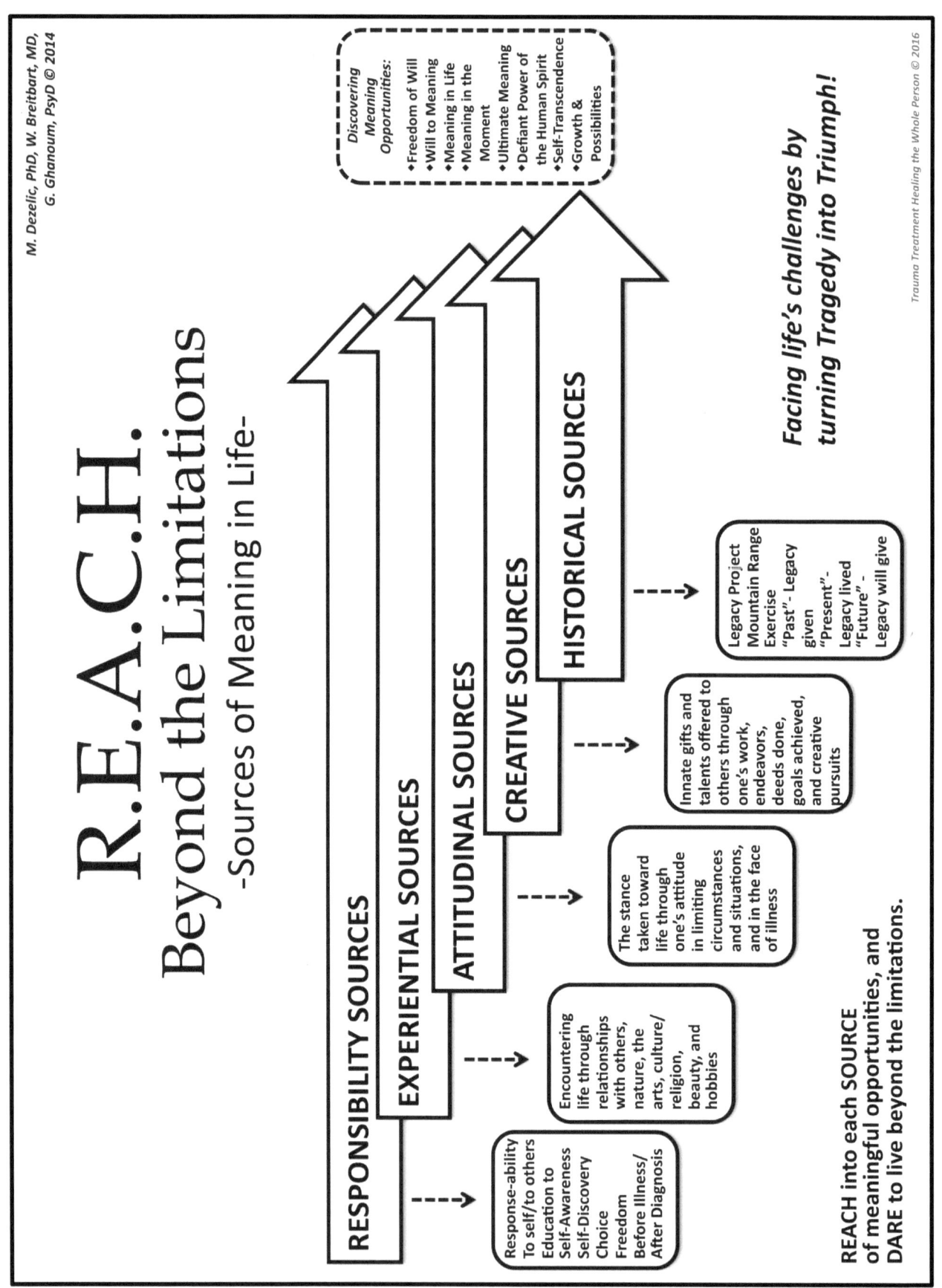

CONNECT—CREATE—CONVEY
Living Life with Meaning and Purpose

M. Dezelic, PhD & G. Ghanoum, PsyD © 2014

Create:
- Access your inner strengths and resources, discovering your natural talents and gifts, and possibilities to bring your uniqueness to the world.
- Be in your life creatively; discover how you bring your unique creativity to tasks, to projects, to your work, to your hobbies, to all of your relationships.

Connect:
- With others who inspire you, motivate you, lift you up, support you, whom you can help, and give of yourself to.
- You can connect with great thinkers, writers, actors, people you look up to, role models (from the past or present).
- You can connect with nature, the arts, culture.

Convey:
- Teach it, give it, bring it, write it, play it, paint it, say it, sing it, dance it; offer your unique creativity in your work, hobbies, causes you serve, and in all of your relationships.
- Convey to the world who you are and live your greater purpose with passion and meaning.

"By connecting we create, by creating we convey, by conveying we connect and create...
By connecting, creating, and conveying we can experience purpose and meaning in life..."

REFERENCES

Barnes, R. C. (1994). Finding meaning in unavoidable suffering. *The International Forum for Logotherapy,* 1(2), 20-26.

Barnes, R. C. (2005). *Franklian psychology: An introduction to logotherapy.* Abilene, Texas: Viktor Frankl Institute of Logotherapy.

Batthyany, A. & Levinson, J., (Eds.). (2009). *Existential psychotherapy of meaning.* Phoenix, AZ: Zeig, Tucker & Theisen, Inc.

Batthyany, A., (Ed.). (2010). *Viktor Frankl, the feeling of meaninglessness: A challenge to psychotherapy and philosophy.* Milwaukee, WI: Marquette University Press.

Blaustein, M. E., & Kinniburgh, K. M. (2010). *Treating traumatic stress in children and adolescents: How to foster resilience through attachment, self-regulation, and competency.* New York: The Guilford Press.

Boon, S., Steele, K., & van der Hart, O. (2011). *Coping with trauma-related dissociation: Skills training for patients and their therapists.* New York: W. W. Norton & Company, Inc.

Borysenko, J. (1988). *Minding the body, mending the mind.* NY: Bantam.

Bowlby, J. (1961). Processes of mourning. *International Journal of Psychoanalysis,* 42, 317-340.

Bowlby, J. (1980). *Attachment and loss: Loss, sadness, and depression.* New York: Basic Books.

Breitbart, W., Rosenfeld, B., Gibson, C., Pessin, H., Poppito, S., Nelson, C., Tomarken, A., et al. (2010). Meaning-centered group psychotherapy for patients with advanced cancer: a randomized controlled trial. *Psycho-Oncology, 19,* 21-28.

Breitbart, W., Poppito, S., Rosenfeld, B., Vickers, A. J., Li, Y. Abbey, J., Olden, M., et al. (2012). Pilot randomized controlled trial of individual meaning-centered psychotherapy for patients with advanced cancer. *Journal of Clinical Oncology, 30,* 1304-1309.

Breitbart, W. S. & Poppito, S. R. (2014a). *Meaning-centered group psychotherapy for patients with advanced cancer, a treatment manual.* NY: Oxford University Press.

Breitbart, W. S. & Poppito, S. R. (2014b). *Meaning-centered individual psychotherapy for patients with advanced cancer, a treatment manual.* NY: Oxford University Press.

Breitbart, W., Rosenfeld, B., Pessin, H., Applebaum, A., Kulikowski, J., & Lichtenthal, W. G. (2015). Meaning-centered group psychotherapy: An effective intervention for improving psychological well-being in patients with advanced cancer. *Journal of Clinical Oncology, 33,* 749-754. doi: 10.1200/JCO.2014.57.2198.

Clements, P., Vigil, G., et al., (2003). Cultural perspectives of death, grief and bereavement. *Journal of Psychosocial Nursing,* 41(7).

Curran, L. A. (2010). *Trauma competency: A clinician's guide.* Eau Claire, WI: PESI, LLC.

Curran, L. A. (2013). *101 trauma-informed interventions: Activities, exercises and assignments to move the client and therapy forward.* Eau Claire, WI: PESI, LLC.

Davis Bush, A. (1997). *Transcending loss: Understanding the lifelong impact of grief and how to make it meaningful.* New York: The Berkley Publishing Group.

Dezelic, M. S. (2014). *Meaning-centered therapy workbook: Based on Viktor Frankl's logotherapy and existential analysis.* San Rafael, CA: Palace Printing and Design.

Dezelic, M. S. & Ghanoum, G. (2015). *Meaning-centered therapy manual: Logotherapy & existential analysis brief therapy protocol for group & individual sessions.* Miami, FL: Presence Press International.

Dezelic, M. S. & Ghanoum, G. (2016). *Meaning in life in palliative care: Bio-psycho-social-spiritual approach in healthcare.* Miami, FL: Presence Press International (in press).

Fabry, J. (1988). *Guideposts to meaning: Discovering what really matters.* Oakland, CA: New Harbinger Publications, Inc.

Fabry, J. B. (2013). *The pursuit of meaning: Viktor Frankl, logotherapy, and life.* Birmingham, AL: Purpose Research.

Fisher, S. F. (2014). *Neurofeedback in the treatment of developmental trauma: Calming the fear-driven brain.* New York: W. W. Norton & Company, Inc.

Foa, E. B., Keane, T. M., Friedman, M. J., & Cohen, J. A. (Eds.) (2009). *Effective treatments for PTSD: Practical guidelines from the International Society for Traumatic Stress Studies, Second Edition.* New York: The Guilford Press.

Frankl, V. E. (1978). *The unheard cry for meaning: Psychotherapy and humanism.* New York: Simon and Schuster, Inc.

Frankl, V. E. (1986). *The doctor and the soul: From psychotherapy to logotherapy (2nd Vintage Books Ed.).* New York: Random House, Inc.

Frankl, V. E. (1988). *The will to meaning: Foundations and applications of logotherapy (Expanded Ed.).* New York: Penguin Books USA Inc.

Frankl, V. E. (2000). *Man's search for ultimate meaning.* New York: Perseus Publishing.

Frankl, V. E. (2004). *On the theory and therapy of mental disorders: An introduction to logotherapy and existential analysis (James M. Dubois, Translation).* New York: Brunner-Routledge.

Frankl, V. E. (2006). *Man's search for meaning.* Boston, Massachusetts: Beacon Press.

Graber, A. V. (2004). *Viktor Frankl's logotherapy: Method of choice in ecumenical pastoral psychotherapy* (2nd Ed.). Lima, Ohio: Wyndham Hall Press.

Graber, A. V. (2009). *The journey home: Preparing for life's ultimate adventure.* Birmingham, Alabama: LogoLife Press.

Heller, L., & LaPierre, A. (2012). *Healing developmental trauma: How early trauma affects self-regulation, self-image, and the capacity for relationship.* Berkeley, CA: North Atlantic Books.

Herman, J. (1997). *Trauma and recovery: The aftermath of violence—from domestic abuse to political terror.* New York: Basic Books.

Johnson, S. (2008). *Hold me tight: Seven conversations for a lifetime of love.* New York: Little, Brown and Company.

Kubler-Ross, E. (1969). *On death and dying.* New York: Scribner.

Kubler-Ross, E., & Kessler, D. (2005). *On grief and grieving: Finding the meaning of grief through the five stages of loss.* New York: Scribner.

Levine, P. A. (1997). *Waking the tiger: Healing trauma.* Berkeley, CA: North Atlantic Books.

Levine, P. A. (2005). *Healing trauma: A pioneering program for restoring the wisdom of your body.* Boulder, CO: Sounds True.

Levine, P. A. (2010). *In an unspoken voice: How the body releases trauma and restores goodness.* Berkeley, CA: North Atlantic Books.

Levine, A. & Heller, R. S. F. (2010). *Attached: The new science of adult attachment and how it can help you find—and keep—love.* New York: Jeremy P. Tarcher/Penguin.

Lukas, E. (2000). *Logotherapy textbook: Meaning-centered psychotherapy consistent with the principles outlined by Viktor E. Frankl, MD, Concept of human beings and methods in logotherapy* (Theodor Brugger, Translation). Toronto, Canada: Liberty Press.

Lukas, E. (2014). *Meaning in suffering: Comfort in crisis through Logotherapy (Joseph Fabry, Translation).* Birmingham, AL: Purpose Research.

May, R., Angel, E. & Ellenberger, H. F. (Eds). 1958. *Existence.* New York: Rowman & Littlefield Publishers, Inc.

May, R. (1994). *The courage to create.* New York: W. W. Norton & Company Ltd.

Mendelsohn, M., Herman, J. L., Schatzow, E., Coco, M., Kallivayalil, D., & Levitan, J. (2011). *The trauma recovery group: A guide for practitioners.* New York: The Guilford Press.

Merriam-Webster (2005). *Merriam-Webster's Collegiate Dictionary.* Springfield, MA: Merriam-Webster Inc.

Neimeyer, R. A. (Ed.). (2001). *Meaning reconstruction and the experience of loss.* Washington, DC: American Psychological Association.

Neimeyer, R. A. (2006). *Lessons of loss: A guide to coping.* Memphis, TN: Center of the Study of Loss and Transition.

Neimeyer, R. A. (Ed.) (2012). *Techniques of grief therapy: Creative practices for counseling the bereaved.* New York: Routledge.

Ogden, P., Minton, K., & Pain, C. (2006). *Trauma and the body: A sensorimotor approach to psychotherapy.* New York: W. W. Norton & Company, Inc.

Parnell, L. (2013). *Attached-focused EMDR: Healing relational trauma.* New York: W. W. Norton & Company.

Pattakos, A. (2008). *Prisoners of our thoughts: Viktor Frankl's principles for discovering meaning in life and work.* San Francisco, CA: Berrett-Koehler Publishers, Inc.

Pattakos, A. & Dundon, E. (2015). *The OPA! way: Finding joy & meaning in everyday life & work.* Dallas, TX: BenBella Books, Inc.

Porges, S. W. (2011). *The polyvagal theory: Neurophysiological foundations of emotions, attachment, communication, and self-regulation.* New York: W. W. Norton & Company, Inc.

Rainer, J. (2013). *Life after loss: Contemporary grief counseling and therapy.* Eau Claire, WI: PESI Publishing and Media.

Raja, S. (2012). *Overcoming trauma and PTSD: A workbook integrating skills from ACT, DBT, and CBT.* Oakland, CA: New Harbinger Publications, Inc.

Rando, R. A. (1993). *Treatment of complicated mourning.* Champaign, IL: Research Press.

Rice, G. E., Graber, A. V., Sjolie I., Pitts, M. A., & Rogina, J. M. (2004). *Franklian psychology: Meaning-centered interventions.* Abilene, Texas: Viktor Frankl Institute of Logotherapy.

Rogina, J. M. (2013, June). Importance of second-order change in clinical practice of logotherapy and existential analysis (LTEA), Presentation, *XIX World Congress V. Frankl's Logotherapy,* Dallas, TX. jmrogina@sbcglobal.net.

Rothschild, B. (2000). *The body remembers: The psychophysiology of trauma and trauma treatment.* New York: W. W. Norton & Company, Inc.

Scaer, R. (2005). *The trauma spectrum: Hidden wounds and human resiliency.* New York: W. W. Norton & Company, Inc.

Schwartz, R. C. (1995). *Internal family systems therapy.* New York: The Guilford Press.

Shapiro, F. (2001). *Eye movement desensitization and reprocessing: Basic principles, protocols, and procedures.* New York: The Guilford Press.

Shapiro, R. (2010). *The trauma treatment handbook: Protocols across the spectrum.* New York: W. W. Norton & Company, Inc.

Shore, A. (1994). *Affect development and the origin of the self: The neurobiology of emotional development.* Hillsdale, NJ: Lawrence Erlbaum.

Siegel, D. J. (2011). *Mindsight: The new science of personal transformation.* New York: Bantam Books Trade Paperbacks.

Siegel, D. J. (2012). *Pocket guide to interpersonal neurobiology: An integrative handbook of the mind.* New York: W. W. Norton & Company, Inc.

Siegel, R. D. (2010). *The mindfulness solution.* New York: The Guildford Press.

Simon Gunn, J. & Potter, B. (2015). *Borderline personality disorder: New perspectives on a stigmatizing and overused diagnosis.* Santa Barbara, CA: ABC-CLIO, LLC.

Solomon, M. F., & Siegel, D. J. (Eds.) (2003). *Healing trauma: Attachment, mind, body, and brain.* New York: W. W. Norton & Company, Inc.

Somov, P. G. (2008). *Choice awareness: Logotherapy and mindfulness training for treatment of addictions.* I-Catching Books.

Somov, P. G. (2013). *Anger management jumpstart: A 4-session mindfulness path to compassion and change.* Eau Claire: WI: PESI Publishing and Media.

Sunoo, B.P. (2002). Cultural Diversity and Grief. *The Forum newsletter, Association for Death Education and Counseling*, March/April issue, 1-4.

van der Kolk, B., McFarlane, A. C., & Weisaeth, L. (Eds.) (2006). *Traumatic stress: The effects of overwhelming experience on mind, body, and society.* New York: The Guilford Press.

van der Kolk, B. (2014). *The body keeps the score: Brain, mind, and body in the healing of trauma.* New York: Viking.

Van Dernoot Lipsky, L. & Burk, C. (2009). *Trauma stewardship: An everyday guide to caring for self while caring for others.* San Francisco, CA: Berrett-Koehlher Publishers, Inc.

van Deurzen-Smith, E. (1997). *Everyday mysteries: Existential dimensions of psychotherapy.* New York: Routledge.

Welter, P. R. (2005). *Franklian psychology: Attitudinal change.* Abilene, Texas: Viktor Frankl Institute of Logotherapy.

Williams, M. B., & Poijula, S. (2002). *The PTSD workbook: Simple, effective techniques for overcoming traumatic stress symptoms.* Oakland, CA: New Harbinger Publications, Inc.

Winokuer, H. R., & Harris, D. L. (2012). *Principles and practice of grief counseling.* New York: Springer Publishing Company.

Worden, J. W. (1991). *Grief counseling and grief therapy: A handbook for the mental health practitioner*. New York: Springer.

Yalom, I. D. (1980). *Existential Psychotherapy.* New York: Basic Books.

Yalom, I. D. & Leszcz, M. (2005). *Theory and practice of group psychotherapy, (5th Ed.).* New York: Basic Books.

SPECIAL RECOGNITION
Information adapted from and embodied within this Workbook from:

Meaning-Centered Therapy Manual:
Logotherapy & Existential Analysis Brief Therapy Protocol
For Group & Individual Sessions
8-Session Format
Marie S. Dezelic & Gabriel Ghanoum (2015)

Meaning-Centered Therapy Workbook:
Based on Viktor Frankl's Logotherapy &
Existential Analysis
Marie S. Dezelic (2014)

Viktor Frankl's Logotherapy:
Meaning-Centered Counseling
Ann V. Graber (2004)

CLINICAL TRAINING RESOURCES

Viktor Frankl Institute of Logotherapy
Abilene, Texas, USA
www.viktorfranklinstitute.org

Viktor Frankl Institute Vienna, Austria
Scientific Society for Logotherapy & Existential Analysis
www.viktorfrankl.org

International Network on Personal Meaning and Meaning of Life
Toronto, ON, Canada
www.meaning.ca

Trauma Center at Justice Resource Institute
Boston, Massachusetts, USA
www.traumacenter.org

International Association of Trauma Professionals
Tampa, Florida, USA
www.traumapro.net

The Addictions Academy
Miami, Florida, USA
www.theaddictionsacademy.com

Marie S. Dezelic, PhD, MS, LMHC, CCTP, NCLC, CFRC, NCAIP, Diplomate in Logotherapy, is an author, workshop presenter and educator, and has a private psychotherapy practice in South Florida. Dr. Dezelic sees adolescents, adults, couples, and families, and travels nationally and internationally for crisis intervention. Her clinical research and work focuses on trauma, grief, spirituality, and psycho-oncology through an integrative Existential framework. Dr. Dezelic holds a PhD in psychology, a Master of Science degree in mental health counseling, a Diplomate in Logotherapy and Existential Analysis, is a Certified Clinical Trauma Professional, Certified in EMDR treatment, holds a Certificate in Traumatic Stress Studies from the Trauma Center at JRI, is a Certified Grief Recovery Specialist, a Certified Life Coach/ Family Recovery Coach/ and Interventionist, is an internationally accredited member of the Viktor Frankl Institute in Vienna, Austria, and holds several advanced training certifications in various treatment modalities, including Couples and Family Systems. She offers numerous psychology and healthcare presentations on mental health topics, staff education, and implementing programs and support teams on the holistic patient-centered approach to patient care such as: Mental Health in Healthcare, Trauma-Informed Treatment, Meaning within Illness, Positive Psychology, Palliative Care, Psycho-Spiritual Oncology Treatment, Compassion Fatigue, Grief and Loss Support, Traumatic Grief, Dimensions of Pain, Pastoral Care, Staff Motivation, and Spirituality. Dr. Dezelic also offers workshops on Relationships, Parenting, and Mind-Body-Spirit Integrative Health. Dr. Dezelic has published a Workbook on Existential Psychology, *Meaning-Centered Therapy: Based on Viktor Frankl's Logotherapy & Existential Analysis;* and has co-authored *Meaning-Centered Therapy Manual: Logotherapy & Existential Analysis Brief Therapy Protocol for Group & Individual Sessions.* Additionally, she has published a book of poetry, has designed several clinical treatment models, a bio-psycho-social-spiritual assessment screening instrument used in healthcare, writes articles and presents in various venues nationally and internationally on mental health and spirituality topics. Dr. Dezelic is actively involved in promoting clinical psychoeducational initiatives, cultural awareness, education, and medical support for cultures and groups facing traumatic stress around the world.

Visit:
www.DrMarieDezelic.com

Gabriel Ghanoum, PsyD, MDiv, GCC, BCC, CFRC, NCAIP, Diplomate in Logotherapy, is an author, workshop presenter, educator and the Director of Pastoral Care and Palliative Care Services for a network of hospitals in South Eastern Florida. He holds various degrees in Psychology, Theology, and Business, is a Certified Grief Therapist, Certified Grief Recovery Specialist, Certified Family Recovery Coach and Interventionist, is an internationally accredited member of the Viktor Frankl Institute in Vienna, Austria, and holds several advanced training certifications in various therapy modalities. Dr. Ghanoum is passionate about bringing spiritual and psychological awareness through his national and international lectures and retreats on Relationships, Parenting, Spirituality, Positive Psychology, Mind-Body-Spirit Integrative Health, and the Psycho-Spiritual approach to oncology and healing. He offers health-care staff psycho-educational seminars on various topics, such as Implementing Palliative Care Programs, Pastoral Care, Psycho-Spiritual Approach to Oncology, Spiritual Well-Being, Compassion Fatigue, Staff Satisfaction and Motivation in Healthcare, Trauma and Grief Support. Dr. Ghanoum has co-authored *Meaning-Centered Therapy Manual: Logotherapy & Existential Analysis Brief Therapy Protocol for Group & Individual Sessions,* has designed several clinical treatment models, a bio-psycho-social-spiritual assessment screening instrument used in healthcare, and presents in various venues nationally and internationally on mental health and spirituality topics. Dr. Ghanoum is a chairman and member on various non-profit boards, and is deeply involved in promoting the mental health perspective within several charity programs around the world, including aiding the homeless of South Florida through bio-psycho-social-spiritual care.

www.ingramcontent.com/pod-product-compliance
Lightning Source LLC
Chambersburg PA
CBHW041150290426
44108CB00002B/24